Grands Crus of Bordeaux

Sixth Edition

Copyright © 1996 by Hans Walraven

Published in the United States by
The Wine Appreciation Guild Ltd.
155 Connecticut St.
San Francisco CA 94116
(415) 864-1202

ISBN 0-932664-94-6

All rights reserved. No part of this book may be reproduced
or copied in any form or by any means graphic, electronic, or
mechanical, including photocopying, taping or information
storage and retrieval systems without written permission of
the publisher.

LIBRARY OF CONGRESS No. 95-061102

Grands Crus of Bordeaux

by
Hans Walraven

Sixth Edition
The Wine Appreciation Guild
San Francisco

Contents

Introduction to the Sixth Edition   7
Why This Guide?   11
The Wines   13
Assessment and development   21
Market Value   23
Auction Prices   26
Value and Quality Indication of Old Vintages   28
Grand Cru in Use   38
Wine as an Investment   40
Wine Auctions   43
Analytical Tasting   46
Grands Crus and your health   51
Top Ten 1993 - 1977   55
The Grands Crus - Alphabetically   83
Supplement   255

Introduction to the Sixth Edition

Market value

The most remarkable change in this edition of *Grands Crus of Bordeaux* compared to the two previous editions concerns the market value. In 1991, the prices of the 1990 and earlier vintages was unchanged. The markets stagnated because the gap between offer and demand was growing too wide. The reason was that, on the one hand, the producers were asking increasingly higher prices for their wine without wondering if wine lovers were willing to pay, and, on the other hand, the turnover was stagnating at the consumer level because the cost of replacing Grands Crus was growing out of proportion. Oenophiles were thinking more in terms of investment than enjoyment. Their wine cellars were filling up, resulting in a decrease in demand.

High prices, low demand. This summarizes the situation we have known for the last four years. The wines from the 1990 and earlier vintages have kept their value on paper. For these vintages, the turnover of large batches of wine was possible only if they were offered at a 30% discount compared to the market price.

The '91, '92 and '93 vintages were sold "in primeur" at such a discount. Yet, notwithstanding the 30% discount compared to the 1990 wines, sales of more recent vintages were sluggish.
However, a slight change occurred at the end of 1994. After many 1992 wines had been dumped in French supermarkets for prices as low as 50% of the 1990 market value, the offer started to shrink. At the same time, some space became available in the cellars of wine lovers.
This resulted in a rather active sales campaign for the 1994 vintage. This, and the good quality of the 1994 wines, had a positive effect on the older and better vintages, whose inventories were shrinking while the demand experienced a slight rise.
This is the background of the remarkable change in market value reflected in this guide, compared to the two previous

editions.

Two extra vintages
Compared to the previous editions, this sixth edition also includes the 1992 and 1993 vintages. With the addition of these two new vintages, we are introducing an extra dimension in the evaluation and evolution of wines, by distinguishing between the tasting of Grands Crus from the barrel and from the bottle.

After our first encounter with the 1991 vintage, we were very disappointed by the quality of the samples from the barrel. We therefore decided to give it another try. The wines were assessed once more, this time not on the basis of a sample from the barrel, but rather on a sample from the bottled end product. We used this double evaluation also for the 1992 and 1993 vintages.

Not all the 1991, 1992 and 1993 wines were assessed twice. The wines of which the final product was tasted twice are printed in bold. The wines for which our scores are based only on a taste from the barrel are not printed in bold.

Most cases show that the barrel samples were not as good as the Grand Cru bottle samples. Obviously, most château owners had made a subsequent selection from their cellars, so that the quality of the end product had improved, especially that of recent vintages.

This conclusion only applies to the last three years. It is proof of a growing concern with quality on the part of the producers. Obviously, we don't know if this will last. In this particular case it might simply be the result of the stagnating market for Grands Crus in recent years.

Le Bon Pasteur, a new addition to the supplement
As you know, Pomerol does not have an official classification. For that reason, the Pomerols are included as a supplement in this guide. These are Pomerols which are sold at the Grand Cru level and for comparable prices. I have added a wine to this new edition, Château Le Bon Pasteur, Pomerol, which you will find in the supplement. The château belongs to the oenologist, Michel Rolland.

In 1991, the Wine Exchange nominated Michel Rolland winemaker of the year because of his innovative influence on the entire Bordeaux region. You will see his name regularly under "oenologist" in the technical data. Many of the Grands

Crus for which he acted as consulting oenologist made it to the top ten of recent years. For that reason I have included Le Bon Pasteur, Michel Rolland's own wine, in this guide. It is a Pomerol which is selling at the level of the top category III wines, comparable with Belair, Talbot and La Gaffelière.

Cellaring potential

I receive questions regularly about the maturation and cellarability of the Grands Crus. Let me put it this way, as a rule, soup is served hotter than it is eaten. In other words, if the guide indicates a certain wine as passé, many believe that it has reached its peak.

Here is an example. For the 1973 Château Pétrus, Pomerol, the period for drinking was 1978-1983. Recently we tasted the wine again and the panel was unanimous in its opinion that this wine was still a special experience. Though this Pétrus may have been in its full glory in 1983, it continues to command respect in its golden years.

The fact that our prognoses for cellarability are cautious, is not only a matter of playing it safe, it is also due to a professional bias on the part of the tasting panel. Indeed, we are used to tasting very young wines and our preference is for young rather than old wines. Feel free to accuse us of a certain degree of subjectivity in our prognoses.

Grands Crus and your health. Enjoy, but drink in moderation

Alcohol is harmful to your health. Because anti-alcohol campaigns, though very useful, are not always very subtle, it seemed to make sense to listen to seek advice from an expert.

I asked Tim Overtoom, the famous radiologist from Sint-Antonius Hospital in Nieuwegein, the Netherlands, for his opinion. Although it is best for everyone to rely on his or her own physical and mental responses, we can all benefit from the views of a specialist. This may lead one person to uncork his bottles more rapidly, while someone else may let his Grands Crus rest a bit longer.

Why this Guide?

Grands Crus of Bordeaux answers the questions which keep wine connoisseurs and collectors busy, and these questions are:

– What is the quality that lies hidden behind that Grand Cru label of a certain vintage?
– When will the wine be ripe for drinking?
– How long can the wine be kept and will it improve?
– What is a sound price, or what should the asking price be when selling?
– When buying and selling at auctions what should be done with the price indication of all wines and vintages?

As those questions are hardly ever answered by the existing wine literature this biannual guide fills an obvious need. In this sixth edition of *Grands Crus of Bordeaux* practical and actual information is given, thereby enabling the real wine lover and collector to attune his or her buying and selling policies. The information contained in this handbook does not express the opinion of only one person. It is based on the expertise of a team of professionals.

At every confrontation with a Grand Cru, whether it be in a restaurant, at a retailer's, wine merchant's or auction, this Grand Cru guide is a handy reference book. The answer to the question: is the wine offered sound? can be found unfailingly. A helping hand to let you know straight away if it is indeed desirable to have a few bottles or cases delivered from the restaurant owner or wine merchant.

The tasting panel

The indications given in this booklet with respect to quality, drinking ripeness and cellaring possibilities of the Grands Crus are extremely valuable.

Each wine is rated with a score of between 0 and 20, the result of ratings given during blind, comparative tastings. For each tasting the panel consisted of at least three experts associated with the American Wine Exchange.

The core of the panel was formed by the tasters Pieter, Paul and Hans Walraven, Franz Lampe and Erik Boelen.
The ratings given in this guide therefore express the opinions of a number of experts specialized in the field of the Grand Crus.

The Wines

As every connoisseur or professional will conclude from the title, it is the 61 Crus Classés du Médoc which are the subject of this handbook. A classification dating from 1855, constituted by the Bordeaux Chamber of Commerce.
This classification was made by order of Napoleon III on the occasion of the first World Exhibition in Paris. Just like the Eiffel Tower, this classification of over 135 years of age still endures in the world of today. It is the only classification to enjoy worldwide recognition. Classifications set up since by other regions outside the Médoc, have not as yet succeeded in gaining the same prestige as that of the famous, although on many points antiquated, 1855 classification.

To this day, when the subject of Grands Crus comes up, it is these 61 selected red wines of Médoc châteaux which are understood; including the Graves, Château Haut-Brion.
Although at the time Sauternes and Barsacs, sweet white wines very much in fashion then, were also included in the classification, they have not been taken into consideration in this guide.

The focus of this booklet is on the 61 Médoc châteaux. Next to the 61 Grands Crus 'par excellence' we have featured a number of other wines and those are the Premiers Grands Crus A and B from Saint-Emilion and the Grands Crus from the Graves. In the supplement one can find some of the best known Pomerols (this region does not have a classification) and a few châteaux who, after often years of struggle, have achieved not only the same ranking but also the same recognition as the Grands Crus du Médoc.

The Médocs classified in 1855

Premiers Crus Classés
Château Lafite-Rothschild	Pauillac
Château Latour	Pauillac
Château Margaux	Margaux
Château Mouton-Rothschild	Pauillac
Château Haut-Brion	Pessac, Graves

Deuxièmes Crus Classés
Château Rausan-Ségla	Margaux
Château Rauzan-Gassies	Margaux
Château Léoville-Las-Cases	Saint-Julien
Château Léoville-Poyferré	Saint-Julien
Château Léoville-Barton	Saint-Julien
Château Durfort-Vivens	Margaux
Château Gruaud-Larose	Saint-Julien
Château Lascombes	Margaux
Château Brane-Cantenac	Margaux
Château Pichon-Longueville-Baron	Pauillac
Château Pichon-Longueville (Comtesse de Lalande)	Pauillac
Château Ducru-Beaucaillou	Saint-Julien
Château Cos d'Estournel	Saint-Estèphe
Château Montrose	Saint-Estèphe

Troisièmes Crus Classés
Château Kirwan	Margaux
Château d'Issan	Margaux
Château Lagrange	Saint-Julien
Château Langoa-Barton	Saint-Julien
Château Giscours	Margaux
Château Malescot Saint-Exupéry	Margaux
Château Boyd-Cantenac	Margaux
Château Cantenac-Brown	Margaux
Château Palmer	Margaux
Château La Lagune	Haut-Médoc
Château Desmirail	Margaux
Château Calon-Ségur	Saint-Estèphe
Château Ferrière	Margaux
Château Marquis d'Alesme-Becker	Margaux

Quatrièmes Crus Classés
Château Saint-Pierre	Saint-Julien
Château Talbot	Saint-Julien
Château Branaire-Ducru	Saint-Julien
Château Duhart-Milon-Rothschild	Pauillac
Château Pouget	Margaux

Château La Tour Carnet	Haut-Médoc
Château Lafon-Rochet	Saint-Estèphe
Château Beychevelle	Saint-Julien
Château Prieuré-Lichine	Margaux
Château Marquis de Terme	Margaux

Cinquièmes Crus Classés

Château Pontet-Canet	Pauillac
Château Batailley	Pauillac
Château Haut-Batailley	Pauillac
Château Grand-Puy-Lacoste	Pauillac
Château Grand-Puy-Ducasse	Pauillac
Château Lynch-Bages	Pauillac
Château Lynch-Moussas	Pauillac
Château Dauzac	Margaux
Château d'Armailhac	Pauillac
Château du Tertre	Margaux
Château Haut-Bages Libéral	Pauillac
Château Pédesclaux	Pauillac
Château Belgrave	Haut-Médoc
Château Camensac	Haut-Médoc
Château Cos Labory	Saint-Estèphe
Château Clerc Milon	Pauillac
Château Croizet-Bages	Pauillac
Château Cantemerle	Haut-Médoc

Saint-Emilions classified in 1954

For Saint-Emilion these are made up of the leaders of the classification published in October, 1954, namely the Premiers Grands Crus Classés A and B.

Premiers Grands Cru Classés A
Château Ausone
Château Cheval Blanc

Premiers Grands Crus Classés B
Château Beauséjour Duffau-Lagarrosse
Château Beau-Séjour – Bécot
Château Belair
Château Canon
Château Figeac
Château La Gaffelière
Château Magdelaine
Château Pavie
Château Trotte Vieille
Clos Fourtet

Crus Classés de Graves classified in 1959

Grands Crus Classés
Château Bouscaut
Château Carbonnieux
Domaine de Chevalier
Château de Fieuzal
Château Haut-Bailly
Château La Tour Martillac
Château Malartic-Lagravière
Château La Mission Haut-Brion
Château Olivier
Château Pape Clément
Château Smith-Haut-Lafitte
Château La Tour Haut-Brion

Supplement

A number of well-known Bordeaux wines which do not fall under the theme of this guide are listed in the Supplement: The best-known Pomerols (a region for which no classification exists), and also the Crus Bourgeois du Médoc of the most renowned châteaux. They are wines of appellations which fall under the Bordeaux region and on account of their quality are often named in the same breath as the Grand Crus. These wines are:

Château Chasse-Spleen, Moulis, Cru Bourgeois du Médoc
Château La Conseillante, Pomerol
Château Le Bon Pasteur, Pomerol
Château Gloria, Saint-Julien, Cru Bourgeois du Médoc
Château Pétrus, Pomerol
Vieux Château Certan, Pomerol

Comments Saint-Emilion

Contrary to the Médoc classification of 1855 to which no periodic adjustments may be made, the regulations of the Saint-Emilion classification state that the classification should be reviewed every 10 years. Once every ten years, a test should be made of the quality of the wines and any changes in the size of the vineyard noted. However, the adjustment determined in 1954 took considerably longer than the proposed ten years to implement, and it was 1985 before those measures were carried out.

The only change that has taken place, within the theme of this guide, is the downgrading of Château Beau-Séjour – Bécot. As the owner of this château, Monsieur Bécot, is fighting the ruling of the classification committee. There is every possibility of the decision being revoked.

When the tasting results of Château Beau-Séjour – Bécot are compared with those of its counterparts, it will be clear that the reason for downgrading this château does not lie in a decline of quality. The downgrading does however, have everything to do with the changed circumstances of the vineyard (see Château Beau-Séjour – Bécot).

Comments Médoc

In spite of entreaties which came in 1855 from the Châteaux not included in the classification and from Grands Crus which felt themselves to have been ranked too low, nothing has changed in the classification. There is one exception however: Château Mouton-Rothschild. This château, ranked with the second Crus in 1855, was given a ranking with the first Crus in 1973. To make this possible the French Government had to amend the law. In the early seventies then, many Château owners who felt themselves to be under-ranked hoped that this amendment would lead to a Government review of the entire classification. Unfortunately for them but happily for the firmly established 61 Grands Crus, this exception applied only to the Rothschild family.

For Rothschild the door was opened a crack to allow Mouton to pass through to the first Crus. And by that single exception it has remained.

Although no changes have taken place in the classification itself, a few Grands Crus have undergone a change in name. In order to prevent misunderstandings the following is a summary of those Grands Crus.

Original Name	*New Name*	*Comments*
Château Lafite	Château Lafite-Rothschild	The Family name of the owner, James Rothschild, was added.
Château Mouton	Château Mouton-Rothschild	This was also the case here with the name Rothschild Another branch of the family though.
Château Rauzan	Château Rauzan-Gassies Château Rausan-Ségla	Split up into Rauzan-Gassies and Rausan-Ségla by the heirs. Note the different spellings of Rauzan with an s and a z.
Château Léoville	Château Léoville-Las-Cases Château Léoville-Poyferré Château Léoville-Barton	In the 1855 document the names of the three owners were mentioned. However the three wines do not appear individually in the classification. The owners' names are now coupled to that of the château.
Château Vivens Durfort	Château Durfort-Vivens	
Château Gruau-Laroze	Château Gruaud-Larose	Previously Gruaud without d and Larose with z instead of s.
Château de Camensac	Château Camensac	
Château Cantenac	Château Brane-Cantenac	Now coupled to the name of Baron Brane.
Château Pichon-Longueville	Château Pichon-Longueville Comtesse de Lalande Château Pichon-Longueville-Baron	Broken up by an inheritance. One part for the Baron and one part for the Comtesse.

19

Château Ducru Beau Caillou	Château Ducru-Beaucaillou	Previously three words, now merged into two.
Château Saint-Exupéry	Château Malescot Saint-Exupéry	Malescot has been added.
Château Boyd	Château Boyd-Cantenac	The addition of the name of the county 'Cantenac'.
Château Dubignon		A name that has disappeared completely.
Château Calon	Château Calon-Ségur	Ségur has has been added.
Château Becker	Château Marquis d'Alesme-Becker	The owner's name, Marquis d'Alesme, has been added.
Château Saint-Pierre	Château Saint-Pierre	Previously split up into Saint-Pierre-Bontemps-Dubarry and Château Saint-Pierre-Sevaistre. In 1982, when the new owner took over, Sevaistre was uncoupled from the original name. The new name is now the same as the old.
Château Duluc	Château Branaire-Ducru	
Château Duhart	Château Duhart-Milon-Rothschild	First the name Milon was added. Then, when the Rothschild family took over, the name Rothschild was added.
Château Pouget	Château Pouget	Was originally two châteaux, which have merged into one.

Château Carnet	Château La Tour Carnet	The name La Tour has been added, which refers to the old tower of this château.
Château Rochet	Château Lafon-Rochet	
Château Le Prieuré	Château Prieuré-Lichine	Has become been combined with the name of the owner, the Lichine family.
Château Canet	Château Pontet-Canet	
Château Batailley	Château Batailley Château Haut-Batailley	Was divided between two brothers and split up into two estates 45 years ago.
Château Grand-Puy	Château Grand-Puy-Lacoste	
Château Artiques Arnaud	Château Grand-Puy-Ducasse	
Château Lynch	Château Lynch-Bages	
Château d'Armailhac(q)	Château d'Armailhac	Has undergone four changes of name. First, it was Mouton d'Armailhac(q) (until 1956) then Mouton Baron Philippe, next the château was called after the Baroness and finally it resumed its old name with the 1989 vintage.
Château Haut-Bages	Château Haut-Bages Libéral	
Château Coutenceau	Château Belgrave	

Assessment and Development

How were the tastings carried out?

All assessments given in this guide were arrived at during blind, comparative tastings. The only correct method to judge a wine objectively, is blind tasting. Every taster, even the skilled professional, can be influenced during a tasting by the smallest hint in the form of a cork, the corner of a label, or the shape of a bottle, and this could stand in the way of his making an objective judgement. A château Margaux or a Pétrus is, to give an example, expected to be a top wine and connoisseurs are only human. They too have their prejudices. To prevent this, tastings must be done without knowing which wine is in the glass. Next to blind tasting, comparison with other wines of a similar quality is essential in order to form an objective and well-founded judgement.

The assessments published in this guide are based therefore on the distinct relationship existing between all Grands Crus.

Scores from 0 - 20

The scoring system employed gives an overall picture of the structure of the wines. Impressions of color, aroma and flavor are reflected in the total score. A maximum of 3 points was given for color, for aroma a maximum of 7 points, and for flavor a maximum of 10 points. A perfect wine would therefore score a total of 20 points. The fact that in *Grands Crus of Bordeaux* not one single wine scored the full 20 points, with the exception of 1961 Château Palmer, is the result of minute differences in the assessment of the panel of tasters. After all, the scores given here represent the opinions of at least three experts.

Regarding the great wines that were not rated so highly, they seldom scored less than 10 points; the wines cataloged in this guide are ranked among the best wines to be found on earth today.

Development

With regard to the development of the wine a prognosis was given by the panel per wine tasted for the moment when the wine would be ripe enough to drink (column 'drink from'). The potential for aging is given in a separate column ('cellaring potential').

Drink from

The prognosis for drinking ripeness is based on the intensity and on the complexity of the wine's flavors. It is a prognosis of the moment when all aromas and flavors are first recognizable in harmony. The indication 'mature' does not mean that the wine has reached full maturity, or the peak of its development. A wine that is only just ready to drink, has barely left adolescence. It is recognizable as an adult. Whether it is granted a short or a long life will depend upon its health and constitution.

Cellaring potential

No matter how good a wine might be one can be sure an end will come to its golden age. An end announced beforehand by all wines. Contrary to the many old wives' tales of wines turning into vinegar overnight, a wine turns slowly. A process comparable to that of reaching maturity. The period of youth and that of old age often correspond. The richer the wine is in alcohol, tannin and acids, the longer its youth and period of maturity will be. The wine's way of taking leave too, will be quieter and more dignified in 'old age'.

The notion that the quality of a wine can turn within a few months or even weeks under normal circumstances is nonsense.

Gossip launched because the wine has been handled badly. Inexperience in the drinking of old wines can be at the root of such inventions as well. It is precisely with the older wines that a bad bottle presents itself more often. Just as infirmities are more noticeable in people growing old, so it is with a wine with the taste of cork or a 'bad' bottle. This has nothing to do with turning.

Aging is a broad concept of course. The one likes the tannins in his wine fully resolved, while the other appreciates the roughness of unresolved tannin. The information given in this guide about aging is a prognosis of the period during which the wine is at its peak; the moment when no further improvement in quality is to be expected.

Market Value

The value of Grands Crus and comparable wines is determined daily by supply and demand. The precise value can be gauged only at the moment when a purchase or sale becomes definite. Next to supply and demand many other factors that have an influence on the price play a role, such as the size of the order, the prospects of the new harvest, payment and packaging (cartons and wooden cases). With older wines, the stage of development, the rarity, and the conditions under which the wine has been matured must all be taken into consideration.

In view of all those factors it is not possible to give an exact value per wine. The prices quoted in this Grand Cru guide give only an indication as to the value; recommended prices, grouped together as much as possible, by which prices and values can be compared.

Market value, Summer 1995

As a basis for the value of especially the young wines (the vintages back to and including 1985) the prices of the free Bordeaux market are the most representative. A château of a certain vintage is, however, offered on that market for various prices. Just as deposit interest can vary from bank to bank, the prices for one and the same wine can vary too. The quotations, upon which the value of the Grands Crus are based in this guide, are made up out of an average taken from the current prices applicable on the French market of a number of prominent Bordeaux negotiants. The years from 1980 and before are no longer current and are therefore very highly priced indeed.

The quotations in this guide, listed under the heading "Market Value, Summer 1995", have been converted according to a uniform formula into American dollars. Under this section you will find the price, including Federal Tax and Duty and ocean freight, for a purchase of a minimum of 25 cases of one type. As Grands Crus are offered by several merchants at various prices, an average of those prices has been used as basis.

Finally, it is important that you realize that the prices mentioned above may vary from day to day.
They reflect a situation at a specific point in time, based on the market prices in Bordeaux in the summer of 1995. Nevertheless, the example may be viewed as a real basis for Grand Cru values for an entire year, provided the harvest in Bordeaux does not fail.

Calculation of the market value by means of an example.
Assume that you buy 25 cases of wine from a château in Bordeaux for a price of 35 French Francs per bottle FOB château. The calculation is as follows:
(Exchange rate: U.S. $ 1 = F. frs. 4.80)

Price FOB château		
F. frs. 35 per bottle	$ 7.30	F. frs 35
Additional cost	2.10 *	10.10
Landed cost	9.40 **	45.10

* Includes: Overseas handling, ocean freight, Federal duties, Customs bond, insurance, handling U.S.A.
** Does not include inland freight, State taxes and wholesale, retail mark-ups (where applicable).

* Additional cost calculation:

Pick-up at château, inland freight plus consolidation	$ 0.50	F. frs 2.40
Ocean freight	1.20	5.80
Fed. tax and duty	0.30	1.40
Customs broker/miscellaneous	0.05	0.25
Insurance	0.05	0.25
Total cost per bottle	2.10	10.10

Price changes in percentages
The alphabetical Grand Cru index in this guide contains a column which indicates price changes over the past years. These changes are indicated in percentage points and refer only to the most recent vintages, i.e., 1977 to 1993.

The percentages are calculated as follows. The market value in France for the summer of 1995 is compared to the market value of the summer of 1993 from the previous Grand Cru edition.

For the 1992 and 1993 vintages, the market value of the summer of 1995 is compared with the Première Tranche price.

Although the list with price changes expressed in terms of percentages is interesting to many people, it is unfortunately the column in which only the most recent years can be entered. In fact, many wines are sold out in Bordeaux so that they are no longer available for this comparison.
Similarly, no percentage is given for the vintages before 1977 because the Bordeaux market quoted exorbitant prices for these vintages which might lead to the impression that enormous price increases are to be expected for older wines. Certainly where old vintages are concerned, the Bordeaux market presents a mixed price picture often involving simply prices on paper. The inventories concerned are very small. Consequently, the quotations of old vintages in Bordeaux barely provide realistic data.

Auction Prices

To predict the value of Grands Crus which are not traded on the free Bordeaux market, exclusive products of some mercantile houses and wines older than 1985, the price development at international wine auctions offers probably the most effective basis. Indeed, the prices asked for old wines in Bordeaux are exorbitant.

The real value of Grands Crus older than 1985 can be derived with greater accuracy from the prices being offered at various auctions. The fact that the Bordeaux market often quotes higher prices for older wines than those realized at auctions is justified.
The auction offer is unstructured, one has to see what is being offered for sale. The Bordeaux market, on the other hand, is capable of supplying Grands Crus of the desired year at any desired moment. The prices are high because the offer is small. As a result, the lion's share of the old and antiquarian wines enters the market by way of auctions. If Bordeaux is the market where the value for young wines from 1985 onward is being determined, auctions constitute the price thermometer for old vintages.

The auction price mentioned per wine and per vintage can be used as a guideline for purchasing and selling at auctions. The prices include the commission for the auction house but not the costs of transportation to or from the auction place. When selling, these prices offer an indication for setting your limits. When purchasing, they serve to check that you are not bidding too high. For old vintages it is advisable to consult with the auction house or another expert before bidding.

The auction prices provided per château are the most recent and current offerings quoted in recent years at international wine auctions. These offerings were achieved at various branches of Christie's, i.e., Amsterdam, London, Chicago (now out of business), Geneva and Bordeaux, and at the auction house Sotheby's in London and Geneva.

The auction prices listed in this guide are partly based on the 9th edition of "The Wine Price File" by William H. Edgerton.

This publication contains 70,000 auction and retail prices of more than 14.000 wines.
(Wine Price File. P.O. Box 1007 / Darien, Connecticut 06820. Tel: (203) 655-2448. Fax: (203) 655-8066. Price: $39 postpaid in the US. Add $9 for UPS blue label, (2nd day). Foreign orders: Add $10 seamail or $22 airmail postage for Europe, $31 elsewhere; for Canada and Mexico add $9. Credit cards accepted.)

The auction prices are listed separately. They include a 15% auction fee, but do not include transportation costs. This summary offers the auction prices for the last four years. If a vintage is accompanied by a *, the price is the auction price of the last two years. This offers a clear picture of the interest a certain Cru enjoys at international wine auctions.

For vintages for which no quality assessment has been included or no market value or auction prices are known, we refer to the chapter "Value and Quality Indication of Old Vintages". In this chapter, the wines have been divided into four categories, according to quality and market value. For each château, we refer to the category in question.

Major American wine auctions

Butterfield and Butterfield
220 San Bruno Avenue
San Francisco, CA 94103
(415) 861-7500

Chicago Wine Company
5663 Howard Street
Niles, IL 60648
(708) 647-8789

Davis and Company, Wine Auctioneers Ltd.
361 West Chestnut
Chicago, IL 60610
(312) 587-9500

Morell and Company, Fine Wine Auctions
535 Madison Ave
New York, NY 10022
(212) 688-9370

Major wine auctions in London, England

Christie's
8 King Street
London SW1Y 6QT
(71) 839 9060

Sotheby's
34 New Bond Street
London W1A 2AA
(71) 493 8080

Value and Quality Indication of Old Vintages

Value
The market value in Bordeaux and the offerings at recent auctions constitute the soundest basis for a prognosis of the value of a Grand Cru. To help provide an indication of the current value, this guide only includes the offerings of the last two years. In the last two years, no complete series of any of the Grand Cru vintages has been auctioned off. It is therefore impossible to present a complete summary. In order to give some kind of indication, we offer a general prognosis hereafter., i.e., a prognosis for the current value of the Grands Crus based on recent offerings at auctions. It offers general guidelines, to be used for a rough assessment of the Grands Crus of the vintage years 1928 through 1986.

According to their reputation or the demand on the wine market, the Grands Crus are subdivided into 4 categories, with Category I being the category with the most requested and best known wines and Category IV being the category with the least known wines.

Calculation of value indication

The value indication given here is an average of the auction prices and market values within a category.

The sequence observed in the categories is based on the prices achieved per wine. The wine with the highest price is mentioned first and the wine with the lowest price last.

For example, within Category I, the prices for Château Pétrus are 30 to 40% above the average value indications for this category. The prices for Château La Mission Haut-Brion, the last wine in category I, are generally 20 to 30% below the value indication given.

N.B. No value indication is given for vintages for which it may be stated with virtual certainty that they are really passé.

Quality
Besides the value indication, some rough guidelines can be provided per category with regard to the quality of each vintage. They indicate what you may expect on the average from the quality of the wine of a certain year, and how long it will keep.

The classification can only be viewed as a guideline. It is an average of the quality standard which applies to the vintage in question.

The decision as to whether a wine is good or bad, and its stage of development, can be assessed with certainty only for each wine individually.

Subdivided by Vintage Quality
1 - top year
2 - very good
3 - good
4 - fair
5 - bad

Subdivided by Stage of Development
1 - do not drink yet
2 - drinkable now
3 - on its return
4 - passé

(see under cellaring potential also)

Category I
Château Pétrus, Pomerol
Château Lafite-Rothschild, Pauillac, 1er Cru
Château Ausone, Saint-Emilion, Grand Cru Classé A
Château Mouton-Rothschild, Pauillac, 1er Cru
Château Latour, Pauillac, 1er Cru
Château Cheval Blanc, Saint-Emilion, Grand Cru Classé A
Château Margaux, Margaux, 1er Cru
Château Haut-Brion, Pessac, Graves Rouge, 1er Cru
Château La Mission Haut-Brion, Graves Rouge

Category I - Value and Quality Indications for Vintages

Vintage	Quality	Stage of Development	Value Indication U.S. $	F. frs
1928	Top	Drinkable now/On its return	471.00	2355
1929	Top	Drinkable now/On its return	671.00	3355
1930/31/32	Bad	Passé	-	-
1933	Fair	On its return	240.00	1200
1934	Good	Drinkable now/On its return	300.00	1500
1935	Bad	Passé	-	-
1936	Fair	On its return	129.00	645
1937	Fair	On its return	283.00	1415
1938	Bad	Passé	111.00	555
1939	Bad	Passé	171.00	855
1940	Fair	Drinkable now/On its return	200.00	1000
1941	Fair	Drinkable now	200.00	1000
1942	Bad	Passé	-	-
1943	Good	Drinkable now	-	-
1944	Fair	Drinkable now/On its return	171.00	855
1945	Top	Drinkable now	858.00	4290
1946	Bad	Passé	-	-
1947	Top	Drinkable now	489.00	2445
1948	Very good	Drinkable now	229.00	1145
1949	Top	Drinkable now	449.00	2245
1950	Fair	On its return	160.00	800
1951	Bad	Passé	-	-
1952	Good	Drinkable now	139.00	695
1953	Top	Drinkable now	343.00	1715
1954	Bad	Passé	-	-
1955	Good	Drinkable now	246.00	1230
1956	Bad	Passé	-	-
1957	Fair	Drinkable now	94.00	470
1958	Fair	On its return	106.00	530
1959	Top	Drinkable now	445.00	2225
1960	Fair	On its return/Passé	57.00	285
1961	Top	Drinkable now	507.00	2535
1962	Good	Drinkable now	170.00	850
1963	Bad	Passé	-	-
1964	Good	Drinkable now	163.00	815
1965	Bad	Passé	43.00	215
1966	Very good	Drinkable now	192.00	960
1967	Fair	Drinkable now	57.00	285
1968	Bad	Passé	-	-
1969	Fair	Drinkable now	49.00	245
1970	Top	Drinkable now	194.00	970
1971	Good	Drinkable now	113.00	565
1972	Bad	On its return	29.00	145
1973	Fair	On its return	69.00	345
1974	Bad	On its return	46.00	230
1975	Good	Do not drink yet/Drinkable now	169.00	845
1976	Good	Drinkable now	88.00	440
1977	Fair	On its return	46.00	230
1978	Very good	Do not drink yet	123.00	615
1979	Good	Drinkable now	93.00	465
1980	Fair	Drinkable now	80.00	400
1981	Good	Do not drink yet	130.00	650
1982	Top	Do not drink yet	223.00	1115
1983	Very good	Do not drink yet	91.00	455
1984	Fair	Drinkable now	46.00	230
1985	Very good	Do not drink yet	114.00	570
1986	Very good	Do not drink yet	119.00	595
1987	Fair	Drinkable now	65.00	325
1988	Very good	Do not drink yet	107.00	535
1989	Very good	Do not drink yet	122.00	610
1990	Good	Do not drink yet	120.00	600
1991	Fair	Do not drink yet	67.00	335
1992	Fair	Do not drink yet	49.00	245
1993	Good	Do not drink yet	54.00	270

Category II
Château Palmer, Margaux, 3me Cru
Château Léoville-Las Cases, Saint-Julien, 2me Cru
Domaine de Chevalier, Graves
Château Cos d'Estournel, Saint-Estèphe, 2me Cru
Château Pichon-Longueville Comtesse de Lalande, Pauillac, 2me Cru
Château Pichon-Longueville-Baron, Pauillac, 2me Cru
Château Pape Clément, Graves, Cru Classé
Château Ducru-Beaucaillou, Saint-Julien, 2me Cru
Vieux Château Certan, Pomerol
Château La Conseillante, Pomerol
Château Magdelaine, Saint-Emilion, 1er Grand Cru Classé B
Château Lynch-Bages, Pauillac, 5me Cru
Château Canon, Saint-Emilion, 1er Grand Cru Classé B
Château Beychevelle, Saint-Julien, 4me Cru
Château Pavie, St.-Emilion, 1er Grand Cru Classé B
Château Montrose, Saint-Estèphe, 2me Cru
Château de Fieuzal, Léognan, Grand Cru Classé de Graves

Category II - Value and Quality Indications for Vintages

Vintage	Quality	Stage of Development	Value Indication U.S. $	F. frs
1928	Top	Drinkable now/On its return	303.00	1515
1929	Top	Drinkable now/On its return	286.00	1430
1930/31/32	Bad	Passé	-	-
1933	Fair	On its return	93.00	465
1934	Good	Drinkable now/On its return	97.00	485
1935	Bad	Passé	-	-
1936	Fair	On its return/Passé	80.00	400
1937	Fair	On its return	114.00	570
1938	Bad	Passé	-	-
1939	Bad	Passé	-	-
1940	Fair	Drinkable now/On its return	171.00	855
1941	Fair	Drinkable now/On its return	171.00	855
1942	Bad	Passé	-	-
1943	Good	Drinkable now/On its return	85.00	425
1944	Fair	On its return	57.00	285
1945	Top	Drinkable now	182.00	910
1946	Bad	Passé	-	-
1947	Top	Drinkable now	222.00	1110
1948	Very good	Drinkable now	100.00	500
1949	Top	Drinkable now	223.00	1115
1950	Fair	Passé	-	-
1951	Bad	Passé	-	-
1952	Good	Drinkable now	65.00	325
1953	Top	Drinkable now	130.00	650
1954	Bad	Passé	-	-
1955	Good	Drinkable now	97.00	485
1956	Bad	Passé	-	-
1957	Fair	Drinkable now	51.00	255
1958	Fair	On its return	30.00	150
1959	Top	Drinkable now	139.00	695
1960	Fair	On its return/Passé	29.00	145
1961	Top	Drinkable now	184.00	920
1962	Good	Drinkable now	60.00	300
1963	Bad	Passé	-	-
1964	Good	Drinkable now	49.00	245
1965	Bad	Passé	-	-
1966	Very good	Drinkable now	78.00	390
1967	Fair	Drinkable now	34.00	170
1968	Bad	Passé	-	-
1969	Fair	Drinkable now	29.00	145
1970	Top	Drinkable now	75.00	375
1971	Good	Drinkable now/On its return	33.00	165
1972	Bad	Passé	14.00	70
1973	Fair	On its return	25.00	125
1974	Bad	Drinkable now/On its return	23.00	115
1975	Good	Drinkable now	54.00	270
1976	Good	Drinkable now	39.00	195
1977	Fair	On its return	19.00	95
1978	Very good	Drinkable now	57.00	285
1979	Good	Drinkable now	39.00	195
1980	Fair	Drinkable now	25.00	125
1981	Good	Drinkable now	38.00	190
1982	Top	Do not drink yet/Drinkable now	77.00	385
1983	Very good	Do not drink yet/Drinkable now	43.00	215
1984	Fair	Drinkable now	26.00	130
1985	Very good	Do not drink yet	50.00	250
1986	Very good	Do not drink yet	48.00	240
1987	Fair	Drinkable now	27.00	135
1988	Very good	Do not drink yet	39.00	195
1989	Very good	Do not drink yet	44.00	220
1990	Good	Do not drink yet	46.00	230
1991	Fair	Do not drink yet	27.00	135
1992	Fair	Do not drink yet	22.00	110
1993	Good	Do not drink yet	23.00	115

Category III
Château Figeac, St.-Emilion, 1er Grand Cru Classé B
Château Gruaud-Larose, Saint-Julien, 2me Cru
Château Léoville-Barton, Saint-Julien, 2me Cru
Château Calon-Ségur, Saint-Estèphe, 3me Cru
Château Talbot, Saint-Julien, 4me Cru
Château Léoville-Poyferré, Saint-Julien, 2me Cru
Château La Tour Haut-Brion, Talence, Grand Cru Cl. Graves
Château Le Bon Pasteur, Pomerol
Château Giscours, Labarde, 3me Cru
Château Belair, Saint-Emilion, 1er Grand Cru Classé B
Château Beauséjour (Duffau-Lagarrosse), Saint-Emilion
Château d'Armailhac, Pauillac, 5me Cru
Château Boyd-Cantenac, Margaux, 3me Cru
Château Branaire-Ducru, Saint-Julien, 4me Cru
Château Brane-Cantenac, Margaux, 2me Cru
Château Cantemerle, Macau, 5me Cru
Château Cantenac-Brown, Cantenac, 3me Cru
Château Clerc Milon, Pauillac, 5me Cru
Château Duhart-Milon-Rothschild, Pauillac, 4me Cru
Château La Gaffelière, Saint-Emilion, 1er Gr. Cru Classé B
Château Grand-Puy-Lacoste, Pauillac, 5me Cru
Château Haut-Bailly, Léognan, Grand Cru Classé de Graves
Château Langoa-Barton, Saint-Julien, 3me Cru
Château Rausan-Ségla, Margaux, 2me Cru
Château Saint Pierre, Saint-Julien, 4me Cru
Château Trotte Vieille, Saint-Emilion, 1er Gr. Cru Classé B
Château Haut-Batailley, Pauillac, 5me Cru
Château d'Issan, Cantenac, 3me Cru
Château Lagrange, Saint-Julien, 3me Cru
Château Lascombes, Margaux, 2me Cru
Château La Lagune, Ludon, 3me Cru
Château Marquis de Terme, Margaux, 4me Cru
Château Rauzan-Gassies, Margaux, 2me Cru
Château Beau-Séjour - Bécot, Saint-Emilion, 1er Gr. Cru B
Château Prieuré-Lichine, Cantenac, 4me Cru
Château Smith-Haut-Lafitte, Martillac, Gr. Cru Cl. Graves

Category III - Value and Quality Indications for Vintages

Vintage	Quality	Stage of Development	Value Indication U.S. $	F. frs
1928	Top	On its return	157.00	785
1929	Top	On its return	302.00	1510
1930/31/32	Bad	Passé	-	-
1933	Fair	Passé	-	-
1934	Good	On its return	77.00	385
1935	Bad	Passé	-	-
1936	Fair	Passé	-	-
1937	Fair	Passé	57.00	285
1938	Bad	Passé	-	-
1939	Bad	Passé	-	-
1940	Fair	On its return	54.00	270
1941	Fair	On its return	54.00	270
1942	Bad	Passé	-	-
1943	Good	On its return	63.00	315
1944	Fair	On its return	51.00	255
1945	Top	On its return	153.00	765
1946	Bad	Passé	-	-
1947	Top	On its return	119.00	595
1948	Very good	On its return	82.00	410
1949	Top	Drinkable now	100.00	500
1950	Fair	Passé	-	-
1951	Bad	Passé	-	-
1952	Good	Drinkable now	86.00	430
1953	Top	On its return	57.00	285
1954	Bad	Passé	-	-
1955	Good	Drinkable now/On its return	57.00	285
1956	Bad	Passé	-	-
1957	Fair	Drinkable now/On its return	33.00	165
1958	Fair	Passé	26.00	130
1959	Top	Drinkable now/On its return	77.00	385
1960	Fair	Passé	-	-
1961	Top	Drinkable now	86.00	430
1962	Good	Drinkable now/On its return	41.00	205
1963	Bad	Passé	-	-
1964	Good	Drinkable now	43.00	215
1965	Bad	Passé	-	-
1966	Very good	Drinkable now	60.00	300
1967	Fair	Drinkable now/On its return	31.00	155
1968	Bad	Passé	-	-
1969	Fair	Drinkable now/On its return	16.00	80
1970	Top	Drinkable now	46.00	230
1971	Good	Drinkable now/On its return	26.00	130
1972	Bad	Passé	13.00	65
1973	Fair	On its return	21.00	105
1974	Bad	On its return	14.00	70
1975	Good	Drinkable now	37.00	185
1976	Good	Drinkable now	27.00	135
1977	Fair	On its return	16.00	80
1978	Very good	Drinkable now	35.00	175
1979	Good	Drinkable now	30.00	150
1980	Fair	On its return	17.00	85
1981	Good	Drinkable now	29.00	145
1982	Top	Drinkable now	46.00	230
1983	Very good	Drinkable now	31.00	155
1984	Fair	Drinkable now	21.00	105
1985	Very good	Drinkable now	30.00	150
1986	Very good	Do not drink yet	33.00	165
1987	Fair	Drinkable now	21.00	105
1988	Very good	Do not drink yet	30.00	150
1989	Very good	Do not drink yet	28.00	140
1990	Good	Do not drink yet	30.00	150
1991	Fair	Do not drink yet	19.00	95
1992	Fair	Do not drink yet	17.00	85
1993	Good	Do not drink yet	18.00	90

Category IV
Château Durfort-Vivens, Margaux, 2me Cru
Château Kirwan, Cantenac, 3me Cru
Château Chasse-Spleen, Moulis, Cru Bourgeois
Château Gloria, Saint-Julien, Cru Bourgeois
Château Malescot Saint-Exupéry, Margaux, 3me Cru
Clos Fourtet, Saint-Emilion, 1er Gr. Cru Classé B
Château Marquis d'Alesme-Becker, Margaux, 3me Cru
Château Desmirail, Margaux, 3me Cru
Château Pontet-Canet, Pauillac, 5me Cru
Château Batailley, Pauillac, 5me Cru
Château Lafon-Rochet, Saint-Estèphe, 4me Cru
Château du Tertre, Margaux, 5me Cru
Château Pouget, Cantenac, 4me Cru
Château Malartic-Lagravière, Léognan, Gr. Cru Cl. Graves
Château Grand-Puy-Ducasse, Pauillac, 5me Cru
Château Haut-Bages Libéral, Pauillac, 5me Cru
Château La Tour Martillac, Martillac, Gr. Cru Cl. de Graves
Château Lynch-Moussas, Pauillac, 5me Cru
Château Dauzac, Margaux, 5me Cru
Château Cos Labory, Saint-Estèphe, 5me Cru
Château La Tour Carnet, Saint-Laurent, 4me Cru
Château Belgrave, Saint-Laurent, 5me Cru
Château Bouscaut, Léognan Grand Cru Classé de Graves
Château Camensac, Saint-Laurent, 5me Cru
Château Croizet-Bages, Pauillac, 5me Cru
Château Carbonnieux, Léognan, Grand Cru Classé de Graves
Château Olivier, Léognan, Grand Cru Classé de Graves
Château Pédesclaux, Pauillac, 5me Cru
Château Ferrière, Margaux, 3me Cru

Category IV - Value and Quality Indications for Vintages

Vintage	Quality	Stage of Development	Value Indication U.S. $	F. frs
1928	Top	On its return	100.00	500
1929	Top	On its return	100.00	500
1930/31/32	Bad	Passé	-	-
1933	Fair	Passé	-	-
1934	Good	On its return	57.00	285
1935	Bad	Passé	-	-
1936	Fair	Passé	-	-
1937	Fair	Passé	-	-
1938	Bad	Passé	-	-
1939	Bad	Passé	-	-
1940	Fair	On its return	43.00	215
1941	Fair	On its return	43.00	215
1942	Bad	Passé	-	-
1943	Good	On its return	49.00	245
1944	Fair	On its return	37.00	185
1945	Top	On its return	71.00	355
1946	Bad	Passé	-	-
1947	Top	On its return	57.00	285
1948	Very good	On its return	34.00	170
1949	Top	Drinkable now	86.00	430
1950	Fair	Passé	-	-
1951	Bad	Passé	-	-
1952	Good	On its return	43.00	215
1953	Top	On its return	57.00	285
1954	Bad	Passé	-	-
1955	Good	On its return	63.00	315
1956	Bad	Passé	-	-
1957	Fair	On its return	31.00	155
1958	Fair	Passé	-	-
1959	Top	On its return	40.00	200
1960	Fair	Passé	-	-
1961	Top	Drinkable now	79.00	395
1962	Good	On its return	51.00	255
1963	Bad	Passé	-	-
1964	Good	On its return	33.00	165
1965	Bad	Passé	-	-
1966	Very good	Drinkable now	32.00	160
1967	Fair	On its return	23.00	115
1968	Bad	Passé	-	-
1969	Fair	On its return	11.00	55
1970	Top	Drinkable now	27.00	135
1971	Good	On its return	25.00	125
1972	Bad	Passé	-	-
1973	Fair	Passé	14.00	70
1974	Bad	On its return	9.00	45
1975	Good	Drinkable now	26.00	130
1976	Good	Drinkable now	21.00	105
1977	Fair	On its return	11.00	55
1978	Very good	Drinkable now	25.00	125
1979	Good	Drinkable now	23.00	115
1980	Fair	On its return	11.00	55
1981	Good	Drinkable now	20.00	100
1982	Top	Drinkable now	27.00	135
1983	Very good	Drinkable now	23.00	115
1984	Fair	Drinkable now	13.00	65
1985	Very good	Drinkable now	25.00	125
1986	Very good	Do not drink yet	23.00	115
1987	Fair	Drinkable now	12.00	60
1988	Very good	Do not drink yet	22.00	110
1989	Very good	Do not drink yet	23.00	115
1990	Good	Do not drink yet	23.00	115
1991	Fair	Do not drink yet	15.00	75
1992	Fair	Do not drink yet	14.00	70
1993	Good	Do not drink yet	15.00	75

Grand Cru in Use

Which wines are and which aren't sound? Considered on the basis of data per château.

Assessment score
The most essential factor for determining just how sound a wine is, is the quality, or rather the assessment score. It doesn't matter how low the price might be, if the wine has an insufficient standard of quality it is never a good buy. It only makes sense to relate quality and price with wines that have a rating of 12 points and upwards.
An example: a 1987 Pavie good for 13 points with a market value of U.S. $ 25.50 (122 F. frs) per bottle is for that price not sound. However, should this wine be offered for U.S. $ 12.00 (58 F. frs) per bottle then it is a very good buy.

Market value
In a few cases you will find that the market value is significantly higher than the price the wine merchant on the corner is asking.
What is the reason for this and are those wines always sound? To start with, the reason behind those often differ considerably. The route the Grands Crus cover before reaching the consumer is important.

According to the traditional distribution pattern, the wine is taken from the producer to the mercantile house in Bordeaux from where it is shipped to the importer. The next step is shipment to the wholesaler and then on to the wine merchant or restaurant, finally ending its journey on the table of the consumer. It goes without saying that the source of this chain of distribution, together with the first link, has the greatest insight into supply and demand. It is at the source that the actual value of a wine is determined, because that is where the demand is concentrated. It is also the place where, in the short term, sizable fluctuations in price could take place. For example, if prospects for the new harvest are unfavorable, then the owner of the château either locks his cellar or raises his prices. These price increases are not immediately felt further along the chain however. Thus an importer can maintain his price-list for six months, which also has an impact on the sub-

sequent links in the chain of distribution.
So it can happen that Grands Crus might occasionally be bought more economically at their final destination than at the château itself.

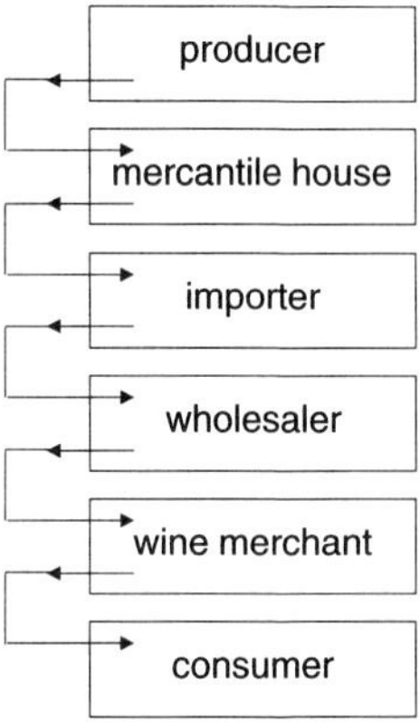

```
producer
   ↓↑
mercantile house
   ↓↑
importer
   ↓↑
wholesaler
   ↓↑
wine merchant
   ↓↑
consumer
```

Chain of distribution

Should you buy the wine from a wine merchant whose prices are based on the replacement value, then the price will vary according to his profit margin.
However, a little market research of a couple of wine merchants or liquor stores should be undertaken before deciding to buy. Should one of the links in the chain of distribution not base the calculations on the replacement value, but adjust his cost price once-only by a fixed margin, there is a chance that you will be able to buy even below the replacement value, or the market value in Bordeaux.

Wine as an Investment

A constant rise in value over a long period of time inspires confidence and attracts investors and speculators. At the beginning of the seventies the wine prices rose so sharply that quite a few speculators fell under the spell of wine. Just like other commodities, stocks or real-estate, wine was regarded as a safe, stable investment.

The oil crisis of 1972 brought with it a drastic change. Wine prices plummeted along with the stock market. This 'crash' had disastrous consequences for the wine market, especially in Bordeaux. Large lots of wine were dumped at auctions all over the world. In 1973, as a result of the speculators' massive flight from this newly discovered commodity, the traditional Bordeaux market was left out in the cold.

For a long time, in the period known in wine circles as the 'Bordeaux Crisis', the most celebrated wines were disposed of at cost price. Only at the end of 1975, at the same time as the introduction of the good quality 1975 vintage,
did things change. The speculators who dared invest in wine around 1975 and even up to five years later, managed to realize a nice return. However, since the 1982 harvest, the moment when the price drop of the Bordeaux crisis underwent a correction, investment in wine has barely offered any perspective for speculators.

The producers who used to offer wine connoisseurs a considerable discount in Première Tranche on their young wines have changed their policy.

Because of their cozy financial position, they no longer need advance sales as a source for financing the latest vintage. They continue to sell in Première Tranche, but at prices 20 to 30% higher than in the past.

These high prices reduce the opportunities for profit on the part of speculators. An investment in Grands Crus with the aim of making a profit is not advisable at this time. However, this is just the personal opinion of the author. Undoubtedly, there will be people willing to take a risk. We list a number of factors hereafter which should be kept in mind when making such an investment.

Which wines are suitable?

Throughout the world there is a greater variety of wines than there are stocks to buy. The success of the venture rests with the right choice of stock. How ever great the offer of wine might be, the choice of suitable wine for investment purposes is extremely limited. A choice limited to the wine region in France, Bordeaux, where the market structure offers wine a chance as a commodity. Once one realizes that only 5% of the total wine production of Bordeaux lends itself for such an investment, then it will be clear just how narrow the base is of this fashionable commodity. When making a choice out of that five percent of Bordeaux wines, a number of criteria should be borne in mind. They are:
a. Name recognition of the château;
b. Reputation of the vintage;
c. Quality and cellar life of the wine.

In the selection of the château, it is safest to pick one of the five Premiers Crus. These wines classified in Category I may be viewed as the main funds. The wines with a lower classification will constitute the less current funds.

The first criterion name recognition of the château is the most important when one has to decide on the investment of capital. This guide provides a classification of Grands Crus according to name recognition (see the chapter on value indication).

Negative issues for speculators

As stated, the fast growing issue prices, the Première Tranche* prices, further reduce the opportunities for profit with regard to recent harvests. In addition, the small allocations by the châteaux per country continue to make it difficult to invest in wine. Take for example Château Latour: only a few hundred cases (of 12 bottles each) are made available for the Netherlands at a relatively attractive initial price. If you insist on buying more, the purchase price will increase drastically, further reducing any opportunity for profit. Accordingly, wine is not an option for small investors.

Finally, when you go to Bordeaux to sell, you will find that the local merchants are not very inclined to buy back the wine, especially if only a few cases are involved. A sale will go smoothly only with a discount of at least 25% on the current quotation. Indeed, sales in old vintages are very limited in Bordeaux. Bordeaux quotations are often simply prices on paper.

The question remains as to whether any profit will be left after a 25% discount. Although 5 years ago an investment in wine could lead to a handsome profit, it is now a rather doubtful venture. The high Première Tranche prices at which the châteaux are currently selling their young wine means that the producers are pocketing the profits themselves. Speculators have do make do with what's left.

Profit opportunities for "investors in pleasure"

Considering the exceptionally high prices of the Bordeaux 1ers Crus, this sector is not very attractive from the point of view of investing in pleasure. The wines with a lower classification offer better perspectives at this point in time. Their quality/price ratio is very favorable.

The most suitable wines for investors in pleasure are Category IV wines at Première Tranche prices. These are often wines of the same quality level as the much more expensive Categories I and II. Category IV offers "investors in pleasure" a reasonable quality/price ratio, and includes also a nice increase in value.

* Première Tranche
Typical for Bordeaux wines, and especially for the Grands Crus, is that the châteaux sell their wines long before delivery can take place. It is a somewhat strange way of doing things, a function with origins in the trade's long history. Originally the Grands Crus were delivered in the barrel and shipped the moment fermentation had been completed, about 6 months after the harvest. The châteaux put some of their wines on the market. This first offer was referred to as Première Tranche which is a term and sales technique that in spite of changed circumstances is still in use today.

At the end of the fifties most Grands Crus started bottling for themselves, but the habit of bringing their 'Première Tranche' on to the market after the second fermentation stuck. The châteaux undertake to bottle and care for the wine. They reserve the right for final responsibility for their product, thereby preventing a great deal of tampering with the wine and misuse of the reputation of the Grands Crus.

Until recently, there has always been a difference of 30% or more between the Première Tranche price and the price at which the wine was later offered on the market. Now that this difference no longer exists, opportunities for making a successful investment in wines have dwindled considerably.

Wine Auctions

As the information given in this Grand Cru guide is partly directed at being able to determine the value of wines, on the basis of which a well-founded decision of whether to buy or sell may be made, information is also given about a somewhat unusual distribution channel, the wine auction. A distribution channel not so well known, but which in some instances can be useful.

Advantages and disadvantages of auctions

Advantages
As a distribution channel for old wines, which are not to be found in the production region or in the trade, auctions offer a solution for the buyer as well as for the seller.
Auctions are especially interesting for the collector looking for that rare bottle. For the well-informed wine connoisseur there is always the chance that he will run up against good wine under the market value.

Disadvantages
If one buys without tasting first, there is a risk that the wines have been cellared badly or that they are on their return.
Auctions give no guarantees on wines. The reputable auction houses are of course open to complaints, which should be submitted within a very short time (at the most three weeks after the wine has been released for collection). The specialized wine auctions often have experts who, during logging, can refuse bottles they don't trust.
Buying at an auction is very often time consuming; for some a problem, for others a hobby and a pleasant pastime. Finally: It goes without saying that the advantages mentioned here for the buyer are the disadvantages for the seller. The reverse is of course also true.

Auctions at home or abroad

From the comparison of prices at different auctions it would appear that there is hardly any difference. The prices obtained for Category IV wines are slightly lower in London, but additional costs (transport, excise, import tariffs) are not worth the trouble of making the trip to London. Only for the very exclusive, old Grands Crus is London the right place.

Selling at auctions

The seller often telephones the auction house first. Depending upon the size of the lot an expert from the auction house will pay a visit to the seller, or the seller will be requested to bring the wine to the auction house.

The key question then of course is: what amount were you thinking of. The organizer of the auction naturally wants a free hand in this. The higher the limit is set, the less chance there is of bringing the transaction to a successful conclusion. The prices realized in the past could serve as an indication. The person who sets too high a limit and still wants his wine to be listed, will have a service charge of 5% if the wine is not sold. Should the wines be sold, then the auction costs amount to 10% of the bid received at the auction.

An example follows of the final price you will receive for a wine submitted at auction. The example is based on 5 cases of wine, converted to a price per bottle. Suppose that on the wine brought in by you a bid is made of 50 F. frs per bottle, then you would receive:

Bid	F. frs 50
10% Auction Fee	5
If you bring the wine to the auction house, you receive:	F. frs 45
Projected cost of delivery, (per bottle)	5
You receive per bottle	F. frs 40
In U.S. $ (exchange rate 4.8)	$ 8.33

Buying at auctions

First obtain a copy of the log of the wines to be auctioned. Reading and studying the log well is already half the work of buying the wine. If you have doubts call the auction house beforehand for extra information.

What does a bottle cost bought at an auction house? Added to your bid should be 10% auction costs and the administration costs at the distribution center.

Suppose you buy a lot of 5 cases of 12 bottles, for which you bid 50 F. frs per bottle. What would a bottle have actually cost?

Your bid	F. frs 50
10% auction fee	5
Administration cost	1
Picked up by you at the auction house	F. frs 56
Cost of delivery to you	4
Your cost per bottle	F. frs 60
In U.S. $ (exchange rate 4.8)	$ 12.50

Changed conditions at Christie's, London

Since 1986, selling at the London auction house has become more interesting because Christie has lowered its commission from 15% to 10%. Further reductions have been promised for large orders and interesting lots. In addition, clients who offer wines for sale in the fall will enjoy a reduction in premium. On the other hand, a 10% buyer's premium has been introduced which did not exist before. The idea is to streamline the selling of wine with other departments of the house and with practices at other auctions, e.g., at the competitor, Sotheby's.

Analytical Tasting

'There's no accounting for tastes'. Many people ask themselves to what extent wine assessment can be objective. In the first instance, objectivity and taste assessments cannot be reconciled. An objective appraisal of a wine is possible however, if two factors have been complied with: the assessment should be carried out according to a certain standard and further it should be the average of a tasting panel consisting of at least three people. The clearest standard is that of the analytical tasting, a tasting during which wine is 'analyzed' and assessed on its basic flavors. Moreover, the tasting panel should consist of several people so as to be able to overcome the small differences in taste each one of us has by nature.

Knowledge of the basic flavors
Many people find it unbelievable that differences of opinion exist over even the four basic flavors. The celebrated oenologist, Professor Emile Peynaud, associated with the University of Bordeaux, takes a different view. When talking of tastes he is one of the greatest supporters of authenticity. He starts his lectures, mainly attended by professionals, with the tasting of distilled water. It isn't a tasteless joke, because it shows just what tasteless is. Following this test he doses distilled water with various basic flavors. His reasoning being that it only makes sense to discuss tastes with others after the basics have been agreed upon.

The basic flavors

Sweet
An easy concept not needing much expansion. If you can imagine eating a large mouthful of sugar, then you are thinking in the right direction. Recognizing sweetness in combination with other basic flavors isn't quite so easy as it sounds. It is relatively easy to recognize sweetness in white wines, the sweetness comes chiefly in combination with sourness, for example in German Elzasser and Sautern wines. With dry red wine this taste is more difficult to trace because sweetness is not only combined with a dose of sourness, but also with bitterness which makes the taste of sweetness very distorted,

especially because of the bitterness. Yet an amount of sweetness lies at the base of all red wines, sweetness which is mostly concealed in the alcohol. A wine with a lot of sweetness is experienced as round, supple and smooth.

Professor Emile Peynaud has created a special term for the factors that determine the harmony of the wine: 'l'indice de souplesse'. The higher the 'indice de souplesse', the milder, rounder and easier the red wine will taste.

Sour

Even the thought of squeezing a yellow-green lemon and taking a big gulp of the juice makes your mouth water. A demonstration of the absolute sour taste. This is a basic taste that most people experience as unpleasant but it is a necessary element in all wines. Apart from the fact that acid is a natural preservative, it gives the wines their freshness. For producers of white wine, finding a good harmony between sweet and sour is the key to success.

Bitter

A taste experienced when you bite into an apple seed or raw endive. A taste which makes your mouth pucker, that you even feel in your gums. The saliva production slows down as soon as the 'bitter taste buds' are activated, making you thirsty, which explains the thirst you can have after a dinner where a lot of red Bordeaux wines were poured.

Salt

A taste almost unknown in wine, yet it is a basic flavor of great importance in the combination wine and food. Just like other basic flavors salt, in a concentrated form (straight from the salt-cellar) is unpleasant, but is a flavor that, provided it is dosed correctly, may be added to almost all dishes. It is the catalytic agent which accentuates other flavors by its presence. This basic flavor brings out clarity and brilliance in many wines.

Harmonization of basic flavors in wine

As mentioned sweetness, sourness and bitterness complement each other. Together they form a unity - the wine.
In the wines you buy the flavors are present in various degrees. You will not find a wine with too much or too little of any one of the three basic flavors in the shops.

The decisive factor of whether or not the wine will be good is the harmony in which the three basic flavors are represented in that wine. The broader, deeper and more intense those three flavors seem and the better interwoven they are, the higher the quality of the wine. The more attention you pay to those basic flavors during tasting, the more you will begin to recognize them.

Depth and intensity

To arrive at a pleasant combination of wine and food it is important to know, along with some knowledge of the basic flavors, if the wine comes from a good, fair or a bad harvest. The degrees by which the basic flavors are represented in a wine are dependent upon the success of the harvest and the selection made by the producer. In good wine years, the dry sunny years, the juice of the grapes is more concentrated. The range of sugar (alcohol), acids and tannin (bitter) is much broader in wines of top years. Such wines are richer, deeper, heavier and more intense. Wines from top years could be the wrong choice for light, refined dishes. Choosing an elegant wine to go with a light dish, that's art.

A well thought-out wine list or cellar should also offer a broad choice of the lesser vintages. By only being able to choose from the great vintages, the harmony between food and wine will be at risk.
It is just the wines from the lesser vintages, with the good 'indice de souplesse' (harmony), which add refinement and subtlety to light dishes. Because of the present trend towards predominantly light and refined dishes, a good cellar cannot be imagined without the unremarkable vintages. Next to their somewhat lower alcohol percentage their price is often attractive too.

Old and young wines

Lastly, in connection with the depth and intensity of wines some information about the development phase follows. As you know it is often the wines of top vintages that try our patience. The three basic flavors appear in large quantities and are not yet 'married', giving an impression of discord in young wines from the best vintages. Because the alcohol, acids and tannins still manifest themselves individually, the wines taste unpleasant. Especially the tannin is overpowering. During the ripening process the bitterness of those tannins is absorbed by the acids.
This is rounded off with the wine alcohol and left-over sugars so that the wine finally develops the harmony desired. By combining food and wine well it is possible to lengthen and shorten the period of drinkability.
Should you serve a wine that is a little too young, that is still a little bitter with a piquant, slightly salty cheese then you will notice that the bitter taste of the wine disappears. The

reverse is true for the wine that is a little too ripe. Because the tannins and acids are already too far resolved, such wines lack the power to hold their own against other tastes. By serving such an over-aged wine with a creamy, light and neutral cheese the wine is raised once more to its high standard.

Wine jargon

A concise summary of wine vocabulary, stemming from basic flavors and intensities:

Sweet in a positive sense
round
full
ripe
supple
muscled
charming
velvety
meaty
honeylike
creamy
plump
sensual

Sweet in a negative sense
sweet
heavy
cumbersome
thick
sickly
chaptalized
shallow
feeble
anemic

Sour in a positive sense
fresh
fruity
sparkling
thoroughbred
elegant
nervous
light
spirited

Sour in a negative sense
sour
scrawny
green
aggressive
sharp
vinegar
thin
unripe

Bitter in a positive sense
firm
robust
tannic acid
tannin
cheeky
powerful
tight
manly
sturdy

Bitter in a negative sense
bitter
hard
wooden
sharp
surly
tough
raw
dried out

Intensity in a positive sense
deep
powerful
long
rich
wide
full palate
good substructure
generous
intense - corps, body, full

Intensity in a negative sense
thin
feeble
narrow
no substance
stinted
weak
short
flat
colorless

Grands Crus and Your Health

Medical science has known for some time that drinking wine reduces considerably the risk of cardiovascular disease. The beneficial effect of alcohol in the struggle against the principal cause of death has been demonstrated frequently. Besides alcohol, red wine contains other vasoconstrictive substances. The medical journal The Lancet published a long article on this phenomenon in 1993, which I will refer to later on.

But first I want to discuss some of the effects of alcohol on vasoconstriction. Alcohol inhibits both acute vasoconstriction (thrombosis) and slow vasoconstriction (atherosclerosis).

Alcohol and Thrombosis

Alcohol inhibits coagulation in the blood vessels, which combats thrombosis or acute constriction of the blood vessels. In addition, alcohol promotes the disposal of blood clots (called thrombolysis). To put it briefly in medical terms, alcohol lowers the risk of thrombosis by decreasing the stickiness of the blood platelets, reducing fibrinogen (a coagulation protein which is converted into fibrin during clotting) and, finally, by increasing fibrinolysis (the dissolution of fibrin).

I will not elaborate on the biochemical mechanisms involved.

Alcohol and Atherosclerosis

Alcohol also contributes to the battle against the slow constriction of blood vessels called atherosclerosis. Indeed, alcohol has a favorable effect on fat metabolism in the blood. Everyone knows that a high level of cholesterol in the blood increases the risk of cardiovascular disease. This is also true for a high level of saturated fatty acids (animal fat) in our diet.

The metabolic processes in our blood are very complex. The following is a highly simplified version of what actually happens. Fat (cholesterol and fatty acids) absorbed by our intestines from food is transported mainly through binding to proteins (indeed, fat is not soluble in water). These proteins the carriers of cholesterol belong to two groups:

- High-Density Lipoprotein (HDL), also called the "protective cholesterol";
- Low-Density Lipoprotein (LDL), also called the "harmful cholesterol".

Alcohol helps in two ways: it increases the "protective HDL cholesterol" and decreases the "harmful LDL cholesterol". HDL removes cholesterol from LDL and transports it to the liver from where it is secreted with the bile.

Why is LDL potentially harmful?

LDL may be damaged by oxidation. Macrophages, cells with a disposal function, take the damaged LDL and form "foam cells" in the vascular wall the first sign of atherosclerosis. Accumulation of these "foam cells" will lead to a thickening of the vascular wall and therefore a constriction of the blood vessel. The blood flow will be restricted. In turn, subtotal constriction can lead to coagulation due to a decrease in the blood flow, causing the blood vessel to close.

Damage of LDL through oxidation is often caused by free radicals (negatively charged molecules produced by the vascular wall, amongst others). The body is equipped with defensive mechanisms but these diminish with age. At the same time, the harmful effect of these radicals increases with age. They are partially to blame for the aging process. Substances which bind with these free radicals are important for the health of the blood vessels as we grow older. Vitamin E and beta carotene are natural substances which combat the oxidation effect of negatively charged molecules. It was recently discovered that some substances in red wine are even more effective than vitamin E.

LDL and red wine

These substances which are found in red wine have a strong inhibitory effect on LDL oxidation. They are different phenolic substances, including tannins and anthocyanins. Anthocyanins are the substances that give wine its red color. Thanks to the antioxidation properties of these non-alcoholic phenolic components, red wine may slow down the onset of atherosclerosis (The Lancet, vol. 341, Feb. 20, 1993).

This is a partial explanation of the "French paradox". Medical research has shown that relatively few people in France die from heart attacks caused by atherosclerosis of the coronary blood vessels, notwithstanding the copious and rich eating habits of the French. One explanation of this apparent contradiction is the high consumption of red wine in France.

How many glasses a day?

How many glasses of alcoholic beverages may we consume per day before the disadvantages outweigh the advantages? The curve used to describe alcohol consumption is U-shaped, with the lowest point corresponding to 2 to 4 glasses a day (see diagram). As far as the alcohol content is concerned, one glass of wine corresponds to 100 cl. Compared to other alcoholic beverages, the lowest point in the diagram is located probably more towards the right for red wine, and also a bit lower because of its antioxidation properties.

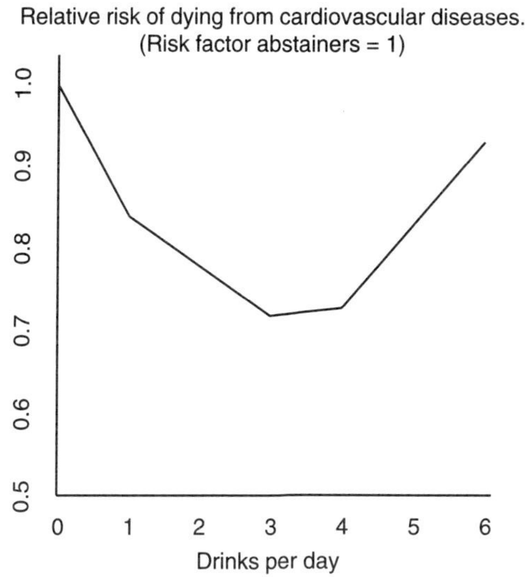

Relative risk of dying from cardiovascular diseases.
(Risk factor abstainers = 1)

The conclusion of our reflections is therefore (with a wink of the eye): the toast "to your health" may have extra meaning when we raise a glass filled with a beautiful Grand Cru. Indeed, most Grands Crus are deeply colored, concentrated wines with an abundance of phenolic substances.

T.Th.C. Overtoom, M.D. radiologist

Dr. Overtoom is radiologist in the biggest heart- and vessel hospital in the Netherlands (The St-Anthonius Hospital in Nieuwegein), where his main occupation is the treatment of vessel diseases such as stenosed and occluded vessels.

Top Ten 1993 - 1977

Top 10 Vintage 1993

In 1993, the vegetation cycle was almost perfect and there were expectations for a top harvest. However, hopes were dashed when it started to rain during the harvest. Nevertheless, the quality was often remarkably good. The grapes were fully ripe and because of their sturdy, thick skin they absorbed very little rain water and preserved their concentration. Because the Merlots ripen before the Cabernets, they could be harvested mainly before the rains started to fall.

The better 1993 wines have a solid color, nicely ripe tannins and a lot of fruit. The top wines are broad, roundly ripe wines with substance, soft tannins, fruit and a supple fullness. These are wines with a strong structure, depth and length.

The Merlot, which is always synonymous with creamy, gentle and elegant wines, adds this year the extra dimension of strength, meaty richness, depth and concentration.

To be remembered
- The 1993 vintage is of a good quality. It is not a top year but it has produced many good wines.
- 1993 is a Merlot year. In the Médoc, about 40% belongs to the better wines, in Saint-Emilion and Pomerol, the figure is 70%.
- The best Merlots are reminiscent of the 1985 vintage, while the top wines from the Médoc bring 1978 and 1988 to mind. Those of middling quality are comparable with the 1979 vintage.

The 10 best '93s in order of appreciation
Château Ausone, Saint-Emilion
Château Le Bon Pasteur, Pomerol
Château Cheval Blanc, Saint-Emilion
Château La Conseillante, Pomerol
Château Montrose, Saint-Estèphe
Château Mouton-Rothschild, Pauillac
Château Léoville-Las-Cases, Saint-Julien
Château Latour, Pauillac
Château Pichon-Longueville-Baron, Pauillac
Château De Fieuzal, Graves

Below the line
Château Croizet-Bages, Pauillac
Château Brane-Cantenac, Margaux
Château Rauzan-Gassies, Margaux
Château Boyd-Cantenac, Margaux
Château Giscours, Margaux
Château La Tour Carnet, Haut-Médoc

Top 10 Vintage 1992

Three records were broken in 1992: it was the wettest summer in fifty years with the fewest hours of sunshine since 1980 and the largest volume ever harvested. All three records are at odds with the concept of quality. In addition, the harvest month of October was wet and cold. The results were as might be expected: irregular blossoms, a slow and incomplete ripening of the grapes, followed by a rained-out and diluted harvest. What counted in 1992 was therefore a restriction of production and a strict selection of the harvest. The good 1992 wines were made in the vineyard, not in the cellar.

Only the better 1992 wines reach the 16 point mark. These are balanced, elegant wines which have a certain amount of body and a soft, ripe tannin structure, besides juicy fruit. They are comparable to the 1973 and 1969 vintages. They are followed immediately by a group of pleasant wines for quick consumption. These are light, succulent, supple and refined wines. Friendly lunch wines for the short term.

The wines which do not live up to their Grand Cru status in 1992 are insipid and thin, with a transparent red color and a lack of concentration. They are comparable with 1972 and 1965.

To be remembered
- 1992 is very inconsistent in quality. Only 10% of the harvest is worth the effort.
- The quality wines are found at producers who kept the harvest volume small by being selective and using only the best grapes for vinification.
- The 1992 differences in quality do not stop at the boundaries of the appellations. Nor are they linked to the grape species. There are good and bad wines everywhere.

The 10 best '92s in order of appreciation
Château Mouton-Rothschild, Pauillac
Château Léoville-Las-Cases, Saint-Julien
Château Cos d'Estournel, Saint-Estèphe
Château Latour, Pauillac
Château Pichon-Longueville-Comtesse de Lalande, Pauillac
Château Le Bon Pasteur, Pomerol
Château Haut-Brion, Graves
Château Cheval-Blanc, Saint-Emilion
Château Léoville-Poyferré, Saint-Julien
Château Talbot, Saint-Julien

Below the line
Château Rauzan-Gassies, Margaux
Château Durfort-Vivens, Margaux
Château Giscours, Margaux
Château Lascombes, Margaux
Château Rausan-Ségla, Margaux

Top 10 Vintage 1991

The night of April 20 to 21, 1991 was decisive for the volume of the 1991 vintage. A devastating night frost reduced the Bordeaux harvest by an average of 50%.
The second catastrophe for the 1991 wines was the weather at harvest time. Rain and cold are ideal conditions for mold. So-called Black Rot determined the quality of the 1991 wines for up to 80 to 90%. Although the color and intensity of most 1991 wines seem to suggest a top year, most of them do not really fulfill the promise of their color as far as their bouquet and flavor is concerned.
The majority of the 1991 wines lack balance in flavor due to an excess in acids and/or hard tannins.

Keep in mind
– 1991 is a very irregular vintage.
– The vintage is small in volume, 57% less than in 1990.
– The wines are drinkable early on, within one to two years, but do not keep long.
– The good wines with scores of 15/16 are supple, light and elegant. They are ideal lunch wines.

The 10 best '91s in order of appreciation
Château Mouton-Rothschild, Pauillac
Château Margaux, Margaux
Château Latour, Pauillac
Château La Lagune, Haut-Médoc
Château Cos d'Estournel, Saint-Estèphe
Château Lynch-Bages, Pauillac
Château Pichon-Longueville-Baron, Pauillac
Château Lafite-Rothschild, Pauillac
Château Léoville-Poyferré, Saint-Julien
Château Pontet-Canet, Pauillac

Below the line
Château Rauzan-Gassies, Margaux
Château La Tour Haut-Brion, Graves
Château La Tour Carnet, Haut-Médoc
Château Croizet-Bages, Pauillac
Château Ferrière, Margaux
Château Pédesclaux, Pauillac

Top 10 Vintage 1990

1990 has the ingredients for a top vintage: a record number of hours of sun, a record number of average temperatures, moderate precipitation, and very favorable weather during harvesting.
Two factors determine the quality of this vintage. The first is the overwhelmingly rich must and the high sugar content. The second factor is the large volume of the 1990 harvest. Many producers did not prune enough in the vineyards, so that the must which finally wound up in the fermentation tanks was insufficiently concentrated.

Because the first factor had a positive effect on the quality while the second had a negative effect, the total picture for the 1990 vintage is irregular.
The successful '90s, the wines with scores of 17 and higher, are deep in color, very broad-based and will keep a long time. They invite comparison with the 1976, 1982 and 1986 vintages.

Other 1990, on the other hand, are also deep in color, but the color seems to promise more structure, grain, depth and content than the wines actually possess. Many wines lack fresh, crisp fruit acids and structure. The lack of structure points to an excessive production per acre, causing quality to be sacrificed to volume.

Keep in mind
– 10 to 15% of the wines is of top quality
– The top wines age well.
– The Grands Crus of the Graves score relatively high.
– The wines with a score of 16 and lower are drinkable early on.

The 10 best '90s in order of appreciation
Château De Fieuzal, Graves
Château Pichon-Longueville-Baron, Pauillac
Château Cheval-Blanc, Saint-Emilion
Château Lynch-Bages, Pauillac
Château Léoville-Las-Cases, Saint-Julien
Château Margaux, Margaux
Château Belair, Saint-Emilion
Château Bouscaut, Graves
Château Cantenac-Brown, Margaux
Château Grand-Puy Lacoste, Pauillac

Below the line
Château Haut-Batailley, Pauillac
Château Camensac, Haut-Médoc

Top 10 Vintage 1989

Like 1990, 1989 was a record year as far as the vegetation cycle is concerned. High average temperatures and low precipitation were typical for the growing season. The harvest took place under excellent weather conditions and was completed on September 26, a date on which in other years the harvest often hasn't even started. The grapes were extremely rich, almost perfect, with an excellent must and tannin contents, and sufficient acids. Irregular ripening occurred in a number of vineyards, and the high production per acre affected the quality of a number of Grand Crus in a negative sense.

Although the conditions for a record year were present for all the Grands Crus, only 25% of the wines managed to produce a quality which can equal the '61 wines or may be qualified as "the vintage of the century". These are Grands Crus which score 17 points or more.

Keep in mind
- Cabernet and Merlot score equally high.
- 1989 was an overripe vintage which required great technical know-how on the part of the wine producers.
- 25% of the '89s is of top level and will keep a long time.
- Most of the '89s will keep less long and will be drinkable earlier.

The 10 best '89s in order of appreciation
Château Pétrus, Pomerol
Château Haut-Brion, Graves
Château Mouton-Rothschild, Pauillac
Château Pichon-Longueville-Baron, Pauillac
Château Talbot, Saint-Julien
Château Lynch-Bages, Pauillac
Château La Conseillante, Pomerol
Château La Mission Haut-Brion, Graves
Château Ausone, Saint-Emilion
Château De Fieuzal, Graves

Below the line
No real failures or wines scoring 13 points or less.

Top 10 Vintage 1988

Apart from the spring of 1988 which was particularly rainy, the vegetation cycle for this vintage exceeded expectations. From August through November, weather conditions in Bordeaux were optimal. The splendid weather during harvesting yielded overripe grapes. The must was sound, with a lot of grape sugar and tannins. The heat at harvest time caused problems for some châteaux. The wines scoring 14 points or less are not properly balanced although they are well-structured. Only those producers who were capable of controlling the temperature during fermentation succeeded in making top wines, in which the excess of soft tannins agrees harmoniously with the wealth in fruit and alcohol.

Keep in mind
- 1988 is a real year for aging.
- The Merlot and Cabernet reach the same high level of quality.
- The quality of the Grands Crus in the Graves is a touch better than in the rest of the Bordeaux region.

The 10 best '88s in order of appreciation
Château Mouton-Rothschild, Pauillac
Château Lynch-Bages, Pauillac
Château Pétrus, Pomerol
Château Pape Clément, Graves
Château Pichon-Longueville-Baron, Pauillac
Château Pichon-Longueville-Comtesse de Lalande, Pauillac
Château La Mission Haut-Brion, Graves
Château Gruaud-Larose, Saint-Julien
Château Talbot, Saint-Julien
Château Lafite-Rothschild, Pauillac

Below the line
Château La Tour Carnet, Saint-Laurent
Château Latour Martillac, Graves
Château Ferrière, Margaux
Château Lascombes, Margaux
Château Croizet-Bages, Pauillac
Château Kirwan, Margaux

Top 10 Vintage 1987

The stars under which the 1987 vintage was born pointed to a minor vintage. This is entirely due to the vegetation cycle which was characterized by a cold spring and a predominantly wet summer. Although the extremely hot month of September revived hopes for a good harvest, thick clouds gathered over Bordeaux during October, the harvest month, and a lot of rain fell. The extremely hot month of September caused the grapes to grow a thick skin, so that the '87s received overall a very promising color. However, though the color creates expectations of intensity and structure, this is precisely what is lacking in most '87s. As a result, the 1987 wines are light and elegant wines which are ready for drinking early on. Thanks to the enormous improvement in vinification during the last decade, many impeccable and acceptable wines were produced in 1987, notwithstanding the poor quality of the must.

Keep in mind
- '87s are light wines ready for drinking early on.
- As far as quality is concerned, '87s may be compared to '84s and in the best cases to '73s.
- The wines will keep for a limited time, maximum 10 years.
- 1987 offers many proper wines, impeccable because of good vinification, but it is absolutely not a top year.
- *N.B.* Midway through 1995: most of the 1987 wines have completely matured and are ready for drinking. Enjoy them now before the quality curve turns downward.

The 10 best '87s in order of appreciation
Château Pétrus, Pomerol
Château Margaux, Margaux
Château Pichon-Longueville-Baron, Pauillac
Château Lynch-Bages, Pauillac
Château Mouton-Rothschild, Pauillac
Château Léoville-Las-Cases, Saint-Julien
Château Léoville-Poyferré, Saint-Julien
Château Cos d'Estournel, Saint-Estèphe
Château La Lagune, Haut-Médoc
Château Ausone, Saint-Emilion

Below the line
Château Rauzan-Gassies, Margaux
Château Dauzac, Margaux
Château Lynch-Moussas, Pauillac
Château Du Tertre, Margaux

Top 10 Vintage 1986

The vegetation cycle for the 1986 harvest went without problem until mid-September when a sudden end came to the stable weather. The grapes were already ripe and that the volume of the 1986 harvest would be considerable was also certain. The producers who had anticipated the fickle weather made good to excellent wines. In addition, with the large volume of the 1986 harvest, the success of the selection depended on the producers themselves. The châteaux who let nature take its course and eliminated neither in the vineyard nor in the cellar, grapes respectively barrels, did not fair so well. The '86s are liberal in their tannins and have a low degree of acidity. They have a deep color. The aging texture of the Crus with 15 points and more is very promising.

Keep in mind
- The best '86s are to be found high up in the Médoc.
- The large volume has watered down much of the quality, especially in Saint-Emilion and Pomerol.
- The high degree of tannin makes the '86 Cabernets sturdy and gives long cellaring potential.
- The '86 Merlots have less cellaring potential.

The 10 best '86s in order of appreciation
Château Margaux, Margaux
Château Mouton-Rothschild, Pauillac
Château Lynch-Bages, Pauillac
Château Pétrus, Pomerol
Château Pichon-Longueville-Baron, Pauillac
Château Pontet-Canet, Pauillac
Château Cheval-Blanc, Saint-Emilion
Château Lafite-Rothschild, Pauillac
Château Pichon-Longueville-Comtesse de Lalande, Pauillac
Château Cos d'Estournel, Saint-Estèphe

Below the line
Château Carbonnieux, Léognan
Château La Tour Carnet, Saint-Laurent

Top 10 Vintage 1985

The weather circumstances under which the 1985 harvest took form were perfect. From the moment the buds showed in April until the moment of harvest the weather gods were extremely well-disposed towards this crop. Characteristic for this vintage is therefore great consistency in the quality which can be said of the entire Bordeaux region.

The Merlot producers had a small advantage from the exceptional vegetation cycle. This very sensitive grape, usually a disrupting influence on the quality front, was perfectly ripe and healthy in 1985. The '85 Crus, especially the Crus with a big percentage of Merlot on the base, are luxurious, robust and round.

Seen as a whole the '85 is a very successful Bordeaux vintage, although the vintage provided only a limited number of wines which scored 19 points; percentage-wise a little disappointing. With such a perfect vegetation cycle the number of real toppers should be much higher. That quality cannot be pinned down to any particular "mathematical" formula is proved by this harvest. Wine remains an unpredictable product of nature.

Keep in mind
- The best '85s can be found at the châteaux with cool cellars, i.e., with equipment with which the high temperatures during harvest can be regulated.
- In the top wines, Merlot and Cabernet are alike.
- In the middleclass wines, Merlot has a little advantage over the Cabernet.
- Many '85s will be drinkable from 1990/95 onward. The top wines should be kept till 2010 or beyond.

The 10 best '85s in order of appreciation
Château Lynch-Bages, Pauillac
Château Margaux, Margaux
Château Mouton-Rothschild, Pauillac
Château De Fieuzal, Graves
Vieux Château Certan, Pomerol
Château Cheval Blanc, Saint-Emilion
Château Pichon-Longueville-Comtesse de Lalande, Pauillac
Château Pétrus, Pomerol
Château Lafite-Rothschild, Pauillac
Château Lagrange, Saint-Julien

Below the line
Château Haut-Brion, Graves
Château Calon-Ségur, Saint-Estèphe
Château Croizet-Bages, Pauillac

Top 10 Vintage 1984

1984 was a year of ups and downs: a good spring, followed by coulure in the Merlots; a reasonable summer that got, however, worse and worse; and finally a few beautiful weeks in October. In spite of a certain inconsistency the majority of the wines appeared to have a good color, a beautiful fruitiness and a firm texture.

The 1984 order of quality of the principal regions in Bordeaux is as follows: Médoc, Graves Rouges, Pomerol, Saint-Emilion. It will be clear from this just how badly hit the Merlot grapes were. 20 to 40% Merlot is usually added to the Cabernet, which gives it suppleness and roundness, but because it was left out many '84 Médocs are strong and manly. That happened to about half of the Grands Crus. They are in fact the better '84 Médocs: strong, but with a reasonable to good cellaring texture. That the Merlot grape was hit hard in 1984, is shown by the fact that no '84s were brought out by the following châteaux: Ausone, Belair, Magdelaine, Canon and Clos Fourtet, among others.

Keep in mind
- The best wines are to be found in the Médoc with the emphasis on the Cabernet.
- Good wines are extremely scarce in Saint-Emilion.
- Only the top wines of 1984 can be aged for 10 to 20 years.
- The majority of the '84s are drinkable from 1988 onwards.
- *N.B.* Midway through 1995: the first signs of drying out and a decline in quality are in evidence. Drink 1984 wines now.

The ten best 1984s in order of appreciation
Château Lynch-Bages, Pauillac
Château Margaux, Margaux
Château Pichon-Longueville-Lalande, Pauillac
Château Saint-Pierre, Saint-Julien
Château Lafite-Rothschild, Pauillac
Château Gruaud-Larose, Saint-Julien
Château Mouton-Rothschild, Pauillac
Domaine de Chevalier, Graves
Château De Fieuzal, Graves
Château Vieux Château Certan, Pomerol

Below the line
Château Pétrus
Château La Mission Haut-Brion, Graves
Château Carbonnieux, Graves
Château Croizet-Bages, Pauillac

Top 10 Vintage 1983

The vegetation cycle of the harvest was changeable: cold in April and May, beautiful in June, almost tropical in August, warm, dry and stable in September and October. The result was a vintage with very obvious differences in quality. Across the board there was talk of a good year with a few outstanding wines.

The quality of the '83s took shape during the last weeks of the vegetation process, just like the harvests of 1978 and 1979. The fall of 1983 was exceptional. For similar weather conditions we have to go as far back as 1961. In comparison with the '82 vintage, the '83s scored on average one point lower. The smaller wines especially are insufficiently balanced: They don't have enough 'meatiness' to compensate for the richness in tannin so characteristic for this vintage. However, the better wines (17 and 19 points) are sufficiently mellow to balance the vigor during the ripening process. They have a very promising aging texture.

Keep in mind
- High average standard of quality of the Merlot producers (Saint-Emilion, Pomerol).
- From the Médoc, the Cabernets harvested late offer the best chances.
- The good '83s have an excellent aging capacity, over 20 years.
- The middle group of the '83s misses the roundness needed to compensate the high tannin content.

The ten best '83s in order of appreciation
Château Margaux, Margaux
Château Cheval Blanc, Saint-Emilion
Château La Conseillante, Pomerol
Château Pétrus, Pomerol
Château Mouton-Rothschild, Pauillac
Château Léoville-Las-Cases, Saint-Julien
Château Lafite-Rothschild, Pauillac
Château Belair, Saint-Emilion
Château Latour, Pauillac
Château Ausone, Saint-Emilion

Below the line
The harvest of 1983 produced no bad Grands Crus. Nevertheless a number of Crus did not live up to their reputation
Château Pontet-Canet, Pauillac
Château Pédesclaux, Pauillac
Château Camensac, Saint-Laurent
Château Croizet-Bages, Pauillac

Top 10 Vintage 1982

The vegetation process for this harvest gave no problems, a vegetation cycle fit for a top year. The beautiful weather during flowering, ripening and harvest resulted in an abundance of ripe, healthy grapes. The description 'Top Year' though does not apply to all '82s. Only a few of the wines can be compared with the vintages 1929, 1945 or 1961.

The majority of the '82s has more of the quality found in large volume, successful vintages. Many '82s can be better compared to the vintages '53 and '59.

The real top wines of this harvest are assessed with 17 points and over. They are deep, compact and balanced wines for aging, showing a lot of meat and roundness (they can be likened to the '29s, '45s and the '61s). The wines with 16 points are, however, not to be scorned. Regarding intensity and aging possibilities they have only a little less to offer (they can be likened to 1953 and 1959).

Keep in mind
- The Cabernet grape had a better crop than the Merlot. The top qualities can therefore be found in the Médoc. On an average Pomerol and St.-Emilion, the areas where the Merlot has the upper hand, score one half point lower.
- Only 25% of the '82s can be ranked with the top wines.
- The wines not ranked with the top, have a somewhat low degree of acidity and miss a little intensity and tannin to be aged for very long.

The ten best '82s in order of appreciation
Château Margaux, Margaux
Château Latour, Pauillac
Château Mouton-Rothschild, Pauillac
Château Cheval Blanc, Saint-Emilion
Vieux Château Certan, Pomerol
Château La Conseillante, Pomerol
Château Cos d'Estournel, Saint-Estèphe
Château Talbot, Saint-Julien
Château Pichon-Longueville-Comtesse de Lalande, Pauillac
Château Magdelaine, Saint-Emilion

Below the line
A vintage where bad buys are almost impossible. 'Below the line' doesn't apply for 1982. However, the wines mentioned here do not come up to the standard befitting the reputation of this vintage.
Château Du Tertre, Margaux
Château Pape Clément, Graves

Top 10 Vintage 1981

The vegetation cycle preceding the 1981 harvest was in no way exceptional. The summer of 1981 was not very warm, nor was the fall invigorating or very sunny. Yet the grapes of most châteaux were very healthy and beautifully ripe. That the harvest produced such a large number of good wines and even a few toppers, is partly due to improvements in vinification methods.

The '81s are rich in tannin and acids. They are quite tight wines that can generally be aged well. The châteaux which score lower than 15 points miss the roundness and suppleness needed to stabilize the sturdy character of this vintage in the long term. In addition, the '81s assessed lower miss intensity. The 1981 vintage offers a good choice of top level wines (16 points). Real toppers of 17 points and more are rare.

Keep in mind
- The best '81s are to be found in the Médoc and the Pomerol.
- The Merlot grape in Saint-Emilion scores on average lower.
- The '81s with their somewhat tight texture can be aged well.

The ten best '81s in order of appreciation
Château Margaux, Margaux
Château Pétrus, Pomerol
Château Mouton-Rothschild, Pauillac
Château Cheval Blanc, Saint-Emilion
Château Léoville-Las-Cases, Saint-Julien
Château Lafite-Rothschild, Pauillac
Château Latour, Pauillac
Château Gruaud-Larose, Saint-Julien
Château Pichon-Longueville-Comtesse de Lalande, Pauillac
Château Chasse-Spleen, Moulis

Below the line
Disappointing '81s:
Château Haut-Brion, 1er Cru (again not a bad wine, but below standard as a 1er Cru)
Château Léoville-Poyferré, Saint-Julien
Château Brane-Cantenac, Margaux
Château Calon-Ségur, Saint-Estèphe
Château Lafon-Rochet, Saint-Estèphe

Top 10 Vintage 1980

The star under which this vintage was born was not very encouraging. A cold, raw and wet spring was followed by temperatures in June and July which were 2°C below the average. The weather during the harvest though was stable and sunny giving the grapes a chance to ripen.
1980 is a typical in-between year. A year without deep, full and richly textured wines. Yet there are a few wines with a good 'indice de souplesse'.

Keep in mind
– An irregular harvest with some good, but also a few doubtful wines.
– The '80s cannot be aged for long.
– On average, the quality of the 1980 Merlots is better than that of the Cabernets. Consequently there is a greater chance of a good wine from the Pomerol and Saint-Emilion than from the Médoc.
– *N.B.* Midway through 1995: fruit, finesse and charm are fading fast. The wines from the '80s are drying out and losing quality.

The ten best '80s in order of appreciation
Château Margaux, Margaux
Château Pétrus, Pomerol
Château Cheval Blanc, Saint-Emilion
Château Latour, Pauillac
Château Léoville-Las-Cases, Saint-Julien
Château Pichon-Longueville-Comtesse de Lalande, Pauillac
Château Cos d'Estournel, Saint-Estèphe
Château Mouton-Rothschild, Pauillac
Château La Conseillante, Pomerol
Château Ausone, Saint-Emilion

Below the line
Château Léoville-Poyferré, Saint-Julien
Château Montrose, Saint-Estèphe
Château Boyd-Cantenac, Margaux
Château Rauzan-Gassies, Margaux
Château Croizet-Bages, Pauillac

Top 10 Vintage 1979

A year which flowered late and was therefore harvested late. The late summer was superb turning the chances around for this harvest, of which expectations were low early on. Volume-wise it was the biggest harvest in Bordeaux since 1934. The theory that volume and quality don't go together, is disproved by the quality of many '79s. This vintage's average standard of quality is high: the '79s do not have outstanding intensity and depth, but they do offer charm and subtlety. Wines with 16 points and more are rather scarce although they are the deepest and most textured wines which with a view to aging can hold their own.

Keep in mind
- The wines from the regions dominated by the Merlot grape, Pomerol and Saint-Emilion, score on average higher than the Médoc where the Cabernet dominates.
- The 1979 Merlot vintage is more consistent.
- '79s assessed with 16 points and more are, in relation to the '78s and '81s, priced low.
- A vintage with a perfect relationship between quality and price.

The ten best '79s in order of appreciation
Château Margaux, Margaux
Château Pichon-Longueville-Comtesse de Lalande, Pauillac
Château Latour, Pauillac
Château Ausone, Saint-Emilion
Château Cos d'Estournel, Saint-Estèphe
Château Canon, Saint-Emilion
Château Ducru-Beaucaillou, Saint-Julien
Château Léoville-Las-Cases, Saint-Julien
Château Pavie, Saint-Emilion
Château Talbot, Saint-Julien

Below the line
Château Calon-Ségur, Saint-Estèphe
Château Brane-Cantenac, Margaux
Château Montrose, Saint-Estèphe
Château Léoville-Poyferré, Saint-Julien
Château Branaire-Ducru, Saint-Julien

Top 10 Vintage 1978

A harvest awaited with great pessimism. The cold, wet spring delayed flowering and reduced the volume. The summer of 1978 too was far from convincing, although the harvest took a turn for the better in an exceptionally beautiful fall. Regarding volume the 1978 harvest was very disappointing. The loss in volume however, was compensated by extra good quality. The average standard of quality of the '78s is high. The wines are luxuriant, rich in color, bouquet and flavor. The '78s have roundness. They are rich, sultry wines. The total degree of acidity of the '78s is quite low, which quickens their drinking ripeness and shortens aging. A vintage which can be likened to that of 1953.

Keep in mind
- A small but fine harvest.
- A harvest with a lot of consistency in quality.

The ten best '78s in order of appreciation
Château Latour, Pauillac
Château Margaux, Margaux
Château Ausone, Saint-Emilion
Château Léoville-Las-Cases, Saint-Julien
Château Pichon-Longueville-Comtesse de Lalande, Pauillac
Château Haut-Brion, Graves
Château Cos d'Estournel, Saint-Estèphe
Château Montrose, Saint-Estèphe
Château La Lagune, Haut-Médoc
Château Ducru-Beaucaillou, Saint-Julien

Below the line
Not applicable. A few wines though, from which more was expected in this top year.
Château Cheval Blanc, Saint-Emilion
Château Branaire-Ducru, Saint-Julien
Château Haut-Batailley, Pauillac
Château Beychevelle, Saint-Julien
Château Lynch-Bages, Pauillac
Château Duhart-Milon-Rothschild, Pauillac

Top 10 Vintage 1977

The harvest with the most unfortunate vegetation cycle of the last few years. It all began with the reduction in volume by 50% by spring frost. Then along came a cold summer and it was to be late fall before the sun started to shine.
Especially the early ripe Merlot grape had a hard time. Saint-Emilion and Pomerol had unprecedented small harvests. The yield of the Merlot plantings in the Médoc was minimum. Even before the harvest the '77s had had bad publicity. A number of reasonably successful '77s never received the rehabilitation they deserved.

Keep in mind
- A harvest dominated by the Cabernet.
- A small and mostly poor harvest. As a result, a lot of wines with too high a degree of acidity.
- Some good wines that develop quite quickly.
- The good wines offer quality for their price.
- *N.B.* Midway through 1995: only the best wines of this vintage still have something to offer. Most of these wines have lost their allure.

The ten best '77s in order of appreciation
Château Margaux, Margaux
Château Lafite-Rothschild, Pauillac
Château Ausone, Saint-Emilion
Château Léoville-Las-Cases, Saint-Julien
Château La Conseillante, Pomerol
Château Prieuré-Lichine, Margaux
Château Talbot, Saint-Julien
Château Chasse Spleen, Moulis
Château Gruaud-Larose, Saint-Julien
Château Ducru-Beaucaillou, Saint-Julien

Below the line
Château Latour, Pauillac
Château Gloria, Saint-Julien
Château Calon-Ségur, Saint-Estèphe
Château Brane-Cantenac, Margaux
Château Croizet-Bages, Pauillac

… *The Grands Crus*

alphabetically

Château d'Armailhac
Pauillac, 5ME CRU CLASSÉ DU MÉDOC

Comments
Château d'Armailhac is the Grand Cru which underwent the most changes. First it was Mouton-d'Armailhac, then Mouton Baron Philippe from 1956 onward, and Mouton Baronne Philippe from the 1974 vintage onward. Since the 1989 vintage, the château bears again its original name.

D'Armailhac used to be sold exclusively by the firm 'La Baronnie' located in Pauillac, also owned by the Rothschilds. In the last two years, this Cru is sold once more on the open market. The Rothschild image, with which this wine is imbued, makes it somewhat more precious than its peers.

Type Indication
A meaty, plump Pauillac. A nicely cared-for wine, rich in fruit and with a good structure for aging.

Technical data

Owner	: Baronne Philippine de Rothschild	
Technical director	: Patrick Léon	
Cellar master	: Joseph Bueno	
Vineyard acreage		: 126 acres
Grape varieties:	Cabernet Sauvignon	: 50%
	Cabernet Franc	: 23%
	Merlot	: 25%
	Other	: 2%
Average age of vines		: 35 years
Average annual production (cases of 12 bottles)		: 16,000

Specifications

Vintage	Assessment and Development			Market Value Summer 1995		Change in % since '93
	0 to 20 rating	drink from	cellaring potential	U.S. $	F. frs	
1993	15	1998	2010	18.00	83	16%
1992	**16**	1996	2002	17.00	77	20%
1991	**14**	1994	2000			
1990	**14**	1995	2005	31.00	142	67%
1989	**17**	1997	2007	31.00	142	36%
1988	**17**	1995	2005			
1987	**16**	1990	1996			
1986	**17**	1995	2015	34.00	155	57%
1985	**16**	1990	2010			
1984	**13**	1988	1994			
1983	**15**	1990	2000			
1982						
1981	**15**	1988	1998			
1980						
1979						
1978						
1977						

Older vintages	0 to 20 rating	drink from	cellaring potential	Market Value	
				U.S. $	F. frs
1976	**15**	1983	1995		
1975	**16**	1985	1997		
1973	**13**	1975	1980		
1970	**17**	1985	1995		
1969	**13**	1974	1980		

Auction prices realized in the last four years

year	U.S. $	F. frs	year	U.S. $	F. frs	year	U.S. $	F. frs
1988*	19.00	106	1970*	21.00	120	1928	166.00	940
1985	13.00	71	1966*	47.00	265			
1983*	16.00	93	1962*	27.00	151			
1982*	22.00	124	1961	69.00	392			
1978*	19.00	109	1949*	89.00	506			
1976*	14.00	77	1945*	107.00	607			
1975*	17.00	98	1941*	72.00	409			
1971*	19.00	108	1934	111.00	62			

* Auction prices since the last two years. For an indication of value and quality of the missing vintages until 1928, see category III, page 34/35.

Château Ausone
Saint-Emilion, 1ER GRAND CRU CLASSÉ A

Comments
This château is one of the top eight of the Bordeaux region. From 1975 to 1992, vinification has taken place under the supervision of the ambitious and extremely competent régisseur Pascal Delbeck. Before the arrival of Pascal Delbeck this 1er Grand Cru didn't always live up to its classification, although since 1975 Ausone has taken its place amongst the best wines of Saint- Emilion.

Type Indication
The intensity and firm compactness is certainly distinctive of the great years. This is the outstanding cellaring wine from Saint-Emilion. The great age of the vines and the low yield per acre guarantee a versatile, deep, and tremendously classy wine of the highest rank. With Ausone, charm comes with the years.

Technical data

Owner	: Mme J. Dubois-Challon and héritiers C. Vauthier
Cellar master	: Mr. Lanau
Oenologist	: Laboratoire C.B.C.

Vineyard acreage			: 17 acres
Grape varieties:	Cabernet Sauvignon	:	
	Cabernet Franc	: 50%	
	Merlot	: 50%	
	Other	:	
Average age of vines			: 50 years
Average annual production (cases of 12 bottles)			: 2,000

Specifications

Vintage	Assessment and Development			Market Value Summer 1995		Change in % since '93
	0 to 20 rating	drink from	cellaring potential	U.S. $	F. frs	
1993	18	2000	2015			
1992	16	1995	2005	75.00	339	
1991						
1990	**17**	1996	2010	161.00	735	16%
1989	**19**	1998	2015	158.00	722	37%
1988	**16**	1995	2015	143.00	653	18%
1987	**16**	1993	2000			
1986	**16**	1995	2010	137.00	626	0%
1985	**17**	1995	2010	167.00	763	20%
1984	Harvest has been declassified					
1983	**18**	1995	2010	146.00	667	0%
1982	**18**	1992	2005	248.00	1131	14%
1981	**17**	1992	2005			
1980	**16**	1987	1995			
1979	**18**	1988	2000			
1978	**18**	1988	2000			
1977	**16**	1985	1995			

Older vintages	0 to 20 rating	drink from	cellaring potential	Market Value	
				U.S. $	F. frs
1976	**17**	1987	2000		
1975				191.00	872
1974					
1973	**15**	1980	1990		
1970				212.00	967
1976	**18**				

Auction prices realized in the last four years

year	U.S. $	F. frs	year	U.S. $	F. frs	year	U.S. $	F. frs
1988*	59.00	332	1976*	61.00	348	1952*	46.00	260
1987*	35.00	201	1975*	62.00	354	1949*	130.00	737
1986*	60.00	343	1971	79.00	450	1947*	115.00	650
1985*	79.00	449	1970*	69.00	392	1945*	345.00	1959
1983*	73.00	417	1967	40.00	227	1934*	278.00	1579
1982*	168.00	951	1966*	71.00	402	1929*	471.00	2676
1979*	72.00	408	1961*	190.00	1077	1928	304.00	1724
1978*	75.00	424	1955*	76.00	431	1906	405.00	2299

Auction prices since the last two years. For an indication of value and quality of the missing vintages until 1928, see category I, page 30/31.

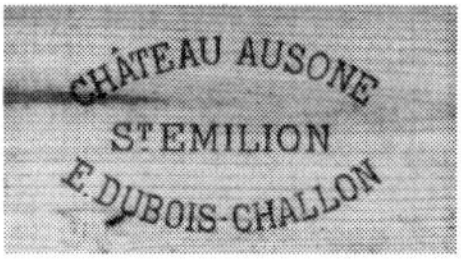

Château Batailley
Pauillac, 5ME CRU CLASSÉ DU MÉDOC

Comments
Château Batailley is distributed exclusively by the firm of Borie-Manoux of Bordeaux. The owners of this business house are connected to the Castéjas, who manage and live in the château. In view of the exclusivity contract with this Bordeaux firm, Batailley is not for sale on the open market. Auction prices are the most sound basis for valuation of this Cru.
Second wine: Château Haut-Bages-Mompelou

Type Indication
Emile Castéja's extremely traditional approach results in tight, robust, somewhat hard wines. With harvests of fully ripe grapes, the tannins are balanced with roundness and meatiness. In poor years the accent lies too heavily on the tannin. Batailley is a wine extremely suitable for cellaring.

Technical data

Owner	: Castéja Family		
Régisseur	: Emile Castéja		
Cellar master	: Mr. Broussy		
Oenologist	: Prof. Pascal Ribéreau-Gayon		
Vineyard acreage		:	111 acres
Grape varieties:	Cabernet Sauvignon	:	70%
	Cabernet Franc	:	5%
	Merlot	:	22%
	Other	:	3%
Average age of vines		:	25 years
Average annual production (cases of 12 bottles)		:	22,500

Specifications

Vintage	Assessment and Development 0 to 20 rating	drink from	cellaring potential	Market Value Summer 1995 U.S. $	F. frs	Change in % since '93
1993	16	1998	2010			
1992	13	1994	1998			
1991	14	1995	2003			
1990	16	1995	2005			
1989	16	1995	2010			
1988	15	1994	2005			
1987	14	1991	1996			
1986	16	1994	2010			
1985	16	1995	2015			
1984	13	1988	1995			
1983	14	1995	2005			
1982	15	1990	2000			
1981						
1980	13	1986	1992			
1979						
1978						
1977						

Older vintages	0 to 20 rating	drink from	cellaring potential	Market Value U.S. $	F. frs
1976	14	1982	1990		
1975	17	1986	2000		
1974					
1973	15	1978	1983		
1970	15	1982	1972		

Auction prices realized in the last four years

year	U.S. $	F. frs	year	U.S. $	F. frs	year	U.S. $	F. frs
1989*	18.00	101	1978	17.00	95			
1988*	18.00	103	1976	22.00	123			
1986	15.00	86	1975*	21.00	117			
1985*	25.00	142	1971*	31.00	177			
1984*	10.00	59	1970*	27.00	150			
1983*	18.00	105	1966	30.00	171			
1982*	32.00	180	1961*	62.00	352			
1979	15.00	86						

* Auction prices since the last two years. For an indication of value and quality of the missing vintages until 1928, see category IV, page 36/37.

CHÂTEAU BATAILLEY
PAUILLAC
GRAND CRU CLASSÉ

Château Beau-Séjour – Bécot
Saint-Emilion

Comments
A few years ago Monsieur Bécot bought 25 acres of vineyard from his neighbors, namely, Château La Carte and Château les Trois Moulins, the wine of which he brought on to the market as Beau-Séjour – Bécot. For that reason, the commission which supervises the St.-Emilion classification has seen fit to take away his "Grand Cru Classé B" status. To expand vineyards in such a way is permitted in the Médoc, because this status is not bound to the situation of the vineyard, but is dependent upon the quality of the wine. That Bécot has been excluded from the classification is simply a case of 'Jalousie de Métier' and is based then more on peevish bickering than it is on the results of his vinification.
(See Comments on classification of Saint-Emilion)
Second wine: Tournelle des Moines

Type Indication
On the nose, Beau-Séjour – Bécot is recognizable by a fine, very characteristic pine aroma. With a successful Merlot crop it is a quite deep, creamy, easily understood Saint-Emilion.

Technical data

Owner	: Michel Bécot et fils.
Régie	: Michel, Gérard & Dominique Bécot
Oenologist	: Michel Rolland

Vineyard acreage		: 42 acres
Grape varieties:	Cabernet Sauvignon :	6%
	Cabernet Franc :	24%
	Merlot :	70%
	Other :	
Average age of vines		: 40 years
Average annual production (cases of 12 bottles)		: 10,000

Specifications

Vintage	Assessment and Development 0 to 20 rating	drink from	cellaring potential	Market Value Summer 1995 U.S. $	F. frs	Change in % since '93
1993	17	1998	2010	23.00	103	8%
1992	14	1995	2000			
1991	**13**	1994	2000			
1990	**17**	1996	2005	28.00	128	27%
1989	**15**	1995	2007	30.00	135	20%
1988	**16**	1994	2005	30.00	135	20%
1987	**15**	1990	1997			
1986	**15**	1992	2007	34.00	155	31%
1985	**15**	1990	2000	34.00	155	11%
1984				18.00	83	0%
1983	**16**	1990	2000	30.00	135	-5%
1982	**17**	1992	2002			
1981	**16**	1990	1998			
1980						
1979	**16**	1987	1995			
1978	**16**	1986	1995			
1977	12	1986	1995			

Older vintages	0 to 20 rating	drink from	cellaring potential	Market Value U.S. $	F. frs
1976	**14**	1982	1988		
1975	**14**	1987	1995		
1974	**13**	1980	1989		
1973	**14**	1980	1988		
1971	**14**	1978	1990		
1970	**15**	1985	1993		

Auction prices realized in the last four years

year	U.S. $	F. frs	year	U.S. $	F. frs	year	U.S. $	F. frs
1983	15.00	84						
1961*	31.00	175						
1952*	21.00	120						
1947*	128.00	724						

Auction prices since the last two years. For an indication of value and quality of the missing vintages until 1928, see category III, page 34/35.

Château Beauséjour
(Duffau-Lagarrosse)
Saint-Emilion, 1ER GRAND CRU CLASSÉ B

Comments
In 1869, when Beauséjour was split up, it was stated in the contract that both new Châteaux were to maintain the right to use the name Beauséjour. The half that fell to Duffau-Lagarrosse, is bordered on the south side by the other Beauséjour and on the north side by Château Canon. The estate is managed by Jean-Michel Dubos. Advising oenologist is Michel Rolland. The methods of vinification are traditional, although new oak barrels are put into use annually.
The excellent location of the vineyard provides a very rich must. Selling rights are held by Ets. Jean-Pierre Moueix in Libourne and Maison Barton & Questier in Blanquefort.
Second wine: Croix de Mazerat.

Type Indication
The mainly traditional methods of vinification provide full wines, that should not be drunk too soon.
In poor years Duffau-Lagarrosse is often a somewhat rigid wine because of its substantial tannin content.

Technical data

Owner	: Héritiers Duffau-Lagarrosse		
Régisseur	: Jean-Michel Dubos		
Cellar master	: Bernard Oizeau		
Oenologist	: Laboratoire Michel & Dany Rolland		
Vineyard acreage		:	17 acres
Grape varieties:	Cabernet Sauvignon	:	15%
	Cabernet Franc	:	30%
	Merlot	:	55%
	Other	:	
Average age of vines		:	35 years
Average annual production (cases of 12 bottles)		:	3,500

Specifications

Vintage	Assessment and Development			Market Value Summer 1995		Change in % since '93
	0 to 20 rating	drink from	cellaring potential	U.S. $	F. frs	
1993	17	1998	2012			
1992	15	1995	2002			
1991	14	1996	2001	This Grand Cru is not		
1990	**17**	1996	2010	being offered for		
1989	**15**	1993	2010	sale on the open		
1988	**16**	1992	2005	market and, therefore,		
1987	**16**	1990	1995	no exact prices are		
1986	**15**	1993	2000	available.		
1985	**15**	1989	1995			
1984	Harvest has been declassified					
1983	**16**	1991	2000			
1982	**16**	1995	2005			
1981	**14**	1990	2000			
1980	**14**	1985	1992			
1979	**13**	1988	1995			
1978						
1977						

Older vintages	0 to 20 rating	drink from	cellaring potential	Market Value	
				U.S. $	F. frs

Auction prices realized in the last four years

year	U.S. $	F. frs	year	U.S. $	F. frs	year	U.S. $	F. frs

Auction prices since the last two years. For an indication of value and quality of the missing vintages until 1928, see category III, page 34/35.

Château Beauséjour
1ᵉʳ Gᴅ CRU CLASSE
Saint Émilion
DUFFAU-LAGARROSSE

Château Belair
Saint-Emilion, 1ER GRAND CRU CLASSÉ B

Comments
Madame J. Dubois-Challon, the owner of this Cru, is also the owner of the famous Château Ausone, where she lives.
Since 1975, she relies upon the extremely competent régisseur Pascal Delbeck. This young, ambitious winemaker made a name for himself in no time at all. Since his arrival at Ausone and Belair, both Crus have undergone a remarkable improvement in quality and belong once more among the very best of the entire Bordeaux region.

Type Indication
Belair and Ausone are brother and sister. The composition of the vineyard shows that Belair has 10% more Merlot than is the case at her big brother's, Ausone. The wines have a lot in common as regards depth and intensity. Although Belair displays a little more roundness and suppleness in its youth, for aging it is almost as good as Ausone.

Technical data

Owner	: Mme. J. Dubois-Challon	
Régisseur	: Pascal Delbeck	
Vineyard acreage		: 32 acres
Grape varieties:	Cabernet Sauvignon	:
	Cabernet Franc	: 40%
	Merlot	: 60%
	Other	:
Average age of vines		: 40 years
Average annual production (cases of 12 bottles)		: 4,000

Specifications

Vintage	Assessment and Development 0 tot 20 rating	drinken from	houdbaar potential	Market Value zomer 1993 U.S. $	F. frs	Change ring in % t.o.v. '89
1993						
1992						
1991						
1990	**18**	1998	2005			
1989	**18**	1997	2010			
1988	**16**	1995	2008			
1987						
1986	**16**	1992	2002			
1985	**15**	1990	1995			
1984	Harvest has been declassified					
1983	**18**	1995	2010			
1982	**16**	1990	2005			
1981	**15**	1992	2000			
1980	**15**	1985	1995			
1979	**17**	1987	1997			
1978	**16**	1987	2000			
1977	**14**	1985	1993			

Older vintages	0 to 20 rating	drink from	cellaring potential	Market Value U.S. $	F. frs
1976	**16**	1987	1995		

Auction prices realized in the last four years

year	U.S. $	F. frs	year	U.S. $	F. frs	year	U.S. $	F. frs
1982	35.00	199						
1979	32.00	180						
1978	28.00	157						
1970	29.00	166						
1959	27.00	154						

* Auction prices since the last two years. For an indication of value and quality of the missing vintages until 1928, see category III, page 34/35.

Château Belgrave
Saint-Laurent, 5ME CRU CLASSÉ DU MÉDOC

Comments
A Cru which was handled very carelessly in the past (up to 1979). Much of the wine was handed over in the barrel, in addition to which the quality was not good enough for the predicate Cru Classé. Fortunately for this château, a number of new owners took over in 1979. Since then things have been straightened out under the management of the owner Dourthe-Kressmann. It is understandable that this Cru will not take up a position at the top of the classification quickly. Although it does seem from the tasting results of the past five years, that the quality is rapidly improving. In particular, the '80s are of a very good standard.
Second wine: Diane de Belgrave

Type Indication
The Belgrave of the last few years is once more a well cared for wine. Not a wine that excels in depth and complexity, but a pure, supple, charming Médoc. The new Belgrave is sparing in tannin and as a consequence will be pleasant to drink quite soon.

Technical data

Owner	: UfG Bank & Dourthe-Kressmann	
Régisseur	: Merete Larsen	
Oenologist	: Michel Rolland	
Vineyard acreage		: 136 acres
Grape varieties:	Cabernet Sauvignon	: 40%
	Cabernet Franc	: 20%
	Merlot	: 35%
	Petit Verdot	: 5%
Average age of vines		: 23 years
Average annual production (cases of 12 bottles)		: 27,500

Specifications

Vintage	Assessment and Development 0 tot 20 rating	drinken from	houdbaar potential	Market Value zomer 1993 U.S. $	F. frs	Change ring in % t.o.v. '89
1993	15	1998	2005	14.00	65	-9%
1992	14	1995	2000			
1991	**16**	1995	2005			
1990	**14**	1995	2005			
1989	**16**	1994	2005	22.00	101	30%
1988	**16**	1995	2008			
1987	14	1991	1997			
1986	**16**	1993	2005			
1985	**16**	1990	2000			
1984	**12**	1988	1996			
1983	**17**	1990	2010			
1982	**15**	1987	1995			
1981	**13**	1988	1995			
1980	**15**	1984	1990			
1979	14	1985	1995			
1978	**15**	1984	1990			
1977						

Older vintages	0 to 20 rating	drink from	cellaring potential	Market Value U.S. $	F. frs
1975	**14**	1982	1987		

Auction prices realized in the last four years

year	U.S. $	F. frs	year	U.S. $	F. frs	year	U.S. $	F. frs
1988*	11.00	60						
1966	20.00	114						
1961	53.00	298						
1948	23.00	129						

Auction prices since the last two years. For an indication of value and quality of the missing vintages until 1928, see category IV, page 36/37.

Château Beychevelle
Saint-Julien, 4ME CRU CLASSÉ DU MÉDOC

Comments
A Cru still thought of as being one of the 2me Crus, as was certainly the case in the sixties. Beychevelle set the tone in the Médoc where care, selection and vinification were concerned and at the start of his career the manager and co-owner, Achille Fould, did everything possible to see to those aspects. Over the last few years though, that management has weakened and this is reflected in the Cru. Recent assessment scores are representative of the state of affairs. At the end of 1983 the château was sold to a big French insurance company. The new owner has brought only a slight improvement in quality.
Second wine: Amiral de Beychevelle

Type Indication
A Beychevelle old style is compact, rich and intense. The flavor is complex and deep, and stays charming because of fruit and roundness. In view of the generous texture, this is a Cru with good aging potential.

Technical data

Owner	: Groupe GMF & Suntory Ltd.	
Régisseur	: Maurice Ruelle	
Cellar master	: Lucien Soussotte	
Oenologist	: Prof. Pascal Ribéreau-Gayon	
Vineyard acreage		: 210 acres
Grape varieties:	Cabernet Sauvignon	: 60%
	Cabernet Franc	: 8%
	Merlot	: 28%
	Petit Verdot	: 4%
Average age of vines		: 20 years
Average annual production (cases of 12 bottles)		: 40,000

Specifications

Vintage	Assessment and Development 0 to 20 rating	drink from	cellaring potential	Market Value Summer 1995 U.S. $	F. frs	Change in % since '93
1993	17	1998	2010	22.00	99	8%
1992	15	1996	2002	20.00	91	
1991	14	1996	2000	26.00	118	26%
1990	16	1995	2005	32.00	146	5%
1989	17	1997	2012	45.00	203	22%
1988	17	1995	2010	42.00	189	30%
1987	16	1990	1995			
1986	16	1993	2010	50.00	228	17%
1985	16	1995	2005			
1984	15	1990	2000			
1983	16	1990	2005	52.00	237	38%
1982	15	1987	1997			
1981	14	1987	1997			
1980	15	1985	1990			
1979	16	1985	1995			
1978	14	1983	1993	70.00	319	
1977	14	1982	1988			

Older vintages	0 to 20 rating	drink from	cellaring potential	Market Value U.S. $	F. frs
1976	15	1983	1994		
1975				85.00	387
1973	16	1980	1989		
1971	16	1976	1986		
1970				115.00	524
1967	16	1972	1983		
1961	17	1975	1990		
1958	11	1963	1976		

Auction prices realized in the last four years

year	U.S. $	F. frs	year	U.S. $	F. frs	year	U.S. $	F. frs
1989*	26.00	147	1978*	29.00	163	1961*	140.00	796
1988*	23.00	131	1976*	37.00	212	1959*	72.00	407
1986*	34.00	193	1975*	30.00	170	1955	60.00	342
1985*	29.00	164	1970*	50.00	282	1949*	214.00	1214
1983*	26.00	147	1967*	28.00	159	1945	191.00	1086
1982*	42.00	237	1966*	49.00	278	1928*	204.00	1158
1981*	22.00	122	1964*	39.00	220	1926*	161.00	916
1979*	26.00	149	1962*	56.00	318	1921*	171.00	970

Auction prices since the last two years. For an indication of value and quality of the missing vintages until 1928, see category II, page 32/33.

Château Bouscaut
Léognan, GRAND CRU CLASSÉ DE GRAVES

Comments
Bouscaut is an attractive newcomer. The estate was bought for one million dollars by a group of Americans in 1969. They spent a small fortune on new plantings and the renovation of the buildings and château. Jean-Bernard Delmas of Château Haut-Brion was brought in to manage and look after the restoration process. In 1980 Bouscaut was bought by the 20th century 'king of the vineyards', Lucien Lurton. He is also the owner of Brane-Cantenac, Durfort-Vivens and Desmirail. Lurton, together with a few of his 10 children, produces good and sound wine at Bouscaut. His vinification and ripening methods are, as he puts it himself, traditional. He attaches great importance to the cellar selection.
Second wine: Château Valoux

Type Indication
Bouscaut is a true-to-type Graves, with a lot of ripe fruit and unaggressive tannin. Often elegant, and in poor years a somewhat delicate wine.

Technical data

Owner	: Lucien Lurton	
Director	: Sophie Lurton	
Régisseur	: Louis Lurton	
Oenologist	: Dominique de Beauregard	
Vineyard acreage		: 111 acres
Grape varieties:	Cabernet Sauvignon	: 35%
	Cabernet Franc	: 5%
	Merlot	: 55%
	Other	: 5%
Average age of vines		: 35 years
Average annual production (cases of 12 bottles)		: 10,000

Specifications

Vintage	Assessment and Development			Market Value Summer 1995		Change in % since '93
	0 to 20 rating	drink from	cellaring potential	U.S. $	F. frs	
1993	14	1997	2005			
1992	13	1996	2001			
1991	14	1994	2000			
1990	18	1996	2005	28.00	128	
1989	14	1995	2005	28.00	128	63%
1988	15	1995	2008			
1987	14	1988	2000			
1986	14	1990	1996			
1985	13	1989	1995			
1984	12	1990	1995			
1983	14	1990	2000	25.00	114	36%
1982	14	1990	2000			
1981	14	1985	1994			
1980	12	1985	1990			
1979						
1978						
1977						

Older vintages	0 to 20 rating	drink from	cellaring potential	Market Value	
				U.S. $	F. frs

Auction prices realized in the last four years

year	U.S. $	F. frs	year	U.S. $	F. frs	year	U.S. $	F. frs
1981	12.00	69						
1975*	19.00	108						
1970	23.00	131						
1966*	22.00	126						
1961	114.00	646						
1959	47.00	266						

Auction prices since the last two years. For an indication of value and quality of the missing vintages until 1928, see category IV, page 36/37.

Château Boyd-Cantenac

Margaux, 3ME CRU CLASSÉ DU MÉDOC

Comments

Monsieur Pierre Guillemet, the owner of Boyd-Cantenac and Château Pouget determines the style of both these Crus. You could say they live under the same roof. His family has managed both châteaux for over fifty years. Their management is open to new developments in the field of oenology which are employed in moderation in both châteaux. The Crus do not stand out in the 1855 classification. Since the harvest of 1984 more investment has been made into barrels, which more than likely accounts for the rise in quality over the past few years.

Type Indication

Boyd-Cantenac is a friendly Margaux. It is a round, supple, honest wine with not a great deal of finesse. A wine generally deserving of its place in the classification.

Technical data

Owner	: Pierre Guillemet		
Régisseur	: Pierre Guillemet		
Oenologist	: Jacques Boissenot		
Vineyard acreage		:	44 acres
Grape varieties:	Cabernet Sauvignon	:	67%
	Cabernet Franc	:	8%
	Merlot	:	20%
	Petit Verdot	:	5%
Average age of vines		:	25 years
Average annual production (cases of 12 bottles)		:	7,000

Specifications

Vintage	Assessment and Development 0 to 20 rating	drink from	cellaring potential	Market Value Summer 1995 U.S. $	F. frs	Change in % since '93
1993	13	1997	2005			
1992	13	1995	2000			
1991	**15**	1995	2002			
1990	**16**	1995	2005	27.00	121	
1989	**17**	1996	2010	28.00	128	35%
1988	**16**	1995	2010	27.00	121	33%
1987	**14**	1990	1995			
1986	**16**	1993	2003			
1985	**16**	1992	2005	33.00	148	0%
1984	**15**	1990	2000			
1983	**15**	1988	2005			
1982						
1981	**14**	1988	1995	30.00	135	-14%
1980	**11**	1983	1988	24.00	107	-7%
1979						
1978	**14**	1983	1993	48.00	217	-9%
1977	**12**	1983	1989			

Older vintages	0 to 20 rating	drink from	cellaring potential	Market Value U.S. $	F. frs
1976				37.00	169
1970	**17**	1986	1996		

Auction prices realized in the last four years

year	U.S. $	F. frs	year	U.S. $	F. frs	year	U.S. $	F. frs
1985*	18.00	99	1970	31.00	173			
1983*	16.00	90	1967*	10.00	56			
1982*	23.00	132	1964	17.00	97			
1981	13.00	74	1961	72.00	406			
1976	25.00	142						
1975*	14.00	80						
1973	13.00	74						
1971	25.00	144						

* Auction prices since the last two years. For an indication of value and quality of the missing vintages until 1928, see category III, page 34/35.

Château Branaire-Ducru

Saint-Julien, 4ME CRU CLASSÉ DU MÉDOC

Comments

In 1988 the families Tapie and Tari (also owners of Giscours) sold Branaire-Ducru to a group of shareholders among whom Sucrerie de Toury, owned by Patrick Maroteaux, held the most shares. The new owners maintain stricter quality standards. The group carried out a thorough restoration of the château and renewed entirely the cuverie and the barrel cellar.

As a direct consequence of the emphasis on quality selection in the cellar, they introduced among others a second wine. The results of this latest initiative of the new shareholders will become clear in the nineties. With a greater investment in new oak barrels this Cru could score better in a short period of time.

Second wine: Château Duluc

Type Indication

A wine vinificated in a wholesome way. Well balanced. Soft tannins, roundness and suppleness have the upperhand in this Cru. Branaire-Ducru is a reasonably good wine for aging.

Technical data

Owner	: Sucrerie de Toury a.o.		
Director	: Ph. Dhalluin		
Oenologist	: Jacques Boissenot		
Vineyard acreage		:	119 acres
Grape varieties:	Cabernet Sauvignon	:	70%
	Cabernet Franc	:	5%
	Merlot	:	22%
	Petit Verdot	:	3%
Average age of vines		:	25 years
Average annual production (cases of 12 bottles)		:	25,000

Specifications

Vintage	Assessment and Development 0 to 20 rating	drink from	cellaring potential	Market Value Summer 1995 U.S. $	F. frs	Change in % since '93
1993	15	1998	2005	20.00	91	12%
1992	13	1994	1998	19.00	87	
1991	15	1994	2000	23.00	105	
1990	16	1995	2005	29.00	132	33%
1989	17	1998	2012	31.00	142	19%
1988	15	1995	2008	28.00	128	13%
1987	14	1990	1992			
1986	15	1993	2003	30.00	135	13%
1985	15	1992	1998			
1984	14	1988	1995			
1983	14	1988	2000			
1982	17	1990	2000			
1981	15	1988	1998			
1980	15	1984	1990			
1979	12	1985	1993			
1978	14	1985	1995			
1977						

Older vintages	0 to 20 rating	drink from	cellaring potential	Market Value U.S. $	F. frs
1973	14	1978	1983		
1964				92.00	421
1959				122.00	558

Auction prices realized in the last four years

year	U.S. $	F. frs	year	U.S. $	F. frs	year	U.S. $	F. frs
1989*	24.00	139	1975*	27.00	151	1945*	147.00	837
1986*	13.00	73	1970*	26.00	147	1934	70.00	399
1985*	20.00	112	1967*	13.00	75	1916	90.00	509
1982*	40.00	226	1966	36.00	207	1899	152.00	862
1981*	15.00	84	1962*	36.00	202			
1979*	24.00	134	1961*	54.00	305			
1978*	25.00	142	1959*	101.00	576			
1976	25.00	144	1947	82.00	466			

Auction prices since the last two years. For an indication of value and quality of the missing vintages until 1928, see category III, page 34/35.

Château Brane-Cantenac
Margaux, 2ME CRU CLASSÉ DU MÉDOC

Comments
Monsieur Lucien Lurton, the owner who was advised by Professor Peynaud, shows his skill with great success. Brane-Cantenac usually produces an outstanding wine. The few poor vintages brought to light in the assessment scores, are a result of new plantings, and also the reason for the quite young average age of the vineyards. (See Château Desmirail)
Second wine: Château Notton

Type Indication
A thoroughbred Margaux. A Cru attesting time and again to having been well taken care of. Brane-Cantenac does not offer that intensity found in the front-runners of the 2mes Crus, yet it is a wine often right up there with the leaders. Suppleness, finesse and roundness are characteristic for this frequently charming Margaux.

Technical data

Owner	: Lucien Lurton	
Régisseur	: Henri Lurton	
Cellar master	: Christophe Caddeville	
Oenologist	: Jacques Boissenot	
Vineyard acreage		: 210 acres
Grape varieties:	Cabernet Sauvignon	: 70%
	Cabernet Franc	: 13%
	Merlot	: 15%
	Other	: 2%
Average age of vines		: 20 years
Average annual production (cases of 12 bottles)		: 29,000

Specifications

Vintage	Assessment and Development			Market Value Summer 1995		Change in % since '93
	0 to 20 rating	drink from	cellaring potential	U.S. $	F. frs	
1993	13	1997	2005	22.00	98	21%
1992	**15**	1996	2001			
1991	**16**	1995	2005			
1990	**15**	1995	2005	36.00	162	38%
1989	**16**	1995	2005	52.00	237	88%
1988	**15**	1995	2008	55.00	251	133%
1987	**16**	1990	1996			
1986	**16**	1992	2005	51.00	230	60%
1985	**15**	1990	2000			
1984	**14**	1988	1998	22.00	101	0%
1983	**16**	1990	2005	33.00	148	0%
1982	**16**	1987	1997	43.00	196	0%
1981	**12**	1987	1992			
1980	**15**	1985	1992			
1979	**14**	1986	1996			
1978	**15**	1987	1997			
1977	**10**	1982	1988			

Older vintages	0 to 20 rating	drink from	cellaring potential	Market Value	
				U.S. $	F. frs
1976	**15**	1984	1994		
1974	**11**	1979	1986		
1973	**14**	1977	1982		
1970	**15**	1980	2000	92.00	421
1967	**12**	1973	1980		
1966				122.00	558
1962				122.00	558
1959				167.00	763

Auction prices realized in the last four years

year	U.S. $	F. frs	year	U.S. $	F. frs	year	U.S. $	F. frs
1985*	24.00	134	1971*	17.00	97	1952*	104.00	588
1983*	23.00	130	1970*	28.00	158	1947	125.00	707
1982*	36.00	204	1967	16.00	91	1938*	41.00	232
1981	16.00	90	1966	50.00	284	1928*	64.00	366
1979*	18.00	102	1964*	34.00	192	1919	253.00	1437
1978*	42.00	239	1961*	55.00	314	1906*	114.00	646
1976*	14.00	80	1959*	127.00	718			
1975*	26.00	146	1955	64.00	362			

Auction prices since the last two years. For an indication of value and quality of the missing vintages until 1928, see category III, page 34/35.

CHATEAU
BRANE CANTENAC
1ᵉʳ VIN

Château Calon-Ségur
Saint-Estèphe, 3ME CRU CLASSÉ DU MÉDOC

Comments
Co-owner and director of this château is Philippe Casqueton, a descendent of a family with the longest service record as propriétaires in the Médoc. Philippe Casqueton is more of a 'gentleman farmer' than a modern manager. He looks for the quality of his wines especially in the vineyards and care of the soil. The traditional vinification is clearly expressed in the quality of the Calon-Ségur. The wine is not altogether as consistent as it should be. The chance of fabulous top wines though is undoubtedly present.

Second wines: Château Marquis de Calon, Château Capbern Gasqueton, Cru Bourgeois

Type Indication
Calon-Ségur from the good years is a compact, exceedingly intense rascal. Especially in youth, it is difficult to fathom because of the large dose of tannin. Fully ripe, if compensated by roundness, the soft tannins and fine acids of this Cru offer a very finely tuned, extremely broad play of sturdy flavors. A Calon-Ségur demands patience.

Technical data

Owner	: S.C.I. Calon-Ségur		
Régisseur	: Philippe Capbern Gasqueton		
Cellar master	: Michel Ellissalde		
Oenologist	: Prof. Pascal Ribéreau-Gayon		
Vineyard acreage			: 232 acres
Grape varieties:		Cabernet Sauvignon	: 65%
		Cabernet Franc	: 15%
		Merlot	: 20%
		Other	:
Average age of vines			: 35 years
Average annual production (cases of 12 bottles)			: 25,000

Specifications

Vintage	Assessment and Development 0 to 20 rating	drink from	cellaring potential	Market Value Summer 1995 U.S. $	F. frs	Change in % since '93
1993	14	2000	2010	19.00	87	20%
1992	14	1997	2003			
1991	15	1994	2000	21.00	94	7%
1990	16	1995	2005	30.00	135	20%
1989	17	1995	2005	30.00	135	0%
1988	15	1995	2010	40.00	183	49%
1987	14	1991	1998			
1986	16	1994	2014			
1985	13	1992	2000	34.00	155	17%
1984	13	1989	1998	21.00	94	0%
1983	14	1990	2005	37.00	169	15%
1982	16	1990	2000	71.00	323	43%
1981	12	1990	1997			
1980	14	1984	1990			
1979	14	1985	1995			
1978	16	1986	1997			
1977	10	1982	1990			

Older vintages	0 to 20 rating	drink from	cellaring potential	Market Value U.S. $	F. frs
1976	14	1985	1995		
1975				78.00	353
1973	17	1978	1985		
1967	14	1975	1985		
1971				78.00	353
1970				100.00	456
1966				115.00	524
1964				87.00	394

Auction prices realized in the last four years

year	U.S. $	F. frs	year	U.S. $	F. frs	year	U.S. $	F. frs
1989*	27.00	155	1978*	27.00	150	1959*	58.00	328
1988*	21.00	118	1976	24.00	138	1949*	244.00	1388
1986	14.00	77	1975	37.00	208	1947*	158.00	898
1985	27.00	152	1970	51.00	287	1945*	223.00	1265
1983	27.00	152	1967*	31.00	175	1934*	85.00	483
1982*	51.00	290	1966*	44.00	250	1929*	208.00	1184
1981*	19.00	105	1962	40.00	226	1928*	180.00	1020
1979	23.00	132	1961*	88.00	499	1916*	92.00	522

Auction prices since the last two years. For an indication of value and quality of the missing vintages until 1928, see category III, page 34/35.

Château Camensac
Saint-Laurent, 5ME CRU CLASSÉ DU MÉDOC

Comments
The Forner Family, which came from Spain by way of Narbonne, has breathed new life in an un-Bordelaise way into the château. They were used to a large-scale approach and they tackled viniculture in the same manner. Vinification takes place in an enormous modern building installed right in the middle of the vineyards, from where the vineyard activities are also managed.
Camensac is a modern company where good wines are made in a responsible fashion.
Note. The name and label changed slightly with the 1988 vintage (previously it was called Château _de_ Camensac).

Type Indication
The Camensac is quite consistent in quality. It is often not the Cru with the most refinement, but it is a healthy, meaty and round wine. A Cru with a standard matching its status of 5me Cru.

Technical data

Owner	: H. Forner Family		
Director	: Gérard Bouquinet		
Cellar master	: José Braz		
Oenologist	: Prof. Guy Guimberteau		
Vineyard acreage		:	161 acres
Grape varieties:	Cabernet Sauvignon	:	60%
	Cabernet Franc	:	15%
	Merlot	:	25%
	Other	:	
Average age of vines		:	30 years
Average annual production (cases of 12 bottles)		:	22,500

Specifications

Vintage	Assessment and Development			Market Value Summer 1995		Change in % since '93
	0 to 20 rating	drink from	cellaring potential	U.S. $	F. frs	
1993	15	1998	2005	17.00	75	
1992	12	1995	1999	16.00	73	
1991	13	1994	2000	16.00	73	41%
1990	13	1995	2005	24.00	107	56%
1989	16	1995	2005	22.00	101	44%
1988	14	1995	2005	27.00	121	60%
1987	14	1990	1995			
1986	14	1991	2000			
1985	14	1989	1997			
1984	12	1987	1995			
1983	13	1987	1997			
1982	15	1987	1995			
1981	13	1988	1995			
1980	12	1983	1988			
1979	14	1985	1993			
1978	15	1983	1994			
1977	15	1983	1990			

Older vintages	0 to 20 rating	drink from	cellaring potential	Market Value	
				U.S. $	F. frs
1976	14	1981	1991		
1975	16	1985	1998		
1974	10	1978	1983		
1973	16	1978	1983		
1971	15	1977	1985		
1970	16	1980	1990		

Auction prices realized in the last four years

year	U.S. $	F. frs	year	U.S. $	F. frs	year	U.S. $	F. frs
1989*	13.00	75	1975*	15.00	84			
1986*	14.00	81	1974	10.00	56			
1985*	13.00	72						
1982	24.00	138						
1981*	14.00	78						
1979*	14.00	82						
1978	20.00	113						
1976*	13.00	71						

Auction prices since the last two years. For an indication of value and quality of the missing vintages until 1928, see category IV, page 36/37.

Château Canon
Saint-Emilion, 1ER GRAND CRU CLASSÉ B

Comments
Owned by the Fournier family which knows how to combine traditional methods of vinification with modern technology. Eric Fournier, the Director, uses modern oenology coupled with classical methods. For example, he prefers cuves made of wood over cuves of stainless steel because he believes that they yield better results. The wooden cuves are not even ten years old and are equipped with electronic temperature controls which regulate the must during fermentation.

In other areas, too, Fournier combines traditional and modern approaches. For example, he uses old vertical grape presses as well as very modern stainless steel machines for stem and leave removal. The fact that in recent years Canon has been doing so well is proof that Fournier has found a happy marriage between modern science and tradition.

Second wine: Clos J. Kanon

Type Indication
Canon is well-constructed, complete and rich. The texture is a bit rigid for a Saint-Emilion which, however, gives the wine a youthful appearance even in maturity.

Technical data

Owner	: Fournier Family	
Régisseur	: Eric Fournier	
Cellar master	: Paul Cazenave	
Oenologist	: Gilles Pauquet	
Vineyard acreage		: 44 acres
Grape varieties:	Cabernet Sauvignon	:
	Cabernet Franc	: 45%
	Merlot	: 55%
	Other	:
Average age of vines		: 35 years
Average annual production (cases of 12 bottles)		: 6,250

Specifications

Vintage	Assessment and Development 0 to 20 rating	drink from	cellaring potential	Market Value Summer 1995 U.S. $	F. frs	Change in % since '93
1993	17	1999	2012	26.00	118	18%
1992	**14**	1995	2002	25.00	113	25%
1991						
1990	**15**	1996	2005	45.00	203	17%
1989	**18**	1997	2010	48.00	217	3%
1988	**17**	1995	2015	54.00	244	13%
1987	**14**	1990	1997			
1986	**17**	1995	2015	49.00	223	11%
1985	**17**	1992	2015	55.00	251	9%
1984	Harvest has been declassified					
1983	**17**	1992	2007	54.00	244	3%
1982	**17**	1990	2000			
1981	**16**	1988	1998			
1980	**15**	1985	1993			
1979	**18**	1985	1998			
1978						
1977						

Older vintages	0 to 20 rating	drink from	cellaring potential	Market Value U.S. $	F. frs
1973	**16**	1977	1981		
1971	**16**	1976	1980		
1970	**14**	1984	1990	100.00	456
1958	**13**	1965	1975		

Auction prices realized in the last four years

year	U.S. $	F. frs	year	U.S. $	F. frs	year	U.S. $	F. frs
1989*	29.00	163	1975*	25.00	142	1947	285.00	1616
1988*	25.00	142	1970*	45.00	253	1945	232.00	1317
1985*	44.00	248	1966*	44.00	251	1934	77.00	435
1983*	31.00	174	1964	55.00	311			
1982*	60.00	339	1961	65.00	368			
1981	26.00	146	1959*	50.00	286			
1979*	31.00	174	1953*	68.00	386			
1978*	41.00	232	1949*	123.00	695			

Auction prices since the last two years. For an indication of value and quality of the missing vintages until 1928, see category II, page 32/33.

CHATEAU CANON
1ᵉʳ GRAND CRÛ CLASSÉ
Sᵗ ÉMILION

Château Cantemerle
Macau, 5ME CRU CLASSÉ DU MÉDOC

Comments
Cantemerle is a Château which up to and including the fifties was one of the better producers. In the sixties and seventies however, the management grew old and the wine deteriorated greatly. The sad list of assessment scores witnesses this fact. Since the arrival of the new owner in 1980, who entrusted Cordier with responsibility for the Cru, times changed for the better for Cantemerle. Congratulations to the competent wine producer Georges Pauli who was the brain behind this impressive rentrée.
Second wine: Villeneuve de Cantemerle

Type Indication
Since 1981, Cantemerle is again a class wine from the Médoc. Vinification by Pauli somewhat changed its character. Where in the past Cantemerle aimed for élan and sophistication, it is now a somewhat 'more robust' and sturdier seigneur.

Technical data

Owner	: Châteaux des Deux Rives S.A.	
Director	: Philippe Dambrine	
Oenologist	: Georges Pauli	

Vineyard acreage		: 163 acres
Grape varieties:	Cabernet Sauvignon	: 45%
	Cabernet Franc	: 10%
	Merlot	: 40%
	Other	: 5%
Average age of vines		: 25 years
Average annual production (cases of 12 bottles)		: 20,000

Specifications

Vintage	Assessment and Development			Market Value zomer 1993		Change ring in % t.o.v. '89
	0 tot 20 rating	drinken from	houdbaar potential	U.S. $	F. frs	
1993	14	1997	2005			
1992	**16**	1995	2000			
1991	**14**	1994	2000	Maison Cordier in		
1990	**15**	1995	2005	Bordeaux has the sole		
1989	**17**	1998	2012	exclusivity to market		
1988	**16**	1995	2010	Cantemerle.		
1987	**13**	1990	1995	Therefore, this wine		
1986	**14**	1993	2010	is not listed on the		
1985	**16**	1995	2015	open market.		
1984	**14**	1988	2000			
1983	**16**	1990	2005			
1982	**17**	1990	2005			
1981	**15**	1988	2000			
1980	**13**	1984	1990			
1979						
1978	**13**	1985	1990			
1977						

Older vintages	0 to 20 rating	drink from	cellaring potential	Market Value	
				U.S. $	F. frs
1976	**12**	1985	1992		
1975	**15**	1995	2005		
1974	**13**	1978	1984		
1973	**12**	1978	1983		
1970	**17**	1990	2000		
1967	**14**	1977	1982		

Auction prices realized in the last four years

year	U.S. $	F. frs	year	U.S. $	F. frs	year	U.S. $	F. frs
1985*	20.00	111	1966*	41.00	233			
1983*	40.00	227	1964*	34.00	192			
1982*	37.00	213	1957	26.00	147			
1981*	16.00	90	1955*	29.00	162			
1978	25.00	142	1938	42.00	239			
1976	22.00	127	1905*	101.00	571			
1975	27.00	151	1900*	214.00	1213			
1970*	34.00	195						

Auction prices since the last two years. For an indication of value and quality of the missing vintages until 1928, see category III, page 34/35.

Château Cantenac-Brown
Cantenac, 3ME CRU CLASSÉ DU MÉDOC

Comments
The château was owned by the Du Vivier family until 1987 when it was sold to the Compagnie du Midi. In 1989, this insurance company merged with AXA Assurance, so that the château came under the sphere of influence of Jean-Michel Cazes. Thanks to the money of AXA and the know-how of Jean-Michel Cazes, this Cru underwent an impressive metamorphosis in a short time. The buildings and cellars were given a new appearance and even the wine received a new "look".
Second wine: Château Canuet

Type Indication
From 1989 onward, the style of this Cru has changed. It used to be a light fragile Margaux. Under the supervision of Cazes it has turned into a broad, juicy Cru with a promising structure for cellaring.

Technical data

Owner	: AXA-Millésimes		
Director	: Jean-Michel Cazes		
Régisseur	: José Sanfins		
Oenologist	: Jaques Boissenot		
Vineyard acreage		:	104 acres
Grape varieties:	Cabernet Sauvignon	:	67%
	Cabernet Franc	:	8%
	Merlot	:	25%
	Other	:	
Average age of vines		:	20 years
Average annual production (cases of 12 bottles)		:	15,000

Specifications

Vintage	Assessment and Development 0 to 20 rating	drink from	cellaring potential	Market Value Summer 1995 U.S. $	F. frs	Change in % since '93
1993	16	1997	2004	19.00	84	18%
1992	**15**	1995	1999	18.00	83	33%
1991	**14**	1994	2000			
1990	**18**	1998	2010	27.00	121	14%
1989	**18**	1996	2010			
1988	16	1995	2005	31.00	140	38%
1987	**13**	1991	1996			
1986	**15**	1995	2003			
1985	**15**	1992	2000			
1984	**13**	1988	1995			
1983						
1982						
1981						
1980						
1979						
1978						
1977						

Older vintages	0 to 20 rating	drink from	cellaring potential	Market Value U.S. $	F. frs
1973	**15**	1978	1983		

Auction prices realized in the last four years

year	U.S. $	F. frs	year	U.S. $	F. frs	year	U.S. $	F. frs
1985*	17.00	95	1947	62.00	351			
1983*	12.00	70	1900*	240.00	1365			
1979	21.00	118						
1978*	21.00	118						
1975*	19.00	105						
1970	30.00	172						
1966	31.00	177						
1953	34.00	194						

Auction prices since the last two years. For an indication of value and quality of the missing vintages until 1928, see category III, page 34/35.

Château Carbonnieux
Léognan, GRAND CRU CLASSÉ DE GRAVES

Comments
Carbonnieux is one of the oldest vineyards in the Graves: the hills were already planted with vines in the days of the 13th century nobleman Ramon Carbonnieu. The present owners, the Perrin family, gained their winemaking experience in Algeria, where they had been winemakers from 1850. The vinification process is traditional; the ripening process takes 18 months to 2 years in oak barrels, 35% of which are renewed annually.

Carbonnieux produces a white wine too, which is not taken into consideration here.

Type Indication
The most striking characteristic of the Carbonnieux wines is the élan they display. Carbonnieux is lean and tight in poor vintages. In good vintages roundness gives this Graves the backbone it sometimes misses.

Technical data

Owner	: Perrin Family		
Régisseur	: Antony Perrin		
Cellar master	: Jean Henquinet		
Oenologist	: Philippe Moureau		
Vineyard acreage		:	111 acres
Grape varieties:	Cabernet Sauvignon	:	55%
	Cabernet Franc	:	10%
	Merlot	:	30%
	Other	:	5%
Average age of vines		:	35 years
Average annual production (cases of 12 bottles)		:	25,000

Specifications

Vintage	Assessment and Development			Market Value Summer 1995		Change in % since '93
	0 to 20 rating	drink from	cellaring potential	U.S. $	F. frs	
1993	15	1997	2005	18.00	83	21%
1992	**14**	1995	2000	22.00	101	7%
1991	**15**	1994	2000	21.00	97	
1990	**15**	1995	2005	37.00	169	53%
1989	**15**	1994	2000	28.00	128	31%
1988	**16**	1995	2005			
1987	**14**	1990	1994			
1986	**12**	1990	1995			
1985	**15**	1992	2000			
1984	**11**	1988	1994			
1983	**16**	1990	2000			
1982	**15**	1987	1995			
1981	**15**	1988	1998			
1980	**12**	1983	1990			
1979	**14**	1985	1995			
1978						
1977	**12**	1983	1990			

Older vintages	0 to 20 rating	drink from	cellaring potential	Market Value	
				U.S. $	F. frs
1975	**16**	1980	1995		
1973	**14**	1977	1983		
1963	**12**	1970	1975		

Auction prices realized in the last four years

year	U.S. $	F. frs	year	U.S. $	F. frs	year	U.S. $	F. frs
1985*	13.00	76						
1982	26.00	150						
1981*	12.00	69						
1978	19.00	109						
1975*	14.00	80						
1970	16.00	90						
1933*	119.00	677						
1928*	133.00	756						

Auction prices since the last two years. For an indication of value and quality of the missing vintages until 1928, see category IV, page 36/37.

Château Cheval Blanc
Saint-Emilion, 1ER GRAND CRU CLASSÉ A

Comments
Although Saint-Emilion is known as a district which has the Merlot grape to thank for its renown, the composition of the Cheval Blanc vineyard is an exception to the rule.
Due to the different composition of the vineyard, this Cru is less vulnerable to night-frost.
Not only the less vulnerable varieties of grape but also the steady management of the owners provides for the exemplary consistency in quality that this Cru displays.

Type Indication
Despite the low percentage of Merlot, Cheval-Blanc is a true-to-type Saint-Emilion. A wine rich in warm subtlety and juicy roundness. Already in its youth this Cru demonstrates a creamy and velvety aroma. Although often quite intense, the Cheval Blanc of the 1ers Crus from Saint-Emilion is not the Cru with the greatest aging potential.

Technical data

Owner	: Héritiers Fourcaud-Laussac		
Régisseur	: Pierre Lurton		
Technical director	: Kees van Leeuwen		
Oenologist	: Gilles Pauquet		
Vineyard acreage		:	89 acres
Grape varieties:	Cabernet Sauvignon	:	1%
	Cabernet Franc	:	60%
	Merlot	:	38%
	Malbec	:	1%
Average age of vines		:	35 years
Average annual production (cases of 12 bottles)		:	11,500

Specifications

Vintage	Assessment and Development 0 to 20 rating	drink from	cellaring potential	Market Value Summer 1995 U.S. $	F. frs	Change in % since '93
1993	18	1998	2015	70.00	319	20%
1992	16	1995	2003	57.00	258	28%
1991	Harvest has been declassified					
1990	18	1996	2010	158.00	722	86%
1989	18	1996	2015	110.00	503	3%
1988	17	1994	2015	128.00	585	29%
1987	16	1990	1997			
1986	17	1992	2010	116.00	531	27%
1985	18	1992	2020	149.00	681	40%
1984	15	1990	1995			
1983	18	1993	2010			
1982	18	1990	2005			
1981	18	1990	2005			
1980	17	1987	1998			
1979	16	1985	1995			
1978	15	1985	1997			
1977	14	1984	1995			

Older vintages	0 to 20 rating	drink from	cellaring potential	Market Value U.S. $	F. frs
1976	18	1985	1998		
1975					
1973	16	1976	1982	272.00	1240
1970	18	1980	1990		
1967	15	1972	1984		
1966	19	1980	2000		
1961	17	1979	1995		

Auction prices realized in the last four years

year	U.S. $	F. frs	year	U.S. $	F. frs	year	U.S. $	F. frs
1989*	72.00	408	1976*	68.00	388	1949*	569.00	3232
1986*	95.00	539	1975*	94.00	532	1948*	211.00	1197
1985*	75.00	423	1971*	75.00	424	1947*	911.00	5172
1983*	78.00	441	1970*	169.00	958	1945*	414.00	2351
1982*	177.00	1966	1966*	151.00	857	1933*	240.00	1365
1981*	62.00	354	1961*	405.00	2299	1928*	319.00	1812
1979*	63.00	359	1959*	241.00	1370	1924*	201.00	1142
1978*	84.00	479	1953*	187.00	1063	1872*	78.00	443

Auction prices since the last two years. For an indication of value and quality of the missing vintages until 1928, see category I, page 30/31.

CHEVAL-BLANC

Domaine de Chevalier
Léognan, GRAND CRU CLASSÉ DE GRAVES

Comments
The name Chevalier is probably a corruption of Chilbaley, the oldest known owner who was most likely the founder of the estate (18th century). In 1865, the estate was bought by Jean Ricard, great-grandfather of the present occupant, Claude Ricard. Just like other Graves (Haut-Bailly, De Fieuzal, La Gravière - now Malartic-Lagravière) Domaine de Chevalier was to profit from the enormous effort and knowledge of the Ricard family. In 1983, the estate was sold to the Bernard family. In 1988, Claude Ricard withdrew. It is to be hoped that he has succeeded in passing on his knowledge and skill to his successors.

Type Indication
In view of the substantial percentage of Cabernet, Domaine de Chevalier normally has a firm and delicate bouquet next to its deep color. The emphasis lies on finesse and élan. It is one of the best Graves to cellar.

Technical data

Owner	: Lucien Bernard Family		
Director	: Olivier Bernard		
Régisseur	: Loïs Grassin		
Oenologist	: Prof. Pascal Ribéreau-Gayon		
Vineyard acreage		:	64 acres
Grape varieties:	Cabernet Sauvignon	:	70%
	Cabernet Franc	:	5%
	Merlot	:	25%
	Other	:	
Average age of vines		:	25 years
Average annual production (cases of 12 bottles)		:	10,000

Specifications

Vintage	Assessment and Development 0 to 20 rating	drink from	cellaring potential	Market Value Summer 1995 U.S. $	F. frs	Change in % since '93
1993	16	1998	2010	25.00	114	14%
1992	15	1995	2000	22.00	101	5%
1991	16	1995	2005	28.00	128	6%
1990	16	1995	2010	45.00	203	25%
1989	18	1997	2015	46.00	210	4%
1988	17	1995	2015	55.00	251	30%
1987	15	1991	1996			
1986	17	1994	2010	48.00	217	3%
1985	16	1992	2005	61.00	278	5%
1984	16	1990	2000			
1983	16	1993	2010	57.00	258	33%
1982	17	1990	2000	81.00	367	41%
1981	17	1988	1998			
1980	15	1985	1990	33.00	148	
1979		1989	2000			
1978		1994	2005			
1977						

Older vintages	0 to 20 rating	drink from	cellaring potential	Market Value U.S. $	F. frs
1976		1987	1995		
1973	16	1977	1985		

Auction prices realized in the last four years

year	U.S. $	F. frs	year	U.S. $	F. frs	year	U.S. $	F. frs
1989*	26.00	147	1970	75.00	428			
1988*	23.00	131	1967*	24.00	136			
1984*	23.00	132	1966*	69.00	389			
1983*	26.00	147	1961*	128.00	729			
1982*	53.00	301	1952	78.00	445			
1981*	32.00	180						
1978*	46.00	263						
1975*	39.00	220						

Auction prices since the last two years. For an indication of value and quality of the missing vintages until 1928, see category II, page 32/33.

Château Clerc Milon
Pauillac, 5ME CRU CLASSÉ DU MÉDOC

Comments
A Cru Classé added to the stable of Philippe de Rothschild in 1970. It is a wine produced along the same lines as that of the Mouton-Rothschild and Château d'Armailhac. The vinification takes place in stainless steel fermentation tanks.

Since the take-over in 1970, the quality of this Cru has improved every year. A château in which responsible financial investment is made.

Type Indication
Clerc-Milon is the most delightful wine in the Philippe de Rothschild stable. For a Pauillac, the wine is strikingly graceful and elegant. The large percentage of Merlot often makes this Cru ripen sooner than its counterparts. In good years Clerc-Milon has sufficient texture to guarantee good aging.

Technical data

Owner	: Baronne Philippine de Rothschild		
Technical director	: Patrick Léon		
Cellar master	: Yves Dupuy		
Vineyard acreage		:	67 acres
Grape varieties:	Cabernet Sauvignon	:	70%
	Cabernet Franc	:	10%
	Merlot	:	20%
	Other	:	
Average age of vines		:	40 years
Average annual production (cases of 12 bottles)		:	10,000

Specifications

Vintage	Assessment and Development 0 to 20 rating	drink from	cellaring potential	Market Value Summer 1995 U.S. $	F. frs	Change in % since '93
1993	16	1998	2008	21.00	97	15%
1992	16	1995	2000	18.00	81	13%
1991	**14**	1994	2000	20.00	88	17%
1990	**14**	1995	2005	33.00	148	
1989	**17**	1996	2015			
1988	**16**	1994	2005			
1987	**15**	1991	1997			
1986	**17**	1994	2015			
1985	**18**	1993	2015			
1984	**15**	1990	2000			
1983	**17**	1993	2010			
1982						
1981	**15**	1988	2000			
1980						
1979	**14**	1985	1995			
1978	**16**	1985	1997	51.00	230	100%
1977	**12**	1983	1988			

Older vintages	0 to 20 rating	drink from	cellaring potential	Market Value U.S. $	F. frs
1973	**15**	1978	1983		
1971	**15**	1980	1990		
1970	**15**	1978	1993		

Auction prices realized in the last four years

year	U.S. $	F. frs	year	U.S. $	F. frs	year	U.S. $	F. frs
1989*	21.00	118						
1988*	19.00	108						
1986*	32.00	180						
1985*	21.00	121						
1982	25.00	142						
1975	19.00	108						
1970	23.00	132						

Auction prices since the last two years. For an indication of value and quality of the missing vintages until 1928, see category III, page 34/35.

Château Cos d'Estournel
Saint-Estèphe, 2ME CRU CLASSÉ DU MÉDOC

Comments
One of the most consistent first-class wines of the Médoc. Monsieur Bruno Prats, who holds the reins here, is an extremely competent and intelligent expert. During fermentation he pays special attention to the development of the tannin content. He endeavors to extract as many soft tannins as possible from the must and skins. Because of this the wine is ready to drink sooner, whilst the period of maturity is not effected.
Second wine: Château de Marbuzet

Type Indication
The large percentage of Merlot and the soft-tannin theory of Bruno Prats often makes this Cru pleasant to drink when still quite young. Cos is moreover a Cru which can hold out for a long period. It is a rich, deep, meaty front runner of the 1855 classification. Intensity and special charm are united in this wine almost every year.

Technical data

Owner	: S.A. des Domaines Prats		
Director	: Bruno Prats		
Cellar master	: Francis Carle		
Oenologist	: Prof. Pascal Ribéreau-Gayon		
Vineyard acreage		:	175 acres
Grape varieties:	Cabernet Sauvignon	:	60%
	Cabernet Franc	:	2%
	Merlot	:	38%
	Other	:	
Average age of vines		:	35 years
Average annual production (cases of 12 bottles)		:	30,000

Specifications

Vintage	Assessment and Development 0 to 20 rating	drink from	cellaring potential	Market Value Summer 1995 U.S. $	F. frs	Change in % since '93
1993	17	1998	2012	28.00	125	9%
1992	**16**	1996	2005	26.00	117	43%
1991	**15**	1994	2000	31.00	142	
1990	**18**	1996	2010	50.00	228	32%
1989	**18**	1997	2015	57.00	258	22%
1988	**17**	1998	2010	57.00	258	38%
1987	**16**	1990	1997	33.00	148	18%
1986	**17**	1995	2010	72.00	326	39%
1985	**17**	1995	2007	66.00	299	24%
1984	**15**	1990	2000	30.00	135	13%
1983	**16**	1990	2008	57.00	258	16%
1982	**18**	1990	2010	130.00	592	42%
1981	**17**	1990	2005			
1980	**16**	1983	1992			
1979	**18**	1987	2000			
1978	**17**	1985	1995			
1977	**14**	1983	1990			

Older vintages	0 to 20 rating	drink from	cellaring potential	Market Value U.S. $	F. frs
1976	**17**	1987	2000		
1975	**18**	1990	2002	81.00	367
1974	**11**	1978	1985		
1973	**14**	1978	1985		
1970	**16**	1985	1995	130.00	592
1967	**12**	1973	1980		
1966	**18**	1972	1992		
1962	**16**	1970	1980		

Auction prices realized in the last four years

year	U.S. $	F. frs	year	U.S. $	F. frs	year	U.S. $	F. frs
1990*	41.00	230	1978*	53.00	299	1961*	177.00	1005
1989*	40.00	229	1976*	35.00	199	1959*	130.00	739
1988*	32.00	180	1975*	48.00	273	1955*	161.00	914
1986*	43.00	243	1970*	73.00	413	1938*	66.00	372
1985*	63.00	359	1966*	70.00	395	1934*	111.00	628
1983*	32.00	180	1964*	25.00	144	1911*	114.00	646
1982*	75.00	424	1963*	21.00	121	1895*	317.00	1801
1981*	45.00	255	1962*	51.00	287	1870*	617.00	3503

Auction prices since the last two years. For an indication of value and quality of the missing vintages until 1928, see category II, page 32/33.

Château Cos-Labory
Saint-Estèphe, 5ME CRU CLASSÉ DU MÉDOC

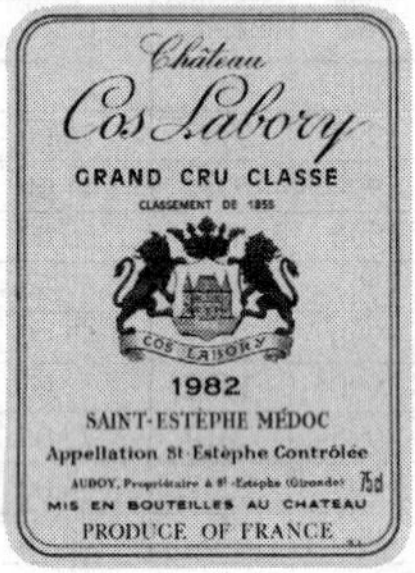

Comments
Cos-Labory is a neighbor of Château Lafite-Rothschild and Château Cos d'Estournel. Strange as it may seem, the wines of Cos-Labory cannot be compared to those of its neighbors. The wine of this château is often taken care of badly. Many Cru Bourgeois in the Médoc produce wines of a much higher standard.

Type Indication
During a tasting with as its theme Lafite-Rothschild and Neighbors, Cos Labory gave a poor rendition of a Grand Cru. The compilers of the 1855 classification would regret their choice. With firm management and purposeful investment, this Cru could once again be restored to its original place of honor.

Technical data

Owner	: S.C.E. Domaines Audoy		
Régisseur	: Bernard Audoy		
Vineyard acreage		:	44 acres
Grape varieties:	Cabernet Sauvignon	:	50%
	Cabernet Franc	:	15%
	Merlot	:	30%
	Petit Verdot	:	5%
Average age of vines		:	25 years
Average annual production (cases of 12 bottles)		:	8,000

Specifications

Vintage	Assessment and Development			Market Value Summer 1995		Change in % since '93
	0 to 20 rating	drink from	cellaring potential	U.S. $	F. frs	
1993	15	1997	2007	18.00	80	25%
1992	**14**	1995	1999	16.00	73	25%
1991	**15**	1994	2000			
1990	**14**	1995	2010	30.00	135	30%
1989	**16**	1995	2005			
1988	**14**	1997	2010			
1987	**13**	1992	1997			
1986	**15**	1993	2005			
1985	**14**	1991	2001			
1984						
1983						
1982						
1981	**14**	1987	1997			
1980						
1979						
1978	**14**	1985	1990			
1977						

Older vintages	0 to 20 rating	drink from	cellaring potential	Market Value	
				U.S. $	F. frs
1974	**7**	1976	1979		
1973	**9**	1977	1978		
1970	**12**	1975	1984		

Auction prices realized in the last four years

year	U.S. $	F. frs	year	U.S. $	F. frs	year	U.S. $	F. frs
1988*	14.00	77						
1985*	19.00	105						
1982*	17.00	98						
1978	17.00	95						
1975	17.00	94						
1970	19.00	108						

* Auction prices since the last two years. For an indication of value and quality of the missing vintages until 1928, see category IV, page 36/37.

Château Croizet-Bages
Pauillac, 5ME CRU CLASSÉ DU MÉDOC

Comments
In spite of the beautiful situation of the vineyards of this Cru, bordering on Château Latour and Château Lynch-Bages, it is not a Cru with a very impressive record.

The quality of the château is very inconsistent. A Cru where a good vintage is a coincidence. For a Cru Classé, Croizet-Bages is cheap. Although there are often better Crus Bourgeois on sale for less.

Starting with the 1992 vintage, owner Jean-Michel Quié, who is also the owner of Rauzan-Gassies, installed a new extensive cuverie so that different types of grapes can be vinified separately and a more careful assembly of the wine will be possible. Time will tell whether the investment will translate into quality.

Type Indication
Croizet-Bages lacks intensity. Although it is a Cru which registers the 'appellation Pauillac' correctly. Often however, the tannins and acids are not resisted enough by the fruit and roundness. Croizet-Bages is not a Cru which can hold out for long.

Technical data

Owner	: Quié Family
Régisseur	: Jean-Michel Quié
Cellar master	: Marc Espagnet

Vineyard acreage		: 62 acres
Grape varieties:	Cabernet Sauvignon	: 70%
	Cabernet Franc	: 10%
	Merlot	: 20%
	Other	:
Average age of vines		: 30 years
Average annual production (cases of 12 bottles)		: 8,000

Specifications

Vintage	Assessment and Development 0 to 20 rating	drink from	cellaring potential	Market Value Summer 1995 U.S. $	F. frs	Change in % since '93
1993	12	1995	2005	15.00	68	32%
1992	**12**	1995	2000	14.00	64	
1991	**12**	1994	2000			
1990	**14**	1995	2005	21.00	94	20%
1989	**14**	1995	2005	21.00	95	17%
1988	**14**	1995	2005			
1987						
1986	**13**	1990	1997			
1985	**11**	1989	1995			
1984	**11**	1989	1995			
1983	**12**	1988	1995			
1982	**15**	1987	1995			
1981	**14**	1986	1990			
1980	**10**	1982	1986			
1979	**14**	1985	1990			
1978						
1977	**10**	1983	1986			

Older vintages	0 to 20 rating	drink from	cellaring potential	Market Value U.S. $	F. frs
1976	**15**	1983	1990		
1975	**16**	1985	1995		
1967	**12**	1974	1980		
1966	**10**	1972	1987		

Auction prices realized in the last four years

year	U.S. $	F. frs	year	U.S. $	F. frs	year	U.S. $	F. frs
1986*	11.00	62	1961	38.00	218			
1983	19.00	107	1959	48.00	273			
1978	19.00	108						
1976	15.00	84						
1975*	18.00	101						
1971*	13.00	75						
1970	27.00	156						
1964*	24.00	139						

* Auction prices since the last two years. For an indication of value and quality of the missing vintages until 1928, see category IV, page 36/37.

Château Dauzac
Labarde, 5ME CRU CLASSÉ DU MÉDOC

Comments
A Cru which has changed hands rather a lot in the past few years and where reconstruction just doesn't seem to get off the ground. The results on the tasting table are as yet not very convincing, although a little confidence in a speedy improvement in quality is justified.

The MAIF insurance company (the social insurance fund of French teachers) is the new owner since 1988. This means that the château enjoyed a more ample budget. The new funds were used to drain the vineyards and modernize the vinification process.

In 1992 the famous wine producer André Lurton became a minority shareholder and was given a management position.
Second wine: La Bastide Dauzac

Type Indication
Although the quality of this Cru has been improving since 1980, the wines from the eighties are a bit light-footed. It is not a reliable wine for aging, nor a wine with real 'Grand Cru' allure.

Technical data

Owner	: Compagnie d'Assurances MAIF / André Lurton	
Management	: André Lurton / Philippe Roux	
Cellar master	: Gabriel Rivéro	
Oenologists	: Prof. Pascal Ribéreau-Gayon, Jacques Boissenot	
Vineyard acreage		: 111 acres
Grape varieties:	Cabernet Sauvignon	: 55%
	Cabernet Franc	: 4%
	Merlot	: 38%
	Petit Verdot	: 3%
Average age of vines		: 25 years
Average annual production (cases of 12 bottles)		: 20,000

Specifications

Vintage	Assessment and Development			Market Value Summer 1995		Change in % since '93
	0 to 20 rating	drink from	cellaring potential	U.S. $	F. frs	
1993	16	1997	2007			
1992	**14**	1995	1998	20.00	91	
1991	**14**	1994	2000			
1990	**15**	1995	2005	28.00	128	63%
1989	**15**	1995	2005	28.00	128	60%
1988	**15**	1995	2010			
1987	**13**	1990	1995			
1986	**16**	1995	2010			
1985	**17**	1993	2003			
1984	**15**	1987	1995			
1983	**15**	1990	2000			
1982						
1981	**14**	1986	1995			
1980	**13**	1983	1989			
1979						
1978						
1977						

Older vintages	0 to 20 rating	drink from	cellaring potential	Market Value	
				U.S. $	F. frs

Auction prices realized in the last four years

year	U.S. $	F. frs	year	U.S. $	F. frs	year	U.S. $	F. frs
1985	12.00	66						
1978	21.00	116						

*Auction prices since the last two years. For an indication of value and quality of the missing vintages until 1928, see category IV, page 36/37.

Château Desmirail

Margaux, 3ME CRU CLASSÉ DU MÉDOC

Comments

The end of the thirties meant for Desmirail the end of its existence. The vineyards, spread over the Cantenac district, were sold to Château Palmer and Brane-Cantenac. The owner of the latter château, Lucien Lurton, decided upon the rebirth of this Cru at the end of seventies. By an exchange he also came into possession in 1980 of the Château Palmer part of the vineyards, so that the old Desmirail was once again complete. In 1981 the first bottling took place of the 3me Cru, risen from the ashes like a phoenix! Concerning the vinification method, Lurton, as he says himself, attaches great importance to the cellar selection. So it is that, among other things, the less successful cuves are not sold under the Desmirail label but are destined for the second wine.

Second wine: Domaine de Fontarney

Type Indication

Desmirail is a classic Margaux. The three vintages since the revival impress by their fine and delicate texture, built up from fruit and soft tannin. Desmirail has good aging potential.

Technical data

Owner	: Lucien Lurton		
Technical director	: Pierre Lafévillade		
Régisseur	: Denis Lurton		
Oenologist	: Jacques Boissenot		
Vineyard acreage		:	67 acres
Grape varieties:	Cabernet Sauvignon	:	80%
	Cabernet Franc	:	9%
	Merlot	:	10%
	Other	:	1%
Average age of vines		:	25 years
Average annual production (cases of 12 bottles)		:	4,000

Specifications

Vintage	Assessment and Development 0 to 20 rating	drink from	cellaring potential	Market Value Summer 1995 U.S. $	F. frs	Change in % since '93
1993	14	1997	2003			
1992	15	1995	2000	16.00	73	
1991	**13**	1994	2000			
1990	**14**	1995	2005	27.00	121	45%
1989	**15**	1997	2007			
1988	**16**	1998	2010			
1987						
1986	**16**	1995	2010			
1985	**15**	1993	2003			
1984	**13**	1990	1997			
1983	**14**	1990	2000			
1982	**13**	1988	1998			
1981	**14**	1987	1997			
1980						
1979						
1978						
1977						

Older vintages	0 to 20 rating	drink from	cellaring potential	Market Value U.S. $	F. frs

Auction prices realized in the last four years

year	U.S. $	F. frs	year	U.S. $	F. frs	year	U.S. $	F. frs
1981	18.00	100						
1929	68.00	384						

Auction prices since the last two years. For an indication of value and quality of the missing vintages until 1928, see category IV, page 36/37.

Château Ducru-Beaucaillou

Saint-Julien, 2ME CRU CLASSÉ DU MEDOC

Comments

The owner of this château, Jean Eugène Borie, is one of the best viticulturists of Bordeaux. The impressive list of evaluation scores is the unmistakable evidence. The list contradicts the reputation of this château somewhat. In poor years, so the legends say, Ducru-Beaucaillou is at its best. In practice, however, the fair years appear to be as successful for this Cru as elsewhere in the region. Modern vinification techniques which have been adopted almost everywhere are putting an end to this legend.

Second wine: Château La Croix

Type Indication

From the large percentage of Cabernet grapes that lie at the base of this wine, one would expect a sturdy, rigid, manly wine. The opposite is true. Ducru is charming, supple and round. A Cru with a beautiful intensity in good years. It is one of the top, first-class wines of the Médoc.

Technical data

Owner	: Jean-Eugène Borie		
Technical director	: François-Xavier Borie		
Cellar master	: René Lusseau		
Oenologist	: Jacques Boissenot		
Vineyard acreage		:	124 acres
Grape varieties:	Cabernet Sauvignon	:	65%
	Cabernet Franc	:	5%
	Merlot	:	25%
	Petit Verdot	:	5%
Average age of vines		:	38 years
Average annual production (cases of 12 bottles)		:	15,500

Specifications

Vintage	Assessment and Development 0 to 20 rating	drink from	cellaring potential	Market Value Summer 1995 U.S. $	F. frs	Change in % since '93
1993	15	1998	2010	27.00	121	16%
1992	16	1996	2000	23.00	105	21%
1991	15	1994	2000	25.00	114	15%
1990	15	1995	2005	43.00	196	17%
1989	17	1998	2015	46.00	210	0%
1988	17	1998	2015	45.00	203	8%
1987	15	1991	1997			
1986	17	1993	2015	54.00	244	0%
1985	16	1992	2010	57.00	258	0%
1984	14	1990	1998			
1983	17	1993	2010	49.00	223	0%
1982	16	1987	1997	95.00	435	3%
1981	16	1990	2000	73.00	333	12%
1980	13	1984	1990			
1979	18	1985	1995	73.00	333	12%
1978	17	1983	1995			
1977	15	1983	1990			

Older vintages	0 to 20 rating	drink from	cellaring potential	Market Value U.S. $	F. frs
1976	16	1987	1998		
1975	19	1990	2005	85.00	387
1974	15	1978	1983		
1973	15	1978	1984		
1972	13	1976	1982		
1971	16	1981	1990		
1970	18	1983	2000	125.00	572
1967	17	1977	1983		

Auction prices realized in the last four years

year	U.S. $	F. frs	year	U.S. $	F. frs	year	U.S. $	F. frs
1990*	37.00	213	1979*	40.00	227	1967*	22.00	124
1989*	43.00	245	1978*	101.00	575	1966*	79.00	449
1988*	37.00	209	1976*	44.00	248	1964*	33.00	185
1986*	55.00	311	1975*	55.00	311	1961*	267.00	1516
1985*	43.00	244	1973*	25.00	144	1959*	98.00	559
1983*	36.00	204	1972*	12.00	69	1945	130.00	739
1982*	87.00	496	1971*	28.00	159	1929	325.00	1846
1981*	42.00	239	1970*	82.00	463	1899	506.00	2873

Auction prices since the last two years. For an indication of value and quality of the missing vintages until 1928, see category II, page 32/33.

Château Duhart-Milon-Rothschild

Pauillac, 4ME CRU CLASSÉ DU MÉDOC

Comments

Since 1962, the owners of this château have been the French branch of the Rothschild family, who also own the 1er Cru Classé Château Lafite-Rothschild. In 1974, the cuverie and the cellars where the wine ripens were entirely renovated. Duhart-Milon is managed by Director Eric Fabre, assisted during vinification by the oenologist, Professor Jacques Boissenot.

Although the evaluation scores of this Cru are not very convincing, it is a Cru to watch. The good score for 1983 is an indication of its potential.

Second wine: Moulin de Duhart-Milon

Type Indication

Duhart-Milon old style is an intense, robust wine with a sturdy aging potential. A wine with a lot of tannin, balanced in good years by fruit and roundness. It is a Pauillac 'par excellence'. By increasing the Merlot share in the vineyards to 30%, the future Duhart-Milon will gain more roundness.

Technical data

Owner	: Domaines Barons de Rothschild	
Technical director	: Eric Fabre	
Régisseur	: Gilbert Rokvam	
Oenologist	: Jacques Boissenot	
Vineyard acreage		: 168 acres
Grape varieties:	Cabernet Sauvignon	: 70%
	Cabernet Franc	:
	Merlot	: 30%
	Other	:
Average age of vines		: 20 years
Average annual production (cases of 12 bottles)		: 20,000

Specifications

Vintage	Assessment and Development 0 to 20 rating	drink from	cellaring potential	Market Value Summer 1995 U.S. $	F. frs	Change in % since '93
1993	15	1998	2010	20.00	90	
1992	15	1995	2000	21.00	94	
1991	14	1994	1998	27.00	121	
1990	15	1995	2005	45.00	203	115%
1989	15	1996	2008	36.00	162	34%
1988	16	1997	2010	45.00	203	79%
1987	14	1992	1997			
1986	16	1993	2010	33.00	148	25%
1985	15	1990	2000	51.00	230	88%
1984	15	1990	2000			
1983	17	1993	2010	57.00	258	64%
1982						
1981	13	1988	1995	40.00	183	0%
1980	15	1983	1990			
1979				33.00	148	
1978	14	1984	1994			
1977						

Older vintages	0 to 20 rating	drink from	cellaring potential	Market Value U.S. $	F. frs
1976					
1975					
1973	13	1977	1982		
1962	11	1970	1977		
1959	17	1970	1990		

Auction prices realized in the last four years

year	U.S. $	F. frs	year	U.S. $	F. frs	year	U.S. $	F. frs
1989*	13.00	72	1975*	27.00	151			
1985	25.00	144	1971	23.00	130			
1983*	22.00	122	1970	31.00	174			
1982*	27.00	151	1962*	21.00	119			
1981*	17.00	98	1940	92.00	521			
1979	25.00	142						
1978	19.00	109						
1976	23.00	132						

Auction prices since the last two years. For an indication of value and quality of the missing vintages until 1928, see category III, page 34/35.

Château Durfort-Vivens
Margaux, 2ME CRU CLASSÉ DU MÉDOC

Comments
Château Durfort-Vivens has the same owner as Château Brane-Cantenac, Lucien Lurton. Both of these châteaux have as advisor, as regards the vinification process, Jacques Boissenot. In their texture therefore, these two wines show a remarkable likeness. Yet there is a clear difference between them, a difference that can be traced back to the different compositions of the vineyards. Durfort-Vivens has more Cabernet at the base.
Second wine: Domaine de Cure-Bourse

Type Indication
The quality is not always consistent. In good years, the wine has depth and intensity and has good aging potential. For a Margaux, the Durfort-Vivens is quite tight.

Technical data

Owner	: Lucien Lurton	
Technical director	: Ludovic Lalande	
Régisseur	: Gonzague Lurton	
Oenologist	: Jacques Boissenot	
Vineyard acreage		: 69 acres
Grape varieties:	Cabernet Sauvignon	: 75%
	Cabernet Franc	: 10%
	Merlot	: 15%
	Other	:
Average age of vines		: 25 years
Average annual production (cases of 12 bottles)		: 5,000

Specifications

Vintage	Assessment and Development 0 to 20 rating	drink from	cellaring potential	Market Value Summer 1995 U.S. $	F. frs	Change in % since '93
1993	13	1998	2005			
1992	12	1995	1998			
1991	**14**	1994	2000			
1990	**16**	1995	2005	33.00	148	
1989	**16**	1996	2010	35.00	158	39%
1988	**17**	1998	2015	33.00	148	43%
1987	**15**	1992	1997			
1986	**15**	1992	2005			
1985	**14**	1990	2000	34.00	155	5%
1984	**13**	1989	1997			
1983	**15**	1990	2000	33.00	148	11%
1982	**15**	1987	1997			
1981	**13**	1987	1995			
1980	**13**	1984	1992			
1979	**16**	1987	1995	36.00	162	-12%
1978	**15**	1986	1996			
1977						

Older vintages	0 to 20 rating	drink from	cellaring potential	Market Value U.S. $	F. frs
1976	**16**	1987	2000		
1967	**11**	1972	1981		

Auction prices realized in the last four years

year	U.S. $	F. frs	year	U.S. $	F. frs	year	U.S. $	F. frs
1978*	18.00	101						
1970*	25.00	144						
1967	12.00	65						
1920*	77.00	435						

* Auction prices since the last two years. For an indication of value and quality of the missing vintages until 1928, see category IV, page 36/37.

Château Ferrière
Margaux, 3ME CRU CLASSÉ DU MÉDOC

Comments
With a small vineyard of 25 acres, Château Ferrière is one of the small Grand Crus Classés. For a long time, the château led an obscure existence. The former owner, Madame André Durand-Feuillerat leased her property to Château Lascombes for 25 years. In the past, Ferrière was therefore considered as a sub-label, Lascombes' second wine.

In 1992, the management was taken over by Jean Merlaut and his nieces Claire and Céline Villars. They are also associated with Chasse-Spleen and Haut-Bages Libéral.

Type Indication
It is clear that the Ferrière is nurtured in the same cellar as the Lascombes. Lascombes however receives the best attention and is a more joyful little Margaux. Especially in the fair vintages both wines are a bit short on depth, more so than their counterparts.

Technical data

Owner	: S.C. du Château Chasse-Spleen	
Director	: Claire and Céline Villars	
Régisseur	: Mr. Sutré	
Cellar master	: M. Fenouillet	
Vineyard acreage		: 25 acres
Grape varieties:	Cabernet Sauvignon	: 80%
	Cabernet Franc	:
	Merlot	: 18%
	Petit Verdot	: 2%
Average age of vines		: 30 years
Average annual production (cases of 12 bottles)		: 2,000

Specifications

Vintage	Assessment and Development			Market Value Summer 1995		Change in % since '93
	0 to 20 rating	drink from	cellaring potential	U.S. $	F. frs	
1993	16	1998	2010	19.00	87	31%
1992	15	1995	2000	18.00	83	
1991	**12**	1994	2000			
1990				23.00	105	
1989				26.00	117	
1988	**13**	1995	2005			
1987						
1986	**15**	1990	1996			
1985	**15**	1990	1995	32.00	146	
1984	**12**	1987	1994			
1983	**13**	1988	1998	32.00	144	
1982	**15**	1990	2000			
1981						
1980						
1979						
1978						
1977						

Older vintages	0 to 20 rating	drink from	cellaring potential	Market Value	
				U.S. $	F. frs
1973	**14**	1978	1985		
1970	**12**	1978	1986		

Auction prices realized in the last four years

year	U.S. $	F. frs	year	U.S. $	F. frs	year	U.S. $	F. frs
1970	20.00	111						

Auction prices since the last two years. For an indication of value and quality of the missing vintages until 1928, see category IV, page 36/37.

Château de Fieuzal

Léognan, GRAND CRU CLASSÉ DE GRAVES

Comments

In 1994 Château de Fieuzal was sold to Fructivie, a life insurance company from the Groupe des Banques Populaires. Michel Dupuy, the Technical Director, who remains responsible for the wine, continues to put his special stamp on a number of Graves wines, including De Fieuzal.

Fifteen years ago, he founded the oenology laboratory of Portets. His philosophy is that first-rate quality goes hand-in-hand with risk-taking during the vinification process. He is an advocate of the highest possible temperature (34/35 °C 93/95°F) at the end of the fermentation process. This is risky because fermentation could stop and turn into production of acetic acid at the drop of a hat and if this happens, there is no alternative but to write it off. Only with optimal supervision of each cuve is such risky vinification safe.

Second wine: L'Abeille de Fieuzal

Type Indication

The new method of vinification was first employed in 1984. The '84s have an unprecedented intensity of color, flavor and bouquet. It is one of the top Graves.

Technical data

Owner	: Gérard Gribelin		
Technical director	: Michel Dupuy		
Régisseur	: Cyril Bourgne		
Cellar master	: Joël Tauzin		
Vineyard acreage		:	106 acres
Grape varieties:	Cabernet Sauvignon	:	60%
	Cabernet Franc	:	5%
	Merlot	:	30%
	Other	:	5%
Average age of vines		:	35 years
Average annual production (cases of 12 bottles)		:	12,000

Specifications

Vintage	Assessment and Development			Market Value Summer 1995		Change in % since '93
	0 to 20 rating	drink from	cellaring potential	U.S. $	F. frs	
1993	17	2000	2015	21.00	94	20%
1992	**15**	1996	2002	19.00	84	33%
1991	**15**	1994	2000	20.00	90	4%
1990	**18**	1996	2010	39.00	176	67%
1989	**18**	1998	2010	31.00	140	18%
1988	17	1995	2015			
1987	**16**	1991	1997			
1986	17	1994	2006			
1985	**18**	1990	2005			
1984	**16**	1989	2000			
1983	**15**	1992	2002			
1982	**15**	1995	2005			
1981	**16**	1988	1998			
1980	**13**	1984	1990	25.00	114	
1979	**16**	1986	1995			
1978						
1977						

Older vintages	0 to 20 rating	drink from	cellaring potential	Market Value	
				U.S. $	F. frs
1976		33.00	148		
1975		42.00	189		
1970		51.00	230		

Auction prices realized in the last four years

year	U.S. $	F. frs	year	U.S. $	F. frs	year	U.S. $	F. frs
1990*	20.00	116	1962	40.00	227			
1989*	18.00	102						
1988*	16.00	90						
1986*	21.00	118						
1985*	27.00	150						
1983	20.00	115						
1978*	16.00	93						
1970	31.00	177						

Auction prices since the last two years. For an indication of value and quality of the missing vintages until 1928, see category II, page 32/33.

CHATEAU DE FIEUZAL
GRAND CRU CLASSÉ

Château Figeac
Saint-Emilion, 1ER GRAND CRU CLASSÉ B

Comments
Of the Premiers Crus Classés from Saint-Emilion, Figeac is the Cru where, relatively speaking, the most Cabernet grapes are cultivated. With regard to position too, Figeac differs with most other 1ers Grands Crus Classés. The majority of the big Saint-Emilions border directly on the old city of Saint-Emilion. Figeac and Cheval Blanc are situated on the border of the district, from where one looks over the vineyards of Pomerol. The owners of this château, the Manoncourt family, are known all over the wine world. Modern developments in vinification have been adopted by Monsieur Thierry Manoncourt, who plays an important role behind the scenes. The daily management of the château is in the hands of Eric d'Aramon, the son-in-law of Monsieur Manoncourt. Second wine: La Grange Neuve de Figeac

Type Indication
Château Figeac is a somewhat refined, elegant Saint-Emilion. The broad sultriness one expects in wines from this district is absent in Figeac and the color also is often not quite as deep. It is a Cru which has an appealing charm and élan.

Technical data

Owner	: Thierry Manoncourt
Director	: Eric d'Aramon
Cellar master	: Jean Albineau

Vineyard acreage		: 96 acres
Grape varieties:	Cabernet Sauvignon	: 35%
	Cabernet Franc	: 35%
	Merlot	: 30%
	Other :	
Average age of vines		: 35 years
Average annual production (cases of 12 bottles)		: 12,500

Specifications

Vintage	Assessment and Development			Market Value Summer 1995		Change in % since '93
	0 to 20 rating	drink from	cellaring potential	U.S. $	F. frs	
1993	16	1997	2007	27.00	121	21%
1992	14	1995	2000	24.00	107	11%
1991						
1990	15	1995	2005	66.00	299	83%
1989	17	1998	2015	54.00	244	17%
1988	17	1994	2010	60.00	271	46%
1987	15	1990	1996			
1986	15	1992	2007	63.00	285	38%
1985	16	1990	2010			
1984	14	1989	1997	33.00	148	5%
1983	16	1988	1998	60.00	271	15%
1982	17	1987	1997			
1981	16	1987	1997	63.00	285	11%
1980	15	1984	1990			
1979	16	1985	1995			
1978	17	1986	1996			
1977	14	1984	1990			

Older vintages	0 to 20 rating	drink from	cellaring potential	Market Value	
				U.S. $	F. frs
1976	16	1987	1995		

Auction prices realized in the last four years

year	U.S. $	F. frs	year	U.S. $	F. frs	year	U.S. $	F. frs
1989*	32.00	180	1977*	14.00	81	1949*	289.00	1641
1986*	26.00	147	1976*	32.00	180	1947	202.00	1149
1985*	48.00	273	1975*	51.00	287			
1983*	38.00	214	1970*	82.00	464			
1982*	88.00	499	1966*	86.00	491			
1981*	30.00	169	1964*	53.00	299			
1979*	31.00	178	1962	74.00	419			
1978*	47.00	269	1959*	145.00	821			

Auction prices since the last two years. For an indication of value and quality of the missing vintages until 1928, see category III, page 34/35.

Clos Fourtet
Saint-Emilion, 1ER GRAND CRU CLASSÉ B

Comments
A Cru which had to go without the necessary care and attention until the mid-seventies. Vinification, as they put it, is traditional. The result is a great deal of hard tannins and an overdose of acids. In some vintages the roundness and suppleness that the Merlot grape naturally has, can compensate for these hard flavors. Clos Fourtet old style was therefore a cellaring wine. But it doesn't matter how long you might cellar an unbalanced wine, it will never become really good. A few years ago the Peynaud method of vinification was introduced, which was the reason behind the pleasant metamorphosis of Clos Fourtet.
Second wine: Domaine de Martialis

Type Indication
The last few years this Cru has a healthy and reasonably deep color, although Clos Fourtet has not yet reached superstar status. A good 'indice de souplesse', which was lacking in this Saint-Emilion, is now noticeable.

Technical data

Owner	: Lurton Frères	
Régisseur	: Tony Ballu	
Vineyard acreage		: 47 acres
Grape varieties:	Cabernet Sauvignon	: 10%
	Cabernet Franc	: 20%
	Merlot	: 70%
	Other	:
Average age of vines		: 22 years
Average annual production (cases of 12 bottles)		: 6,000

Specifications

Vintage	Assessment and Development			Market Value Summer 1995		Change in % since '93
	0 to 20 rating	drink from	cellaring potential	U.S. $	F. frs	
1993	15	1998	2008	23.00	102	10%
1992	**16**	1996	2002			
1991						
1990	**14**	1995	2005			
1989	**15**	1996	2005	32.00	147	2%
1988	**15**	1996	2005			
1987						
1986	**14**	1990	1995	33.00	148	5%
1985	**15**	1991	1997			
1984	Harvest has been declassified					
1983	**15**	1988	2000			
1982	**14**	1987	1995			
1981	**13**	1986	1992			
1980	**13**	1983	1993			
1979	**15**	1984	1994			
1978						
1977						

Older vintages	0 to 20 rating	drink from	cellaring potential	Market Value	
				U.S. $	F. frs
1971	**14**	1978	1988		
1970	**13**	1976	1987		
1966	**14**	1974	1985		
1961	**10**	1971	1981		

Auction prices realized in the last four years

year	U.S. $	F. frs	year	U.S. $	F. frs	year	U.S. $	F. frs
1982	21.00	120	1949*	70.00	395			
1981	16.00	89	1899*	207.00	1177			
1979	19.00	109						
1978	17.00	96						
1975	23.00	131						
1970	27.00	156						
1961*	49.00	279						
1955*	47.00	269						

Auction prices since the last two years. For an indication of value and quality of the missing vintages until 1928, see category IV, page 36/37.

Château La Gaffelière

Saint-Emilion, 1ER GRAND CRU CLASSÉ B

Comments

As recent as in the fifties, this Cru was known under the present name with the addition of 'Naudes', a name referring to one of the vineyards of this château. Previously Château La Gaffelière-Naudes, now simply 'La Gaffelière', is now organized along modern lines. What is special about this Cru is the length of time that the grape must remains in the fermentation tanks. The intention is to give the wine more flavor. Even so La Gaffelière does not excel in the Saint-Emilion classification.

Second wine: Clos la Gaffelière

Type Indication

In spite of the not insignificant percentage of Merlot grapes, which would lead one to expect a quick supple wine, La Graffière is quite rigid and hard for a Saint-Emilion. La Gaffelière is firm in its tannins, which gives the wine a somewhat tight appearance. It is a Cru which can be aged well, and when ready to drink, its hardness is brought into balance with roundness.

Technical data

Owner	: Comte de Malet Roquefort	
Technical director	: Alain Dourthe Larrère	
Cellar master	: Jean-Marie Galeri	
Oenologist	: Prof. Guy Guimberteau	
Vineyard acreage		: 54 acres
Grape varieties:	Cabernet Sauvignon	: 10%
	Cabernet Franc	: 25%
	Merlot	: 65%
	Other :	
Average age of vines		: 40 years
Average annual production (cases of 12 bottles)		: 10,000

Specifications

Vintage	Assessment and Development 0 to 20 rating	drink from	cellaring potential	Market Value Summer 1995 U.S. $	F. frs	Change in % since '93
1993	17	1998	2010	24.00	107	17%
1992	15	1995	2000	21.00	94	8%
1991	14	1995	2000			
1990	17	1996	2010	43.00	196	51%
1989	17	1997	2010	46.00	210	42%
1988	16	1995	2005	45.00	203	56%
1987	13	1991	1996			
1986	16	1992	2007			
1985	16	1990	2000			
1984	13	1988	1993	33.00	148	25%
1983	15	1988	2000	43.00	196	8%
1982	15	1987	1987	75.00	339	50%
1981	15	1987	1997			
1980	13	1985	1990			
1979	14	1984	1994			
1978				78.00	353	0%
1977						

Older vintages	0 to 20 rating	drink from	cellaring potential	Market Value U.S. $	F. frs
1975				57.00	258

Auction prices realized in the last four years

year	U.S. $	F. frs	year	U.S. $	F. frs	year	U.S. $	F. frs
1985*	21.00	118	1967	20.00	114			
1983*	20.00	116	1966*	45.00	254			
1982*	33.00	185	1964	43.00	245			
1978	30.00	172	1962	27.00	154			
1975*	24.00	136						
1973*	12.00	67						
1971	17.00	95						
1970	37.00	209						

Auction prices since the last two years. For an indication of value and quality of the missing vintages until 1928, see category III, page 34/35.

Château Giscours
Labarde, 3ME CRU CLASSÉ DU MÉDOC

Comments
An imposing château with a total acreage of 741 acres planted with vines, 198 acres of which have the right of the 'appellation Margaux'. The château underwent a facelift in the early sixties. The neglected parklands and château are now in perfect condition.

Until 1988, Giscours was a Cru whose sale was exclusively in the hands of the firm of Gilbey in Loudenne, so that the wine was rather isolated from the Grand Cru scene. Now that this Cru is on the open market, it will quickly get a realistic market value.

Type Indication
Giscours is a real Margaux. In successful vintages it has a lovely suppleness but at the same time firm texture. However, it is a Cru lacking a certain consistency in quality. The intense, deep color is striking, even in poor vintages.

Technical data

Owner	: Nicolas Tari Family		
Technical director	: Mr. Vanderpotte		
Régisseur	: Pierre Tari		

Vineyard acreage		:	198 acres
Grape varieties:	Cabernet Sauvignon	:	70%
	Cabernet Franc	:	5%
	Merlot	:	20%
	Petit Verdot	:	5%
Average age of vines		:	35 years
Average annual production (cases of 12 bottles)		:	33,000

Specifications

Vintage	Assessment and Development			Market Value Summer 1995		Change in % since '93
	0 to 20 rating	drink from	cellaring potential	U.S. $	F. frs	
1993	14	1998	2010			
1992	12	1995	2000			
1991	**15**	1994	2000			
1990	**15**	1995	2005	31.00	140	2%
1989	**16**	1995	2010	35.00	158	9%
1988	**16**	1995	2015			
1987	14	1992	2000			
1986	**15**	1993	2007			
1985	**16**	1995	2020			
1984	14	1989	1995			
1983	**15**	1988	1994			
1982	**17**	1995	2010	54.00	247	15%
1981	**16**	1990	2000			
1980						
1979	**15**	1983	1992			
1978						
1977						

Older vintages	0 to 20 rating	drink from	cellaring potential	Market Value	
				U.S. $	F. frs
1976	**16**	1983	1995		
1974	**12**	1978	1986		
1973	**16**	1978	1985		
1970	**17**	1987	2000		
1969	**15**	1976	1987		
1967	**17**	1975	1985		

Auction prices realized in the last four years

year	U.S. $	F. frs	year	U.S. $	F. frs	year	U.S. $	F. frs
1989*	20.00	112	1975*	35.00	201			
1986	18.00	100	1970*	55.00	309			
1983*	24.00	136	1967*	20.00	112			
1982*	32.00	180	1966	58.00	329			
1981	40.00	227	1962	30.00	172			
1979	26.00	150	1961*	43.00	242			
1978*	41.00	230	1959*	38.00	217			
1976	24.00	138	1919	75.00	425			

* Auction prices since the last two years. For an indication of value and quality of the missing vintages until 1928, see category III, page 34/35.

Château Grand-Puy Ducasse
Pauillac, 5ME CRU CLASSÉ DU MÉDOC

Comments
Since 1971, this Cru has been connected to the firm of Mestrezat et Preller of Bordeaux. When they took over the château, only 25 acres were planted with vines. In the meantime another 69 acres have been planted. The vineyard of this château is therefore still quite young.

As the wine and vineyard are taken care of well, this is a château that will have good chances of attractive wines in the near future. With a really reasonable price, it is a Cru giving value for money.

Second wine: Château Artigues-Arnaud

Type Indication
A fine, somewhat light-footed Pauillac. The tight harmony is characteristic. The bouquet, like the flavor, often needs time to develop. A real Pauillac with good aging potential.

Technical data

Owner	: Société Civile de Grand-Puy Ducasse		
Technical director	: Patrice Bandiera		
Cellar master	: Yvon Rautureau		
Oenologist	: Bernard Monteau		
Vineyard acreage		:	94 acres
Grape varieties:	Cabernet Sauvignon	:	62%
	Cabernet Franc :		
	Merlot	:	38%
	Other	:	
Average age of vines		:	25 years
Average annual production (cases of 12 bottles)		:	12,500

Specifications

Vintage	Assessment and Development 0 to 20 rating	drink from	cellaring potential	Market Value Summer 1995 U.S. $	F. frs	Change in % since '93
1993	15	1998	2008	22.00	101	25%
1992	17	1995	2000	23.00	106	17%
1991	14	1994	2000	20.00	88	24%
1990	15	1995	2005	27.00	121	31%
1989	16	1995	2005	26.00	118	34%
1988	15	1994	2010	25.00	114	36%
1987	13	1991	1996	18.00	80	39%
1986	15	1990	2000	27.00	121	29%
1985	17	1990	2005	34.00	155	50%
1984	14	1990	1997			
1983	16	1990	2005	25.00	114	3%
1982	17	1990	2000	42.00	192	36%
1981	15	1988	1995			
1980	14	1986	1992			
1979	15	1987	1997			
1978	15	1987	1997			
1977	15	1983	1987			

Older vintages	0 to 20 rating	drink from	cellaring potential	Market Value U.S. $	F. frs
1969	15	1976	1988		

Auction prices realized in the last four years

year	U.S. $	F. frs	year	U.S. $	F. frs	year	U.S. $	F. frs
1989*	19.00	110	1966*	30.00	173			
1985*	20.00	113	1957*	27.00	155			
1982	28.00	157	1943	100.00	566			
1981*	17.00	94	1899*	151.00	856			
1979*	18.00	102						
1978	20.00	113						
1975	25.00	144						
1970	27.00	152						

Auction prices since the last two years. For an indication of value and quality of the missing vintages until 1928, see category IV, page 36/37.

Château Grand-Puy-Lacoste

Pauillac, 5ME CRU CLASSÉ DU MÉDOC

Comments

In 1978 and then in his eighty-third year, Monsieur Dupin sold the château to Jean-Eugène Borie for a song. He entrusted his so carefully managed château to his friend and skilled winemaker, because he knew that his life's work would be in good hands. François-Xavier, Jean-Eugène Borie's son moved into the château after the death of Monsieur Dupin in 1980. In close cooperation with his father, who manages Ducru-Beaucaillou excellently, François-Xavier now operates Grand-Puy-Lacoste.
Second wine: Château Lacoste-Borie

Type Indication

Château Grand-Puy-Lacoste is a classic example of a Pauillac. The wine is tough, reserved and manly. After sufficient ripening, a gossamer, pure 'mahogany' bouquet develops. A Cru with dignity and distinction, firm but nonetheless elegant and refined. A Cru with good aging potential.

Technical data

Owner	: Borie Family	
Director	: François-Xavier Borie	
Cellar master	: Philippe Gouze	
Oenologist	: Bernard Couasnon	
Vineyard acreage		: 124 acres
Grape varieties:	Cabernet Sauvignon	: 70%
	Cabernet Franc	: 5%
	Merlot	: 25%
	Other :	
Average age of vines		: 38 years
Average annual production (cases of 12 bottles)		: 12,500

Specifications

Vintage	Assessment and Development 0 to 20 rating	drink from	cellaring potential	Market Value Summer 1995 U.S. $	F. frs	Change in % since '93
1993	15	1998	2010	21.00	97	22%
1992	15	1995	2002	17.00	79	6%
1991	16	1997	2009	23.00	105	12%
1990	18	1998	2010			
1989	17	1995	2007	30.00	135	6%
1988	16	1995	2010	28.00	128	9%
1987	15	1990	1996	25.00	114	53%
1986	18	1995	2010			
1985	15	1993	2005	43.00	196	35%
1984	14	1987	1993	20.00	88	-11%
1983	17	1990	2005	33.00	148	5%
1982						
1981	16	1990	2000	36.00	162	0%
1980	16	1985	1990			
1979	16	1985	1995			
1978	16	1985	1997			
1977	15	1983	1992			

Older vintages	0 to 20 rating	drink from	cellaring potential	Market Value U.S. $	F. frs
1976	15	1984	1994		
1974	9	1978	1984		
1973	9	1978	1984		
1970	14	1980	1990		
1967	16	1973	1983		
1958	15	1964	1975		
1953	17	1960	1978		

Auction prices realized in the last four years

year	U.S. $	F. frs	year	U.S. $	F. frs	year	U.S. $	F. frs
1990*	22.00	127	1981*	19.00	110	1953	173.00	980
1989*	24.00	139	1979*	20.00	114	1952	68.00	383
1988*	20.00	114	1978*	35.00	196	1945	172.00	978
1987*	15.00	85	1976*	23.00	130	1936	49.00	275
1986*	22.00	122	1975	36.00	207			
1985*	27.00	155	1970	46.00	259			
1983*	23.00	128	1966	63.00	359			
1982*	46.00	263	1961*	57.00	322			

* Auction prices since the last two years. For an indication of value and quality of the missing vintages until 1928, see category III, page 34/35.

Château Gruaud-Larose
Saint-Julien, 2ME CRU CLASSÉ DU MÉDOC

Comments
In 1994 the firm of Cordier sold Gruaud-Larose to the French telecommunication giant Alcatel Alsthom. It was a purely financial transaction which did not affect the vinification, which remains under the management of the highly capable Georges Pauli. His style of vinification is also evident in the other Cordier properties, Château Meyney and Château Cantemerle.

Typically, Pauli produces good wines in poor years. Especially the wines from these intermediate years are worth buying, considering their often reasonable prices.

Second wine: Sarget de Gruaud-Larose

Type Indication
Gruaud-Larose is a sturdy, stately 'Grand-Seigneur'. The wine has intensity and depth. Even in poor vintages, the color is rich and deep. A Gruaud-Larose is juicy and meaty. The hefty amount of tannin is resisted by fruit and roundness, giving this Cru excellent potential for aging.

Technical data

Owner	: S.C. Château Gruaud-Larose / Domaines Cordier	
Technical director	: Georges Pauli	
Régisseur	: Patrick Fréderic	
Cellar master	: Philippe Carmagnac	
Vineyard acreage		: 203 acres
Grape varieties:	Cabernet Sauvignon	: 65%
	Cabernet Franc	: 7%
	Merlot	: 25%
	Petit Verdot	: 3%
Average age of vines		: 30 years
Average annual production (cases of 12 bottles)		: 40,000

Specifications

Vintage	Assessment and Development			Market Value Summer 1995		Change in % since '93
	0 to 20 rating	drink from	cellaring potential	U.S. $	F. frs	
1993	16	2000	2015			
1992	16	1997	2003			
1991	16	1996	2003	Maison Cordier in		
1990	17	1996	2010	Bordeaux has the sole		
1989	18	2000	2015	exclusivity to market		
1988	18	2000	2010	Gruaud-Larose.		
1987	16	1991	2000	Therefore, this wine		
1986	17	1995	2015	is not listed on the		
1985	17	1995	2020	open market.		
1984	16	1990	2000			
1983	17	1992	2010			
1982	17	1990	2005			
1981	17	1990	2005			
1980	16	1985	1995			
1979	17	1989	2000			
1978	16	1988	1998			
1977	16	1985	1993			

Older vintages	0 to 20 rating	drink from	cellaring potential	Market Value	
				U.S. $	F. frs
1976	16	1985	1995		
1975	17	1987	2000		
1974	14	1979	1986		
1973	16	1977	1984		
1970	16	1978	1990		
1967	13	1973	1981		
1961	17	1976	1995		

Auction prices realized in the last four years

year	U.S. $	F. frs	year	U.S. $	F. frs	year	U.S. $	F. frs
1989*	20.00	113	1978*	47.00	269	1953*	104.00	588
1988*	24.00	134	1976*	27.00	156	1949	211.00	1197
1986*	39.00	218	1975	38.00	218	1945*	153.00	870
1985*	35.00	198	1970	43.00	245	1937*	54.00	308
1983*	34.00	192	1966*	67.00	380	1928*	331.00	1877
1982*	66.00	377	1962	60.00	340	1917	207.00	1175
1981	34.00	192	1961	244.00	1388	1870	925.00	5254
1979*	27.00	155	1959	79.00	451	1865	655.00	3722

Auction prices since the last two years. For an indication of value and quality of the missing vintages until 1928, see category III, page 34/35.

Château Haut-Bages Libéral

Pauillac, 5ME CRU CLASSÉ DU MÉDOC

Comments

Until 1983, this was a château owned by the eight descendants of the Cruse family. Those divided interests did not improve the quality of this Cru. Although little was invested, this 5me Cru brought a reasonable wine out each year. The prospects for this château were promising in 1984. Indeed, the château was being sold to one of the most successful viticulturists of the Médoc, the Merlaut family. A family who has succeeded in bringing the Cru Bourgeois Château Chasse-Spleen up to the standard of a Cru Classé. Thus far, however, this 5me Cru has seen little progress in quality.

Type Indication

A friendly and, for a Pauillac, fast ripening wine but lacking the depth and intensity to be ranked with the great wines of the Pauillac. A more careful selection would give this Cru the potential to score higher.

Technical data

Owner	: S.A. du Château Haut-Bages Libéral	
Management	: Claire and Céline Villars	
Technical director	: M. Sutré	
Oenologist	: Bernard Couasnon	
Vineyard acreage		: 57 acres
Grape varieties:	Cabernet Sauvignon	: 80%
	Cabernet Franc	:
	Merlot	: 17%
	Petit Verdot	: 3%
Average age of vines		: 18 years
Average annual production (cases of 12 bottles)		: 10,000

Specifications

Vintage	Assessment and Development 0 to 20 rating	drink from	cellaring potential	Market Value Summer 1995 U.S. $	F. frs	Change in % since '93
1993	16	1997	2010	18.00	80	35%
1992	13	1995	2000	17.00	75	35%
1991	15	1994	2000	20.00	91	61%
1990	14	1995	2005			
1989	15	1995	2005			
1988	15	1992	1998	28.00	127	40%
1987	14	1990	1995			
1986	15	1992	2002	37.00	169	15%
1985	15	1990	2000			
1984	14	1988	1998			
1983	15	1990	2000	46.00	210	46%
1982	16	1987	1997			
1981	15	1987	1997			
1980	14	1984	1988			
1979	15	1985	1994			
1978	14	1985	1993			
1977	14	1980	1987			

Older vintages	0 to 20 rating	drink from	cellaring potential	Market Value U.S. $	F. frs
1976	14	1983	1990		
1975	15	1982	1992		
1974	13	1978	1985		
1973	12	1976	1982		

Auction prices realized in the last four years

year	U.S. $	F. frs	year	U.S. $	F. frs	year	U.S. $	F. frs
1990*	16.00	90	1975	36.00	207			
1989*	20.00	115						
1986	15.00	87						
1985*	21.00	118						
1983	21.00	119						
1982	13.00	76						
1979	14.00	82						
1976	16.00	90						

* Auction prices since the last two years. For an indication of value and quality of the missing vintages until 1928, see category IV, page 36/37.

CHATEAU
HAUT-BAGES-LIBERAL
PAUILLAC

Château Haut-Bailly
Léognan, GRAND CRU CLASSÉ DE GRAVES

Comments
In 1955, when the property was bought by a Bordeaux wine merchant of Belgian descent, Daniel Sanders, Château Haut-Bailly began to flourish. Recently, Daniel Sanders' son, Jean Sanders, took charge. Profiting from the good composition of the soil and the old age of many of the vines, the Sanders family have boosted Haut-Bailly into an excellent wine. The cellar selection is rigorous. As much as 30% is sometimes destined for the second wine.
Second wine: La Parde de Haut-Bailly

Type Indication
Haut-Bailly is characterized by low acidity and therefore a high degree of suppleness. It is a rather appealing wine with harmony and charm. A Graves with good aging potential.

Technical data

Owner	: Sanders Family		
Director	: Jean Sanders		
Cellar master	: Serge Charritt		
Oenologist	: Prof. Pascal Ribéreau-Gayon		
Vineyard acreage		:	69 acres
Grape varieties:	Cabernet Sauvignon	:	62%
	Cabernet Franc	:	13%
	Merlot	:	25%
	Other	:	
Average age of vines		:	35 years
Average annual production (cases of 12 bottles)		:	10,000

Specifications

Vintage	Assessment and Development 0 to 20 rating	drink from	cellaring potential	Market Value Summer 1995 U.S. $	F. frs	Change in % since '93
1993	15	1998	2007	22.00	99	23%
1992	**15**	1996	2002	21.00	97	18%
1991	Harvest has been declassified					
1990	**16**	1995	2005	48.00	217	92%
1989	**16**	1996	2005			
1988	**17**	1997	2015			
1987	**14**	1992	1997			
1986	**15**	1990	1997	49.00	223	82%
1985	**16**	1992	2010			
1984	**13**	1988	1995	22.00	101	8%
1983	**16**	1990	2000			
1982	**14**	1987	1995	66.00	299	56%
1981	**16**	1990	2000	45.00	203	
1980						
1979	**16**	1985	1995	45.00	203	
1978						
1977						

Older vintages	0 to 20 rating	drink from	cellaring potential	Market Value U.S. $	F. frs
1975				66.00	299
1973	**14**	1977	1981		

Auction prices realized in the last four years

year	U.S. $	F. frs	year	U.S. $	F. frs	year	U.S. $	F. frs
1990*	21.00	117	1975*	19.00	110			
1985	21.00	120	1971*	18.00	103			
1983	17.00	96	1970*	35.00	196			
1982	31.00	178	1967	12.00	65			
1981	22.00	123	1962	36.00	202			
1979	15.00	87	1940	85.00	482			
1978*	24.00	139						
1976	23.00	132						

* Auction prices since the last two years. For an indication of value and quality of the missing vintages until 1928, see category III, page 34/35.

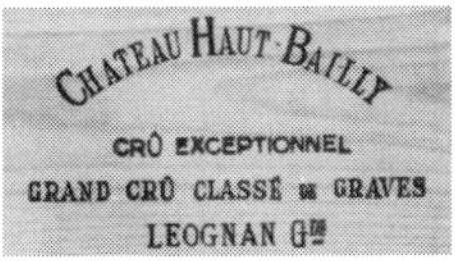

CHÂTEAU HAUT-BAILLY
CRÛ EXCEPTIONNEL
GRAND CRÛ CLASSÉ DE GRAVES
LEOGNAN G^{de}

Château Haut-Batailley

Pauillac, 5ME CRU CLASSÉ DU MÉDOC

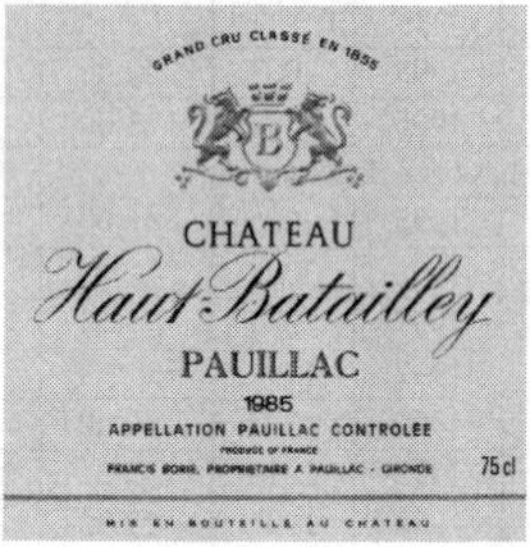

Comments

A property having connections with the Borie family, owners of Château Ducru-Beaucaillou and Château Grand-Puy-Lacoste. Jean-Eugène Borie and his son François-Xavier are in charge of management. Jean-Eugène is one of the best winemakers of the Bordeaux district. Haut-Batailley is, therefore, a very well cared for wine. Of the three châteaux Jean-Eugène Borie is involved in, Haut-Batailley scores the least. Haut-Batailley still compares excellently with the other Grands Crus.

Second wine: Château La Tour l'Aspic.

Type Indication

Haut-Batailley does not have the tight, sturdy firmness that one expects from a Pauillac. However, the wine has a little bit more charm than that of its counterparts and is a supple, delicately balanced Pauillac of high class.

Technical data

Owner	: Madame des Brest-Borie	
Management	: Jean-Eugène and François-Xavier Borie	
Cellar master	: René Lusseau	
Oenologist	: Jacques Boissenot	
Vineyard acreage		: 49 acres
Grape varieties:	Cabernet Sauvignon	: 65%
	Cabernet Franc	: 10%
	Merlot	: 25%
	Other :	
Average age of vines		: 30 years
Average annual production (cases of 12 bottles)		: 9,000

Specifications

Vintage	Assessment and Development			Market Value Summer 1995		Change in % since '93
	0 to 20 rating	drink from	cellaring potential	U.S. $	F. frs	
1993	14	1997	2007	18.00	83	14%
1992	13	1995	1999	18.00	83	6%
1991	13	1994	2000	21.00	94	33%
1990	13	1995	2005			
1989	17	1997	2015			
1988	15	1995	2010			
1987	16	1991	1996			
1986	16	1995	2010	31.00	142	36%
1985	14	1992	2002	34.00	155	24%
1984	15	1988	1995			
1983	15	1988	2000			
1982	16	1987	1995			
1981	15	1990	2000			
1980	12	1983	1988			
1979	16	1985	1995			
1978	14	1983	1993			
1977						

Older vintages	0 to 20 rating	drink from	cellaring potential	Market Value	
				U.S. $	F. frs
1976	14	1986	1996		
1973	15	1977	1983		
1967	15	1974	1984		
1966	12	1975	1990		

Auction prices realized in the last four years

year	U.S. $	F. frs	year	U.S. $	F. frs	year	U.S. $	F. frs
1990*	15.00	86	1979*	14.00	82			
1989*	20.00	114	1978*	23.00	132			
1988*	19.00	108	1976	18.00	100			
1986*	19.00	105	1975*	25.00	144			
1985*	20.00	114	1971*	22.00	126			
1983*	21.00	118	1970*	33.00	186			
1982*	34.00	192	1966	34.00	192			
1981*	19.00	109	1959*	37.00	208			

Auction prices since the last two years. For an indication of value and quality of the missing vintages until 1928, see category III, page 34/35.

Château Haut-Brion
Pessac, Graves, 1ER CRU CLASSÉ DU MÉDOC

Comments
The only Graves in the Médoc classification and also the smallest of the Premiers Crus Classés as far as production is concerned. The château was one of the first Crus in Bordeaux to install stainless steel fermentation tanks in order to better control the temperature during fermentation. Although the cellar installations have been adapted for years to meet modern requirements, the quality of this 1er Cru is not always impressive.

In 1983, this Cru acquired Château La Mission-Haut-Brion, its neighbor across the road. It seems as if this acquisition has given the Premier Cru a shot of quality in the arm.

Type Indication
In successful years, Haut-Brion is powerful, deep and full. This intensity is combined with an abundance of playful fruit. In good years Haut-Brion is creamy and full of nuances.

Technical data

Owner	: Domaine Clarence Dillon S.A.		
Director	: La Duchesse de Mouchy		
Régisseur	: Jean-Bernard Delmas		

Vineyard acreage		:	109 acres
Grape varieties:	Cabernet Sauvignon	:	55%
	Cabernet Franc	:	20%
	Merlot	:	25%
	Other	:	
Average age of vines		:	30 years
Average annual production (cases of 12 bottles)		:	12,000

Specifications

Vintage	Assessment and Development 0 to 20 rating	drink from	cellaring potential	Market Value Summer 1995 U.S. $	F. frs	Change in % since '93
1993	16	2000	2015	72.00	326	36%
1992	**16**	1995	2002	58.00	264	27%
1991	**16**	1995	2005	69.00	312	33%
1990	**17**	1995	2010	103.00	469	24%
1989	**19**	1996	2020	302.00	1377	167%
1988	**17**	1998	2015	87.00	394	4%
1987	**16**	1992	2000			
1986	**17**	1993	2005	92.00	421	0%
1985	**15**	1990	2000	104.00	476	-3%
1984	**15**	1990	2000	60.00	271	6%
1983	**17**	1990	2005	92.00	421	0%
1982	**17**	1990	2005	190.00	865	39%
1981	**15**	1991	2000			
1980	**14**	1985	1992			
1979	**16**	1987	2000	122.00	558	11%
1978	**17**	1985	1995			
1977	**14**	1982	1990			

Older vintages	0 to 20 rating	drink from	cellaring potential	Market Value U.S. $	F. frs
1976	**16**	1985	1995	137.00	626
1975				182.00	831
1973	**13**	1976	1981		
1971	**16**	1978	1990	167.00	763
1970	**16**	1988	2000	227.00	1036

Auction prices realized in the last four years

year	U.S. $	F. frs	year	U.S. $	F. frs	year	U.S. $	F. frs
1990*	66.00	375	1979*	74.00	419	1959*	279.00	1583
1989*	115.00	654	1976*	58.00	330	1949*	304.00	1724
1988*	58.00	329	1975*	69.00	392	1947*	257.00	1459
1986*	54.00	305	1970*	104.00	588	1945*	604.00	3428
1985*	77.00	437	1967*	63.00	359	1928*	336.00	1910
1983*	60.00	339	1966*	177.00	1006	1918*	177.00	1002
1982*	98.00	555	1964*	108.00	611	1896*	490.00	2783
1981*	52.00	293	1961*	388.00	2204	1891*	528.00	2997

* Auction prices since the last two years. For an indication of value and quality of the missing vintages until 1928, see category I, page 30/31.

Château d'Issan

Cantenac, 3ME CRU CLASSÉ DU MEDOC

Comments

A château owned since 1945 by the Cruse family of the Bordeaux firm of the same name.

The production of the château has been distributed exclusively by that Cruse firm, isolating this Cru from the rest of the Grand Cru scene. Château d'Issan has recently been launched on the open market; therefore, within a few years supply and demand will determine the exact value of this Cru.

Second wine: Château de Candale, Haut-Médoc

Type Indication

Château d'Issan is a Cru which beautifully portrays the characteristics of its appellation. A Margaux according to the book; charming because of its roundness and suppleness, but above all well-textured, thus asserting itself as a cellaring wine.

Technical data

Owner	: Mme. Emmanuel Cruse		
Director	: Lionel Cruse		
Cellar master	: M. Deturck		
Oenologist	: M. Couesnon		
Vineyard acreage			: 79 acres
Grape varieties:		Cabernet Sauvignon	: 75%
		Cabernet Franc	:
		Merlot	: 25%
		Other	:
Average age of vines			: 20 years
Average annual production (cases of 12 bottles)			: 12,500

Specifications

Vintage	Assessment and Development			Market Value Summer 1995		Change in % since '93
	0 to 20 rating	drink from	cellaring potential	U.S. $	F. frs	
1993	14	1998	2008	19.00	87	28%
1992	**15**	1995	2000			
1991	**14**	1994	2000	27.00	121	
1990	**16**	1995	2005	33.00	148	61%
1989	**16**	1995	2005	33.00	148	39%
1988	**15**	1996	2008	39.00	176	71%
1987	**15**	1991	1997			
1986	**15**	1995	2005			
1985	**17**	1990	2000			
1984	**14**	1988	1995			
1983	**16**	1990	2005			
1982	**15**	1990	2000			
1981	**15**	1987	1997			
1980				25.00	114	7%
1979						
1978						
1977						

Older vintages	0 to 20 rating	drink from	cellaring potential	Market Value	
				U.S. $	F. frs
1973	**15**	1978	1983		
1967	**15**	1973	1983		
1962	**13**	1969	1976		
1961	**17**	1975	1990		

Auction prices realized in the last four years

year	U.S. $	F. frs	year	U.S. $	F. frs	year	U.S. $	F. frs
1989*	17.00	96	1978	20.00	114			
1987*	12.00	69	1975*	20.00	113			
1986*	19.00	106	1966*	27.00	154			
1985*	24.00	139	1929	86.00	486			
1983*	21.00	118						
1982*	25.00	139						
1981	25.00	144						
1979*	24.00	135						

* Auction prices since the last two years. For an indication of value and quality of the missing vintages until 1928, see category III, page 34/35.

CHATEAU d'ISSAN
MARGAUX

Château Kirwan
Cantenac, 3ME CRU CLASSÉ DU MÉDOC

Comments
Since 1925 this Cru belongs to the firm of Schröder & Schÿler in Bordeaux, a firm which dates back 250 years. In 1994, the Groupe Gan, one of the largest French insurance companies, acquired a 65% share in the firm. The other 35% is in the hands of the Schÿler family.

The wine is distributed exclusively by this firm worldwide. A Cru known only to customers of Schröder & Schÿler and which, as a result, has become a little isolated from the other Crus.

Because the value is not determined on the open market, the closest value indications are the auction limits.

Second wine: Private Margaux-Réserve

Type Indication
A well-cared-for wine; quite smooth, not too deep, a bit short on intensity, but balanced.

Technical data

Owner	: Schröder & Schÿler & Cie		
Director	: Jean-Henri Schÿler		
Cellar master	: Philippe Mottes		
Oenologist	: Michel Rolland		
Vineyard acreage		:	86 acres
Grape varieties:	Cabernet Sauvignon	:	40%
	Cabernet Franc	:	20%
	Merlot	:	30%
	Petit Verdot	:	10%
Average age of vines		:	20 years
Average annual production (cases of 12 bottles)		:	12,500

Specifications

Vintage	Assessment and Development			Market Value Summer 1995		Change in % since '93
	0 to 20 rating	drink from	cellaring potential	U.S. $	F. frs	
1993	17	1998	2012			
1992	15	1996	2002			
1991	15	1994	2000	This Grand Cru is		
1990	14	1995	2005	being marketed		
1989	15	1995	2005	exclusivily by the		
1988	14	1995	2007	Schröder & Schÿler		
1987	14	1992	1998	company and is not		
1986	15	1992	1997	listed on the		
1985	16	1990	2000	open market.		
1984	12	1988	1995			
1983	15	1988	2000			
1982	16	1987	1996			
1981	14	1986	1995			
1980						
1979						
1978						
1977						

Older vintages	0 to 20 rating	drink from	cellaring potential	Market Value	
				U.S. $	F. frs

Auction prices realized in the last four years

year	U.S. $	F. frs	year	U.S. $	F. frs	year	U.S. $	F. frs
1982*	21.00	122						
1981	13.00	73						
1979	15.00	84						
1978	22.00	124						
1971*	13.00	75						
1970	26.00	150						
1865	159.00	902						

* *Auction prices since the last two years. For an indication of value and quality of the missing vintages until 1928, see category IV, page 36/37.*

Château Lafite-Rothschild
Pauillac, 1ER CRU CLASSÉ DU MÉDOC

Comments
From 1972 to 1993, the man responsible has been 'Chef de Culture' Jean Crété. He is a follower of the Emile Peynaud vinification method. Under the management of Jean Crété, several modernizations were realized at the château.
However, the replanting of a number of vineyards in 1975 was done a bit too rigorously. At first, Lafite was somewhat short on depth and texture because of a lack of grapes from old vines. This period of 'anemia' came to an end with the very powerful '81. Thanks to the vineyards which have matured in the meantime, the prospects for Lafite are very promising indeed.
Second wine: Moulin des Carruades

Type Indication
A good Lafite is robust combined with great refinement and subtle distinctions. The bouquet of an especially ripe Lafite has a characteristic 'small flower' by which this 1er Cru can be recognized clearly.

Technical data

Owner	: Domaines Barons de Rothschild	
Technical director	: Eric Fabre	
Régisseur	: Gilbert Rokvam	
Cellar master	: Francis Perez	
Vineyard acreage		: 222 acres
Grape varieties:	Cabernet Sauvignon	: 70%
	Cabernet Franc	: 5%
	Merlot	: 25%
	Other	:
Average age of vines		: 23 years
Average annual production (cases of 12 bottles)		: 22,500

Specifications

Vintage	Assessment and Development 0 to 20 rating	drink from	cellaring potential	Market Value Summer 1995 U.S. $	F. frs	Change in % since '93
1993	17	2000	2020	55.00	251	4%
1992	**16**	1997	2004	54.00	247	18%
1991	**16**	1995	2005	66.00	299	20%
1990	**17**	1996	2010	122.00	558	43%
1989	**18**	1996	2015	122.00	558	7%
1988	**18**	1998	2015	115.00	524	7%
1987	**15**	1991	1995	81.00	367	0%
1986	**17**	1995	2015	143.00	653	25%
1985	**18**	1992	2020	110.00	503	3%
1984	**16**	1990	2000			
1983	**18**	1994	2010	91.00	415	-16%
1982	**17**	1990	2005	227.00	1036	25%
1981	**17**	1990	2005	122.00	558	5%
1980	**15**	1985	1995	107.00	490	6%
1979	**16**	1986	2000	167.00	763	22%
1978	**16**	1987	1998	212.00	967	0%
1977	**16**	1987	1998			

Older vintages	0 to 20 rating	drink from	cellaring potential	Market Value U.S. $	F. frs
1976	**17**	1990	2000		
1975	**18**	1990	2010		
1974	**16**	1980	1990		
1973	**16**	1977	1981		
1970	**18**	1987	1995		
1967	**13**	1975	1982		
1962	**16**	1973	1985		

Gerealiseerde v eilingprijzen sinds de laatste jaren

year	U.S. $	F. frs	year	U.S. $	F. frs	year	U.S. $	F. frs
1990*	78.00	441	1976*	115.00	651	1945*	577.00	3275
1988*	84.00	479	1975*	122.00	691	1944*	283.00	1605
1986*	86.00	491	1970*	121.00	687	1929*	397.00	2253
1985*	90.00	509	1966*	145.00	821	1928*	506.00	2873
1983*	69.00	392	1961*	287.00	1627	1914*	360.00	2043
1982*	138.00	785	1959*	437.00	2481	1898*	481.00	2730
1981*	69.00	389	1949*	257.00	1459	1874*	1581.00	8979
1979*	84.00	479	1947	258.00	1466	1858*	1645.00	9338

Auction prices since the last two years. For an indication of value and quality of the missing vintages until 1928, see category I, page 30/31.

Château Lafon-Rochet
Saint-Estèphe, 4ME CRU CLASSÉ DE MÉDOC

Comments
A weak wine a lot of the time. Bottles of this Cru for sampling have been repeatedly tasted and they leave an ill-cared for impression. The owner, Guy Tesseron, who also owns Château Pontet-Canet has invested a great deal in this Cru since 1961. The quality of the two Tesseron properties was not very convincing for years but since the harvest of 1985 there has been a rise in quality. This is a Cru whose price is rising relatively slower than its quality, which suggests that chances for a good price/quality relationship are increasing for this wine.

Type Indication
Until the beginning of the eighties, Lafon-Rochet lacked the character and depth worthy of a Cru Classé. The wine as it has been presented over the last few years is green and a little short. The youngest versions are performing somewhat better. They are quite sturdy wines, with a satisfactory level and a better foundation.

Technical data

Owner	: Guy Tesseron		
Management	: Alfred and Michel Tesseron		
Régisseur	: Paul Bussier		
Cellar master	: Bernard Franc		
Vineyard acreage		:	99 acres
Grape varieties:	Cabernet Sauvignon	:	55%
	Cabernet Franc	:	5%
	Merlot	:	40%
	Other	:	
Average age of vines		:	30 years
Average annual production (cases of 12 bottles)		:	12,000

Specifications

Vintage	Assessment and Development 0 to 20 rating	drink from	cellaring potential	Market Value Summer 1995 U.S. $	F. frs	Change in % since '93
1993	15	1998	2010			
1992	**14**	1995	2000	16.00	73	0%
1991	**14**	1994	2000			
1990	**16**	1995	2005	24.00	109	48%
1989	15	1995	2005			
1988	**16**	1996	2010	25.00	112	46%
1987	**14**	1990	1995			
1986	**16**	1995	2010	27.00	124	30%
1985	**16**	1992	2000	28.00	128	25%
1984	**14**	1988	1995			
1983	**14**	1988	1996			
1982	15	1987	1995			
1981	**12**	1986	1990			
1980				18.00	80	-17%
1979	**14**	1983	1988			
1978						
1977						

Older vintages	0 to 20 rating	drink from	cellaring potential	Market Value U.S. $	F. frs
1973	**11**	1976	1980		
1970	**14**	1977	1989		

Auction prices realized in the last four years

year	U.S. $	F. frs	year	U.S. $	F. frs	year	U.S. $	F. frs
1985*	12.00	65	1966	25.00	144			
1983*	14.00	81						
1982*	20.00	116						
1981	15.00	87						
1978	21.00	120						
1976	17.00	94						
1975	21.00	120						
1970*	34.00	192						

* Auction prices since the last two years. For an indication of value and quality of the missing vintages until 1928, see category IV, page 36/37.

Château Lagrange

Saint-Julien, 3ME CRU CLASSÉ DU MÉDOC

Comments

Lagrange has been owned by the Japanese beverage concern, Suntory, since December 15, 1983. The Régisseur is Marcel Ducasse, a student of Professor Peynaud. A large-scale and strictly systematically planned new approach is being tried out to remold Lagrange from a somewhat changeable wine into one of the 'greats' from the Médoc. The percentage of Cabernet Sauvignon is being considerably increased at the cost of the Merlot and a new cuvier has been installed that looks more like a vinification laboratory. The men in armor on the label have had to step aside the gothic period belongs to the past. Their strict selection indicates room for a good wine.

Second wine: Les Fiefs de Lagrange

Type Indication

The '84 wine is one of the first to profit from the new approach. The wine has a deep, concentrated color and an intense aroma. On the palate it is powerful but friendly, broad and meaty. It has good aging potential.

Technical data

Owner	: Suntory Ltd		
Director	: Marcel Ducasse		
Cellar master	: Michel Raymond		
Oenologist	: Jacques Boissenot		
Vineyard acreage		:	279 acres
Grape varieties:	Cabernet Sauvignon	:	67%
	Cabernet Franc	:	
	Merlot	:	26%
	Petit Verdot	:	7%
Average age of vines		:	25 years
Average annual production (cases of 12 bottles)		:	20,000

Specifications

Vintage	Assessment and Development			Market Value Summer 1995		Change in % since '93
	0 to 20 rating	drink from	cellaring potential	U.S. $	F. frs	
1993	16	2000	2015	19.00	87	15%
1992	16	1996	2002	17.00	76	5%
1991	16	1995	2000	21.00	94	16%
1990	18	1997	2010	43.00	193	77%
1989	18	1998	2015	32.00	146	38%
1988	17	1995	2010	30.00	135	29%
1987	16	1991	1996			
1986	17	1997	2020	42.00	189	30%
1985	18	1995	2020			
1984	16	1990	1995			
1983	16	1988	2005			
1982	16	1987	2000			
1981	15	1988	2000	30.00	135	20%
1980	15	1984	1990			
1979	14	1985	1995	39.00	176	20%
1978						
1977	13	1983	1987			

Older vintages	0 to 20 rating	drink from	cellaring potential	Market Value	
				U.S. $	F. frs

Auction prices realized in the last four years

year	U.S. $	F. frs	year	U.S. $	F. frs	year	U.S. $	F. frs
1985	20.00	114	1966	50.00	281			
1983*	21.00	119	1964	22.00	123			
1982*	23.00	132	1961*	46.00	260			
1979*	16.00	90	1949	57.00	325			
1978*	16.00	92	1945*	46.00	263			
1975*	15.00	84						
1970*	21.00	121						
1967*	13.00	71						

Auction prices since the last two years. For an indication of value and quality of the missing vintages until 1928, see category III, page 34/35.

CHATEAU LAGRANGE
St JULIEN – MEDOC

Château La Lagune
Ludon, 3ME CRU CLASSÉ DU MÉDOC

Comments
A château which has existed since 1724 and where only 10 acres were planted with vines in 1958.
Between 1958 and 1960, 126 acres were newly planted. The history of La Lagune new style is therefore still quite young when one considers that a vineyard is only regarded as mature after 10 years. Since the seventies, La Lagune has stood for good, healthy wines with intermittent outstanding highlights, e.g., the 1978 vintage. In the coming years, La Lagune is a Cru to follow very carefully indeed as the vineyard has now reached the ideal age.
Second wine: Château d'Agassac

Type Indication
La Lagune is a friendly, supple charmer. With the exception of the most successful vintages, La Lagune is not a reliable wine for aging.

Technical data

Owner	: Jean-Michel Ducellier
Technical director	: Patrick Moulin
Régisseur	: Caroline Desvergnes du Vivier

Vineyard acreage		: 173 acres
Grape varieties:	Cabernet Sauvignon	: 55%
	Cabernet Franc	: 20%
	Merlot	: 20%
	Other	: 5%
Average age of vines		: 24 years
Average annual production (cases of 12 bottles)		: 25,000

Specifications

Vintage	Assessment and Development 0 to 20 rating	drink from	cellaring potential	Market Value Summer 1995 U.S. $	F. frs	Change in % since '93
1993	14	1998	2010	20.00	91	26%
1992	14	1995	2000	18.00	80	11%
1991	16	1995	2005			
1990	15	1995	2005	45.00	203	126%
1989	17	1995	2012			
1988	16	1994	2008			
1987	16	1990	1995			
1986	14	1992	2005	37.00	167	14%
1985	15	1990	2000	51.00	230	28%
1984	14	1980	1997			
1983	14	1989	2000	39.00	176	26%
1982	16	1988	1995	75.00	339	55%
1981	14	1990	2000			
1980	14	1984	1989			
1979	14	1985	1995			
1978	17	1985	1997			
1977	12	1984	1989			

Older vintages	0 to 20 rating	drink from	cellaring potential	Market Value U.S. $	F. frs
1976	14	1985	1997		
1975				67.00	305
1974	13	1977	1987		
1973	15	1978	1983		
1972	11	1975	1979		
1970	17	1988	2000	100.00	456
1969				31.00	142
1966				115.00	524

Auction prices realized in the last four years

year	U.S. $	F. frs	year	U.S. $	F. frs	year	U.S. $	F. frs
1990*	25.00	143	1979*	20.00	116	1961*	52.00	294
1989*	24.00	136	1978*	28.00	159			
1988*	25.00	143	1976*	26.00	147			
1986*	26.00	149	1975*	26.00	147			
1985*	25.00	141	1971*	25.00	142			
1983*	27.00	152	1970*	36.00	202			
1982*	56.00	316	1967*	25.00	144			
1981*	22.00	122	1966	42.00	239			

Auction prices since the last two years. For an indication of value and quality of the missing vintages until 1928, see category III, page 34/35.

Château Langoa-Barton
Saint-Julien, 3ME CRU CLASSÉ DU MÉDOC

Comments
Langoa-Barton and Château Léoville-Barton are brother and sister. They ripen, are bottled and nurtured under one roof. The person in charge is the dedicated owner, Anthony Barton himself. Vinification takes place in the same way as at Château Léoville-Barton.
Second wine: Lady Langoa.

Type Indication
See Léoville-Barton. Langoa-Barton is a somewhat lighter version.

Technical data

Owner	: Barton Family		
Director	: Anthony Barton		
Régisseur	: Michel Raoult		
Oenologist	: Jacques Boissenot		
Vineyard acreage		:	49 acres
Grape varieties:	Cabernet Sauvignon	:	70%
	Cabernet Franc	:	10%
	Merlot	:	20%
	Other	:	
Average age of vines		:	25 years
Average annual production (cases of 12 bottles)		:	8,000

Specifications

Vintage	Assessment and Development 0 to 20 rating	drink from	cellaring potential	Market Value Summer 1995 U.S. $	F. frs	Change in % since '93
1993	16	1998	2010			
1992	**15**	1996	2000			
1991	**15**	1994	2000	This Grand Cru is		
1990	**16**	1995	2005	not being offered		
1989	**16**	1995	2005	for sale on the		
1988	**16**	1998	2010	open market and,		
1987	**14**	1991	1997	therefore, no exact		
1986	**16**	1995	2010	prices are available.		
1985	**16**	1990	2005			
1984	**13**	1988	1995			
1983	**15**	1992	2002			
1982						
1981	**16**	1990	2000			
1980						
1979						
1978						
1977						

Older vintages	0 to 20 rating	drink from	cellaring potential	Market Value U.S. $	F. frs
1973	**14**	1978	1983		
1967	**14**	1974	1981		

Auction prices realized in the last four years

year	U.S. $	F. frs	year	U.S. $	F. frs	year	U.S. $	F. frs
1989*	24.00	135	1975	33.00	187			
1988*	16.00	92	1970*	32.00	183			
1985*	24.00	137	1966	46.00	259			
1983*	18.00	102	1959	31.00	176			
1982*	33.00	188	1949	33.00	187			
1981	21.00	118	1945	149.00	847			
1978*	26.00	147						
1976*	20.00	114						

* Auction prices since the last two years. For an indication of value and quality of the missing vintages until 1928, see category III, page 34/35.

Château Lascombes

Margaux, 2ME CRU CLASSÉ DU MÉDOC

Comments

Until 1988, the wines of Lascombes were traded exclusively by the firm of Lichine, which is why this Cru was not quoted on the open market in Bordeaux. This came to an end with the 1989 vintage, so that the value of this Cru is now determined by supply and demand.

The vineyards of the château are rather split up. Of the 205 acres, 124 acres are used for the Cru, while the others are used for the second wine. Important investments have been made since 1986. The estate and the cuverie are in perfect condition. The château's equipment is excellently suited for the making of a top wine. However, with a somewhat stricter cellar selection, a more robust textured wine could be produced.

Second wine: Château Segonnes

Type Indication

Lascombes is a fragrant, harmonious Margaux with, especially in fair vintages, a somewhat light texture. Overall it is a wine with an average aging texture.

Technical data

Owner	: Bass & Charrington	
Director	: René Vannetelle	
Cellar master	: Serge Ladra	
Vineyard acreage		: 124 acres
Grape varieties:	Cabernet Sauvignon	: 55%
	Cabernet Franc	:
	Merlot	: 40%
	Petit Verdot	: 5%
Average age of vines		: 25 years
Average annual production (cases of 12 bottles)		: 20,000

Specifications

Vintage	Assessment and Development 0 to 20 rating	drink from	cellaring potential	Market Value Summer 1995 U.S. $	F. frs	Change in % since '93
1993	14	1998	2010	22.00	98	17%
1992	13	1995	2000	19.00	87	20%
1991	13	1994	2000	21.00	97	13%
1990	15	1995	2005	25.00	114	14%
1989	15	1995	2005	30.00	135	13%
1988	16	1995	2007	30.00	135	13%
1987	15					
1986	15	1993	2005	36.00	162	25%
1985	16	1992	2002			
1984	14	1989	1997			
1983	15	1990	2000			
1982	16	1992	2002	49.00	223	22%
1981	15	1988	1998			
1980						
1979						
1978						
1977						

Older vintages	0 to 20 rating	drink from	cellaring potential	Market Value U.S. $	F. frs
1973	15	1978	1983		
1970	15	1985	1995		
1967	17	1977	1986		
1961	15	1977	1990		

Auction prices realized in the last four years

year	U.S. $	F. frs	year	U.S. $	F. frs	year	U.S. $	F. frs
1986*	16.00	89	1970*	47.00	269			
1982*	35.00	198	1966	50.00	286			
1979	22.00	124	1964	25.00	144			
1978*	29.00	165	1962*	42.00	238			
1976*	18.00	99	1961*	49.00	278			
1975*	34.00	192	1959	62.00	354			
1973	14.00	81	1953	40.00	227			
1971	17.00	96						

Auction prices since the last two years. For an indication of value and quality of the missing vintages until 1928, see category III, page 34/35.

Château Latour

Pauillac, 1ER CRU CLASSÉ DU MÉDOC

Comments

In June of 1993, Latour returned to French hands when businessman and wine connoisseur François Pinault bought the château back for 129 million dollars from the English group Allied-Lyons Hiram Walker. Until 1986, director Jean-Paul Gardère played an important role at Latour. In a short time he maneuvered the château to the front lines of the great Bordeaux wines. Since he retired in 1986, Gardère has remained only as an advisor. As a result, the quality of recent years is less convincing than that of previous vintages.

The new owner, François Pinault, is determined to improve the quality further. Evidence as to whether he succeeds will be found in the evaluation of future vintages.

Second wine: Les Forts de Latour

Type Indication

Intense, deep, luxurious and firm. Those are the chief characteristics of Latour. Especially in youth Latour is not very appealing. The wines are rich in tannin and have a reserved firmness, characteristic of the Cabernet. Latour is not a lovely wine, but rather a sturdy and distinguished wine.

Technical data

Owner	: François Pinault		
Technical director	: Christian Le Sommer		
Cellar master	: Jean Malbec		
Vineyard acreage		:	161 acres
Grape varieties:	Cabernet Sauvignon	:	80%
	Cabernet Franc	:	3%
	Merlot	:	15%
	Other	:	2%
Average age of vines		:	45 years
Average annual production (cases of 12 bottles)		:	19,000

Specifications

Vintage	Assessment and Development 0 to 20 rating	drink from	cellaring potential	Market Value Summer 1995 U.S. $	F. frs	Change in % since '93
1993	17	2000	2015	63.00	285	18%
1992	**16**	1995	2003	60.00	273	31%
1991	**16**	1995	2005	81.00	367	49%
1990	**17**	1996	2010	242.00	1104	224%
1989	**18**	1996	2015	125.00	572	17%
1988	**17**	1998	2015	107.00	490	17%
1987	14	1992	1997	69.00	312	26%
1986	**16**	1994	2010	107.00	490	0%
1985	**16**	1995	2020	122.00	558	21%
1984	15	1994	2000			
1983	**18**	1992	2005	92.00	421	-8%
1982	**18**	1992	2015	302.00	1377	54%
1981	**17**	1995	2005	97.00	443	-10%
1980	**17**	1985	1995	78.00	353	-17%
1979	**18**	1990	2005	107.00	490	-3%
1978	**19**	1992	2007			
1977	14	1985	1993	60.00	271	-24%

Older vintages	0 to 20 rating	drink from	cellaring potential	Market Value U.S. $	F. frs
1976	**18**	1988	2003		
1975				227.00	1036
1974	15	1980	1990	69.00	312
1973				107.00	490
1970	12	1980	1990		
1965				92.00	421
1961	**16**	1977	1990		
1960	**11**	1968	1978		

Auction prices realized in the last four years

year	U.S. $	F. frs	year	U.S. $	F. frs	year	U.S. $	F. frs
1989*	114.00	646	1979*	60.00	341	1959*	466.00	2647
1988*	50.00	286	1978*	135.00	766	1953*	217.00	1230
1986*	95.00	539	1976*	67.00	382	1949	504.00	2864
1985*	111.00	629	1975*	115.00	651	1945*	886.00	5028
1983*	57.00	321	1973*	47.00	268	1929*	482.00	2738
1982*	24.00	137	1971*	90.00	509	1890*	415.00	2355
1981*	69.00	389	1966*	190.00	1077	1870*	581.00	3297
1980*	35.00	196	1961*	816.00	4632	1865	4181.00	23740

Auction prices since the last two years. For an indication of value and quality of the missing vintages until 1928, see category I, page 30/31.

GRAND VIN DE LATOUR

Château Léoville-Barton
Saint-Julien, 2ME CRU CLASSÉ DU MÉDOC

Comments
Of the three Léoville wines Barton, Las-Cases and Poyferré Léoville-Barton is the most reserved. Whereas the two other Léoville chateaux follow the Peynaud vinification method, the Barton management is guided by the analysis and advice of Jacques Boissenot. It is clear that this Cru is governed by a different vinification philosophy. Léoville-Barton is a wine with its own, beautiful style. The quality is sometimes of an exceptionally high standard. It is a Cru which, especially in recent years, has produced good quality on a regular basis.

Type Indication
A very firm, beautifully perfumed wine. The Cabernet grape dominates the flavor giving the wine a manly character. In successful vintages a wine which develops slowly, but which may reach a high standard.

Technical data

Owner	: Barton Family		
Director	: Anthony Barton		
Régisseur	: Michel Raoult		
Oenologist	: Jacques Boissenot		
Vineyard acreage			: 111 acres
Grape varieties:		Cabernet Sauvignon :	70%
		Cabernet Franc :	8%
		Merlot :	20%
		Petit Verdot :	2%
Average age of vines			: 28 years
Average annual production (cases of 12 bottles)			: 20,000

Specifications

Vintage	Assessment and Development 0 to 20 rating	drink from	cellaring potential	Market Value Summer 1995 U.S. $	F. frs	Change in % since '93
1993	16	1998	2015	30.00	135	53%
1992	**15**	1996	2002	23.00	103	40%
1991	**15**	1994	2000	33.00	148	82%
1990	**16**	1995	2005	58.00	264	118%
1989	**17**	1996	2010	43.00	193	56%
1988	**17**	1997	2010			
1987	**14**	1992	1997			
1986	**16**	1993	2007	51.00	230	39%
1985	**15**	1992	2002	55.00	252	53%
1984	**16**	1988	2000			
1983	**14**	1988	1995	42.00	189	30%
1982						
1981	**15**	1988	1998	40.00	183	0%
1980	**14**	1985	1990			
1979	**16**	1987	1997			
1978						
1977						

Older vintages	0 to 20 rating	drink from	cellaring potential	Market Value U.S. $	F. frs
1976	**12**	1983	1995		
1974	**15**	1978	1990		
1970	**15**	1980	1990		
1961	**16**	1977	1990		
1960	**11**	1968	1978		

Auction prices realized in the last four years

year	U.S. $	F. frs	year	U.S. $	F. frs	year	U.S. $	F. frs
1990*	27.00	152	1981*	17.00	99	1967	34.00	192
1989*	24.00	139	1979	46.00	262	1966	61.00	345
1988*	27.00	153	1978*	33.00	188	1962*	34.00	193
1987*	15.00	82	1976	40.00	225	1961	86.00	490
1986*	40.00	226	1975	42.00	238	1947	72.00	411
1985*	33.00	188	1973	17.00	96	1945*	121.00	686
1983*	22.00	126	1971	20.00	111	1942	66.00	373
1982*	47.00	269	1970*	40.00	225	1871	529.00	3002

Auction prices since the last two years. For an indication of value and quality of the missing vintages until 1928, see category III, page 34/35.

Château Léoville-Las-Cases
Saint-Julien, 2ME CRU CLASSÉ DU MÉDOC

Comments
A 2me Cru which was very badly taken care of in the fifties. When Michel Delon became manager, he immediately appointed Professor Emile Peynaud as his advisor. Léoville-Las-Cases is the Cru with which Professor Peynaud made his name.

An important reason for the splendid list of ratings is the influence of this famous oenologist. Considering its record, Château Léoville-Las-Cases is a wine which can be bought almost blindly, provided Delon remains at the helm.

Second wine: Clos du Marquis

Type Indication
Beautifully textured, rich and deep flavor and color. The Las-Cases has a firm discipline kept in balance by the richness of fruit and roundness, making this Cru a stately aging wine of the highest class.

Technical data

Owner	: S.C. du Château Léoville-Las-Cases	
Director	: Michel Delon	
Technical director	: Jacques Depoizier	
Oenologist	: Jacques Boissenot	
Vineyard acreage		: 235 acres
Grape varieties:	Cabernet Sauvignon	: 65%
	Cabernet Franc	: 13%
	Merlot	: 19%
	Petit Verdot	: 3%
Average age of vines		: 28 years
Average annual production (cases of 12 bottles)		: 30,000

Specifications

Vintage	Assessment and Development 0 to 20 rating	drink from	cellaring potential	Market Value Summer 1995 U.S. $	F. frs	Change in % since '93
1993	17	2000	2015	34.00	155	19%
1992	**17**	1997	2005	30.00	135	15%
1991	**16**	1996	2002	34.00	155	20%
1990	**18**	2000	2010	63.00	285	33%
1989	**18**	2000	2020	57.00	258	0%
1988	**17**	1998	2010	55.00	251	25%
1987	**17**	1992	1998	39.00	176	26%
1986	**17**	1995	2015	84.00	380	35%
1985	**17**	1992	2020	66.00	299	17%
1984	**16**	1992	1997	39.00	176	20%
1983	**18**	1993	2010	63.00	285	25%
1982	**17**	1990	2010	145.00	660	36%
1981	**18**	1990	2005	55.00	251	0%
1980	**16**	1985	1992			
1979	**17**	1987	1997	54.00	244	13%
1978	**18**	1985	1995	87.00	394	12%
1977	**16**	1983	1993			

Older vintages	0 to 20 rating	drink from	cellaring potential	Market Value U.S. $	F. frs
1976	**16**	1985	1995	66.00	299
1975	**18**	1988	2000	104.00	476
1974	**13**	1977	1987	42.00	189
1973	**14**	1978	1985		
1971	**16**	1985	1988	100.00	456
1970	**17**	1985	2000	130.00	592
1967	**16**	1975	1985		
1966	**15**	1976	1990		

Auction prices realized in the last four years

year	U.S. $	F. frs	year	U.S. $	F. frs	year	U.S. $	F. frs
1989*	41.00	235	1979*	37.00	209	1962*	41.00	233
1987*	23.00	131	1978*	49.00	278	1961*	180.00	1020
1986*	44.00	251	1977*	18.00	99	1959*	135.00	766
1985*	52.00	298	1976*	32.00	180	1947*	131.00	744
1984*	26.00	147	1975*	71.00	402	1945*	202.00	1149
1983*	41.00	232	1971*	26.00	147	1943*	57.00	322
1982*	99.00	562	1970*	73.00	417	1929*	111.00	627
1981*	37.00	212	1966*	95.00	542	1878*	302.00	1712

Auction prices since the last two years. For an indication of value and quality of the missing vintages until 1928, see category II, page 32/33.

Château Léoville-Poyferré
Saint-Julien, 2ME CRU CLASSÉ DU MÉDOC

Comments
This château has two progressive neighbors, in the north Château Pichon-Longueville-Comtesse and in the south Léoville-Las-Cases. A château with the same possibilities as its neighbors and for good reason was classified as a 2me Cru in 1855. Unfortunately this Cru does not succeed in producing first-class wines with the same regularity as its neighbors. The quality differs considerably each year. A Cru where you can come across a top wine such as the '82s, while the '81s and '79s were fair.
In 1994, significant investments were made in new equipment, and Michel Rolland was hired as an expert enologist.
Second wines: Pavillon des Connétables, Château Moulin Riche.

Type Indication
Based on the successful '82 vintage: very intense and deep in color. Compact and rich in texture. In youth reserved, although with a lot of fruit and roundness in the background. The good harmony is the guarantee for long and balanced development.

Technical data

Owner	: S.C. des Domaines de Saint-Julien / Propr. Cuvelier	
Director	: Didier Cuvelier	
Cellar master	: Francis Dourthe	
Oenologist	: Jacques Boissenot	
Vineyard acreage		: 195 acres
Grape varieties:	Cabernet Sauvignon	: 65%
	Cabernet Franc	: 2%
	Merlot	: 25%
	Petit Verdot	: 8%
Average age of vines		: 25 years
Average annual production (cases of 12 bottles)		: 23,000

Specifications

Vintage	Assessment and Development 0 to 20 rating	drink from	cellaring potential	Market Value Summer 1995 U.S. $	F. frs	Change in % since '93
1993	15	2000	2010	29.00	131	34%
1992	17	1996	2002	27.00	121	38%
1991	16	1995	2005			
1990	17	1997	2010	36.00	162	43%
1989	17	1996	2008	34.00	155	17%
1988	16	1995	2010			
1987	17	1991	1996			
1986	16	1995	2010	37.00	169	10%
1985	14	1992	2002			
1984	12	1988	1995	21.00	94	0%
1983	15	1990	2005	39.00	176	9%
1982	17	1990	2010	52.00	237	3%
1981	12	1987	1995	39.00	176	20%
1980	12	1984	1989	28.00	128	21%
1979	13	1985	1995	42.00	189	37%
1978	16	1985	1993			
1977	12	1983	1988			

Older vintages	0 to 20 rating	drink from	cellaring potential	Market Value U.S. $	F. frs
1976	14	1985	1994		
1975				72.00	326
1974	10	1977	1982		
1973	15	1978	1983		
1970	16	1980	1995	92.00	421
1967	12	1973	1980	39.00	176
1966	12	1975	1985	122.00	558
1961	16	1977	1990		

Auction prices realized in the last four years

year	U.S. $	F. frs	year	U.S. $	F. frs	year	U.S. $	F. frs
1989*	17.00	95	1976*	24.00	138	1937	84.00	479
1986	15.00	83	1975*	20.00	113	1929	367.00	2086
1985*	20.00	113	1970*	32.00	180	1882	304.00	1724
1983*	31.00	178	1966*	29.00	163	1881	376.00	2133
1982*	58.00	329	1961*	125.00	709	1870	380.00	2155
1981*	18.00	101	1959*	68.00	387			
1979*	30.00	168	1945	108.00	616			
1978*	26.00	147	1943*	51.00	290			

Auction prices since the last two years. For an indication of value and quality of the missing vintages until 1928, see category III, page 34/35.

LÉOVILLE POYFERRÉ

Château Lynch-Bages
Pauillac, 5ME CRU CLASSÉ DU MÉDOC

Comments
It was the grandfather of Jean-Michel Cazes, the current owner, who made this Cru into a glorious wine in the postwar years and succeeded in elevating it well beyond the level of a 5me Cru. Early on, Lynch-Bages gained a reputation for being able to produce good wines even in poor years the mark of great wine producers. Although the father of the current owner was less successful (the '70 series was not the best for this Cru), since the eighties Lynch-Bages can again compete with the second and even the first Crus. In 1990, the cellars and the château were entirely renovated. The château has unique facilities where, besides Lynch-Bages, Ormes de Pez and Cordeillan-Bages are also raised.
Second wine: Château Haut-Bages-Averous

Type Indication
Lynch-Bages is a robust, intense Pauillac, although less firm than its counterparts. Typical for this Cru is the somewhat sultry, round suppleness which supplies wines of successful vintages with a very pleasant after-taste.

Technical data

Owner	: Jean-Michel Cazes		
Technical director	: Daniel Llose		
Cellar master	: Guy Bergey		
Chef de culture	: Jean-Louis Lajoux		
Vineyard acreage		:	210 acres
Grape varieties:	Cabernet Sauvignon	:	75%
	Cabernet Franc	:	10%
	Merlot	:	15%
	Other	:	
Average age of vines		:	35 years
Average annual production (cases of 12 bottles)		:	35,000

Specifications

Vintage	Assessment and Development			Market Value Summer 1995		Change in % since '93
	0 to 20 rating	drink from	cellaring potential	U.S. $	F. frs	
1993	16	1998	2010	26.00	120	14%
1992	15	1995	2000	24.00	110	26%
1991	16	1996	2005	27.00	121	16%
1990	18	1998	2015	49.00	223	41%
1989	19	1998	2020			
1988	18	1997	2015	48.00	217	30%
1987	17	1992	2000			
1986	18	1995	2015	69.00	312	76%
1985	19	1995	2020			
1984	17	1992	2005			
1983	17	1992	2010			
1982	17	1990	2005	145.00	660	188%
1981	14	1988	1998			
1980	13	1984	1989			
1979	15	1985	1995			
1978	14	1983	1993			
1977	12	1982	1988	25.00	114	7%

Older vintages	0 to 20 rating	drink from	cellaring potential	Market Value	
				U.S. $	F. frs
1976	14	1985	1995		
1975	18	1987	2002		
1974	8	1978	1982		
1970	16	1985	1995		
1966	14	1976	1990		
1961	17	1975	1995		

Auction prices realized in the last four years

year	U.S. $	F. frs	year	U.S. $	F. frs	year	U.S. $	F. frs
1989*	44.00	251	1978*	58.00	329	1962	66.00	377
1988*	36.00	204	1976*	28.00	159	1961*	182.00	1034
1986*	42.00	237	1975*	46.00	260	1959	96.00	544
1985*	56.00	320	1973*	25.00	144	1957	47.00	266
1983*	40.00	227	1971*	25.00	140	1955	54.00	304
1982*	91.00	517	1970*	100.00	569	1953	98.00	555
1981*	37.00	209	1966*	73.00	411	1945	106.00	600
1979*	27.00	156	1965	38.00	217	1928	304.00	1724

Auction prices since the last two years. For an indication of value and quality of the missing vintages until 1928, see category II, page 32/33.

LYNCH BAGES
PAUILLAC - FRANCE

Château Lynch-Moussas

Pauillac, 5ME CRU CLASSÉ DU MÉDOC

Comments

A very traditionally managed château but a little neglected in the past. As far as acreage is concerned it is a Cru which could be one of the largest producers of the Médoc. In 1969 only 5% of the 247 acres was planted. This has now been increased to 30%. Lynch-Moussas is now in a phase of building up. The management however, is not very dynamic and vinification is still quite traditional. With a successful vintage, it is Grand Cru which offers good wine for the money.

Type Indication

Lynch-Moussas is tough and not very inviting in its youth. Should it be well-balanced, such as for example the '79s and '82s were, it is a Cru with a very promising future. Patience is rewarded here with the pure, tight and manly flavor patterns; a good Pauillac. A 5me Cru without pretensions.

Technical data

Owner	: Castéja Family
Régisseur	: Emile Castéja
Cellar master	: Mr. Broussy
Oenologist	: Prof. Pascal Ribéreau-Gayon

Vineyard acreage		: 74 acres
Grape varieties:	Cabernet Sauvignon	: 70%
	Cabernet Franc	: 15%
	Merlot	: 15%
	Other :	
Average age of vines		: 20 years
Average annual production (cases of 12 bottles)		: 15,000

Specifications

Vintage	Assessment and Development			Market Value Summer 1995		Change in % since '93
	0 to 20 rating	drink from	cellaring potential	U.S. $	F. frs	
1993	16	1998	2008	15.00	68	14%
1992	**14**	1995	2000			
1991	**14**	1994	2000			
1990	**16**	1994	2000			
1989	**14**	1995	2005	24.00	107	52%
1988	**15**	1996	2010	22.00	101	63%
1987	**11**	1990	1994			
1986	**16**	1995	2015	25.00	114	15%
1985	**14**	1992	2002	28.00	125	19%
1984	**12**	1988	1995			
1983	**14**	1988	1998	27.00	121	14%
1982	**17**	1990	2000			
1981	**15**	1988	1998			
1980	**14**	1983	1989			
1979	**16**	1987	1997			
1978						
1977						

Older vintages	0 to 20 rating	drink from	cellaring potential	Market Value	
				U.S. $	F. frs
1970	**15**	1980	1990		
1967	**13**	1972	1982		
1966	**15**	1972	1984		

Auction prices realized in the last four years

year	U.S. $	F. frs	year	U.S. $	F. frs	year	U.S. $	F. frs
1983	15.00	87	1959*	27.00	153			
1982*	16.00	93	1945*	56.00	316			
1981*	12.00	68						
1978	20.00	113						
1975*	15.00	86						
1970*	14.00	78						
1966	29.00	164						
1961*	30.00	169						

Auction prices since the last two years. For an indication of value and quality of the missing vintages until 1928, see category IV, page 36/37.

Château Magdelaine
Saint-Emilion, 1ER GRAND CRU CLASSÉ B

Comments
Of the 1er Grand Crus of Saint-Emilion this Cru has the largest Merlot vineyard. Since 1953, the château has been the property of the mercantile house of Jean-Pierre Moueix of Libourne, which also owns Château Pétrus. Château Magdelaine is supervised by employees of Pétrus. Like Pétrus harvesting at this château is carried out in the shortest time possible by Moueix' big team of pickers.
But it is understandable that Pétrus comes first.

Type Indication
Château Magdelaine is one of the thoroughbreds of the Merlot wines. It is a very intensely colored wine with a lot of suppleness. The large percentage of Merlot is the cause of the relatively low acid and tannin content. Nonetheless, a wine which doesn't require much patience and which, in view of its robust texture, can also be aged well.

Technical data

Owner	: Ets. J.P. Moueix	
Technical director	: Christian Moueix	
Régisseur	: Michel Gillet	
Cellar master	: François Veyssières	
Vineyard acreage		: 25 acres
Grape varieties:	Cabernet Sauvignon	:
	Cabernet Franc	: 10%
	Merlot	: 90%
	Other	:
Average age of vines		: 35 years
Average annual production (cases of 12 bottles)		: 4,000

Specifications

Vintage	Assessment and Development 0 to 20 rating	drink from	cellaring potential	Market Value Summer 1995 U.S. $	F. frs	Change in % since '93
1993	16	2000	2015			
1992	**16**	1996	2002			
1991	Harvest has been declassified			Maison Moueix in		
1990	**17**	1996	2010	Bordeaux has the sole		
1989	**18**	1997	2010	exclusivity to market		
1988	**16**	1995	2008	Magdelaine.		
1987	**13**	1990	1995	Therefore,		
1986	**16**	1995	2010	this wine is not listed		
1985	**16**	1993	2005	on the open market.		
1984	Harvest has been declassified					
1983	15	1990	2005			
1982	**18**	1995	2010			
1981						
1980	**14**	1985	1993			
1979						
1978						
1977						

Older vintages	0 to 20 rating	drink from	cellaring potential	Market Value U.S. $	F. frs
1975	**17**	1982	1997		
1973	**15**	1978	1983		
1964	**15**	1972	1985		

Auction prices realized in the last four years

year	U.S. $	F. frs	year	U.S. $	F. frs	year	U.S. $	F. frs
1989*	27.00	155	1978	49.00	276	1962	54.00	307
1988*	20.00	114	1976	33.00	184	1961	111.00	629
1986*	24.00	136	1975	44.00	251	1953	91.00	517
1985	36.00	207	1971	37.00	209	1952*	31.00	174
1983*	25.00	143	1970	58.00	329	1945	106.00	603
1982*	47.00	269	1967	27.00	152			
1981	24.00	138	1966*	60.00	343			
1979	30.00	169	1964	44.00	250			

Auction prices since the last two years. For an indication of value and quality of the missing vintages until 1928, see category II, page 32/33.

CHÂTEAU MAGDELAINE
SAINT EMILION
PREMIER GRAND CRU CLASSÉ

Château Malartic-Lagravière
Léognan, GRAND CRU CLASSÉ DE GRAVES

Comments
In 1850, the old domain of the Malartic family fell into the hands of the Ricard family, to whom the former owner, Jacques Marly, is related. Marly is the great advocate of the Graves and founder of the Syndicat des Crus Classés de Graves. The self-willed Marly is convinced of his own vinification methods, that do not always run parallel with what is considered 'normal'. At Malartic, he replaced the vines with a rotation scheme of 30 years: Malartic had therefore a young vineyard for a long time, with a large crop per acre. After being taken over by the Laurent-Perrier group, Jacques Marly's son Bruno became director of Malartic-Lagravière. The château also produces a white wine, which is not taken into consideration here.

Type Indication
Malartic is a very light Graves. The wine lacks sturdy body and for that reason cannot be ranked among the great wines. The big crops and the absence of a second wine could be the cause.

Technical data

Owner	: Groupe Laurent-Perrier	
Director	: Bruno Marly	
Technical director	: Jean Pelatan	
Oenologist	: Prof. Guy Guimberteau	
Vineyard acreage		: 37 acres
Grape varieties:	Cabernet Sauvignon	: 50%
	Cabernet Franc	: 25%
	Merlot	: 25%
	Other	:
Average age of vines		: 20 years
Average annual production (cases of 12 bottles)		: 10,000

Specifications

Vintage	Assessment and Development			Market Value Summer 1995		Change in % since '93
	0 to 20 rating	drink from	cellaring potential	U.S. $	F. frs	
1993	15	1999	2009	19.00	87	45%
1992	**14**	1995	2000	18.00	80	
1991	**12**	1994	2000			
1990	**14**	1995	2005	37.00	169	60%
1989	**14**	1995	2005			
1988	**16**	1996	2008			
1987	**14**	1990	1994			
1986	**16**	1995	2005			
1985	**16**	1992	2002			
1984	**14**	1988	1996			
1983	**14**	1990	2000			
1982	15	1988	1998			
1981	**13**	1986	1996			
1980	**11**	1983	1990			
1979	**13**	1987	1995			
1978						
1977						

Older vintages	0 to 20 rating	drink from	cellaring potential	Market Value	
				U.S. $	F. frs
1971	**15**	1980	1990		
1970	**16**	1985	1995		
1966	**15**	1975	1992		

Auction prices realized in the last four years

year	U.S. $	F. frs	year	U.S. $	F. frs	year	U.S. $	F. frs
1988*	18.00	99	1916	152.00	860			
1983*	13.00	71						
1982*	20.00	114						
1978	16.00	88						
1975	12.00	66						
1970	22.00	122						
1966	30.00	171						
1949*	27.00	155						

Auction prices since the last two years. For an indication of value and quality of the missing vintages until 1928, see category IV, page 36/37.

Château Malescot Saint-Exupéry

Margaux, 3ME CRU CLASSÉ DU MÉDOC

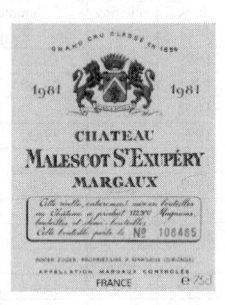

Comments

A château that, just like Château Marquis d'Alesme-Becker, is owned by the Zuger family. They are reputable propriétaires who go their own way in the Médoc. This is also expressed in their sales policy. The Zugers do not sell via the Bordeaux market; they appoint an agent per country. The value that this Cru actually represents is obscure because of that policy. The best criterion for determining the value is the international auction.

Type Indication

A somewhat light-footed, charming Margaux. Well-cared-for, but lacks a little depth and roundness. A wine that relies especially on its finesse. Not a very convincing wine for aging.

Technical data

Owner	: Roger Zuger
Director	: Roger Zuger
Oenologist	: Michel Rolland

Vineyard acreage		:	74 acres
Grape varieties:	Cabernet Sauvignon	:	50%
	Cabernet Franc	:	10%
	Merlot	:	35%
	Petit Verdot	:	5%
Average age of vines		:	30 years
Average annual production (cases of 12 bottles)		:	18,000

Specifications

Vintage	Assessment and Development			Market Value Summer 1995		Change in % since '93
	0 to 20 rating	drink from	cellaring potential	U.S. $	F. frs	
1993	15	1998	2008			
1992	**13**	1995	2001			
1991	**14**	1994	2000	This Grand Cru is		
1990	**15**	1995	2005	not being offered		
1989	**15**	1995	2005	for sale on the		
1988	**17**	1998	2010	open market and,		
1987	**13**	1991	1996	therefore, no		
1986	**15**	1995	2005	exact prices are		
1985	**15**	1990	2000	available.		
1984	**14**	1989	1995			
1983	**15**	1990	2000			
1982						
1981						
1980	**12**	1983	1990			
1979						
1978						
1977						

Older vintages	0 to 20 rating	drink from	cellaring potential	Market Value	
				U.S. $	F. frs
1973	**14**	1978	1983		
1967	**12**	1972	1980		

Auction prices realized in the last four years

year	U.S. $	F. frs	year	U.S. $	F. frs	year	U.S. $	F. frs
1985	13.00	74	1967	13.00	74			
1983	20.00	114	1966	32.00	180			
1982	24.00	135	1961	90.00	511			
1979	23.00	132	1878	248.00	1410			
1978	19.00	110						
1975	28.00	157						
1974	28.00	158						
1970	25.00	139						

* *Auction prices since the last two years. For an indication of value and quality of the missing vintages until 1928, see category IV, page 36/37.*

Château Margaux
Margaux, 1ER CRU CLASSÉ DU MÉDOC

Comments
A 1er Cru neglected until 1976. Quality and price-wise, Margaux found it extremely difficult to keep up with the other Crus. With the sale of the château to the Mentzelopoulos family in 1977, an end came to this troublesome period.
First father Mentzelopoulos and then, after he passed away, his daughter Corinne have shown that good management can change the prospects for the better within a year. It is almost unbelievable, but since the Mentzelopoulos family have been managing Margaux, it is the best 1er Cru.
A white wine, Pavillon-Blanc, is also produced at Margaux, which is not taken into consideration here.
Second wine: Pavillon-Rouge de Château Margaux

Type Indication
The recent Margaux have intensity and depth. They are luxuriant, creamy and fruity wines. Harmony, depth, finesse and élan go hand-in-hand. Wines of the highest class.

Technical data

Owner	: S.C. Château Margaux		
Management	: Corinne Mentzelopoulos		
Technical director	: Paul Pontallier		
Cellar master	: Jean Grangerou		
Vineyard acreage		:	185 acres
Grape varieties:	Cabernet Sauvignon	:	75%
	Cabernet Franc	:	2.5%
	Merlot	:	20%
	Petit Verdot	:	2.5%
Average age of vines		:	30 years
Average annual production (cases of 12 bottles)		:	30,000

Specifications

Vintage	Assessment and Development 0 to 20 rating	drink from	cellaring potential	Market Value Summer 1995 U.S. $	F. frs	Change in % since '93
1993	17	1998	2012	74.00	335	40%
1992	15	1995	2003	63.00	285	37%
1991	17	1995	2005	116.00	531	73%
1990	18	1996	2010			
1989	18	1996	2015	122.00	558	14%
1988	18	1997	2020	128.00	585	31%
1987	17	1991	1995			
1986	18	1995	2015	170.00	776	32%
1985	19	1995	2020	170.00	776	40%
1984	17	1991	2005			
1983	19	1993	2015	158.00	722	41%
1982	19	1992	2007	257.00	1172	70%
1981	19	1990	2005			
1980	17	1985	1995			
1979	19	1988	2000			
1978	19	1987	2002			
1977	17	1987	1995			

Older vintages	0 to 20 rating	drink from	cellaring potential	Market Value U.S. $	F. frs
1976	15	1985	1995		
1975				160.00	729
1973	16	1978	1983		
1970	16	1980	1990	227.00	1036
1967	14	1975	1985		
1966				249.00	1138
1964	18	1974	1995	212.00	967
1953	17	1963	1995		

Auction prices realized in the last four years

year	U.S. $	F. frs	year	U.S. $	F. frs	year	U.S. $	F. frs
1989*	74.00	419	1978*	98.00	555	1947*	206.00	1167
1988*	69.00	389	1970*	86.00	490	1945*	633.00	3592
1986*	100.00	569	1966*	115.00	654	1929*	822.00	4669
1985*	80.00	455	1961*	506.00	2873	1928*	588.00	3340
1983*	86.00	491	1959*	244.00	1388	1921*	327.00	1855
1982*	224.00	1273	1955*	132.00	751	1900*	980.00	5565
1981*	69.00	392	1953*	250.00	1420	1892*	569.00	3232
1979*	111.00	629	1949*	173.00	980	1862*	2530.00	14366

Auction prices since the last two years. For an indication of value and quality of the missing vintages until 1928, see category I, page 30/31.

Château Marquis d'Alesme-Becker

Margaux, 3ME CRU CLASSÉ DU MÉDOC

Comments

This château, which just like Château Malescot-St.-Exupéry belongs to the family Zuger, used to serve as the second wine of Château Malescot. They are reputable propriétaires who go their own way in the Médoc. This is also expressed in their sales policy. The Zugers do not sell via the Bordeaux market; they appoint an agent per country. Because of that, the value that these wines actually represent is a little obscure. For both Zuger wines value is best gauged by auction prices. Since 1979, Marquis d'Alesme-Becker has been following its own course. Although the composition of the Malescot vineyards differs somewhat from that of Alesme-Becker, both wines show some resemblance.

Type Indication

Marquis d'Alesme is quite elegant. For a real Margaux the wine lacks roundness and suppleness. A somewhat tight wine, but which often offers value for the money.

Technical data

Owner	: Jean-Claude Zuger	
Régisseur	: Jean-Claude Zuger	
Cellar master	: Christophe Chabot	
Oenologist	: Jacques Boissenot	
Vineyard acreage		: 25 acres
Grape varieties:	Cabernet Sauvignon	: 30%
	Cabernet Franc	: 30%
	Merlot	: 30%
	Other	: 10%
Average age of vines		: 30 years
Average annual production (cases of 12 bottles)		: 5,500

Specifications

Vintage	Assessment and Development			Market Value Summer 1995		Change in % since '93
	0 to 20 rating	drink from	cellaring potential	U.S. $	F. frs	
1993	13	1997	2004			
1992	12	1995	2000			
1991	13	1996	2002	This Grand Cru is		
1990	15	1995	2005	not being offered		
1989	15	1995	2005	for sale on the		
1988	16	1996	2008	open market and,		
1987	13	1991	1997	therefore, no exact		
1986	14	1992	2002	prices are available.		
1985	14	1990	2000			
1984	13	1989	1997			
1983						
1982						
1981						
1980						
1979	15	1985	1992			
1978						
1977						

Older vintages	0 to 20 rating	drink from	cellaring potential	Market Value	
				U.S. $	F. frs
1976	14	1981	1990		
1974	12	1978	1984		
1973	14	1976	1980		
1972	11	1975	1982		
1967	15	1975	1982		

Auction prices realized in the last four years

year	U.S. $	F. frs	year	U.S. $	F. frs	year	U.S. $	F. frs
1982*	20.00	111						
1981	19.00	107						
1980*	11.00	62						
1979*	13.00	74						
1977*	8.00	46						
1975*	12.00	68						
1971	25.00	141						
1970*	20.00	116						

Auction prices since the last two years. For an indication of value and quality of the missing vintages until 1928, see category IV, page 36/37.

Château Marquis de Terme
Margaux, 4ME CRU CLASSÉ DU MÉDOC

Comments
The Sénéclauze family, wealthy repatriates from Algeria, have owned the château for 25 years. Almost no investment into this property was made for the first twenty years. At the beginning of the eighties, after the death of Sénéclauze Sr., a radical change took place. The young Jean-Pierre Hugon, a perfectionist, was taken on as régisseur. Under his expert direction, the cuverie and the château were renovated. In the meantime, Marquis de Terme has become one of the best cared for Grands Crus in the Médoc. The steady rise in the quality graph makes it crystal clear that the management of Jean-Pierre Hugon is paying off.
Second wine: Château des Gondats

Type Indication
Before 1980 Marquis de Terme was a light, elegant Margaux, of which the quality was not always consistent. During the last 5 years, because of strict quality control, this Grand Cru has grown into a rich, creamy thoroughbred with splendid aging potential.

Technical data

Owner	: Sénéclauze Family	
Régisseur	: Jean-Pierre Hugon	
Cellar master	: Mr. Gouinaud	
Oenologist	: Bernard Couasnon	
Vineyard acreage		: 86 acres
Grape varieties:	Cabernet Sauvignon	: 55%
	Cabernet Franc	: 3%
	Merlot	: 35%
	Petit Verdot	: 7%
Average age of vines		: 35 years
Average annual production (cases of 12 bottles)		: 13,500

Specifications

Vintage	Assessment and Development			Market Value Summer 1995		Change in % since '93
	0 to 20 rating	drink from	cellaring potential	U.S. $	F. frs	
1993	15	1998	2010			
1992	13	1995	2002			
1991	15	1994	2000	This Grand Cru is		
1990	15	1995	2005	not being offered		
1989	16	1995	2005	for sale on the		
1988	17	1997	2010	open market and,		
1987	15	1991	1996	therefore, no exact		
1986	17	1995	2015	prices are available.		
1985	18	1992	2020			
1984	14	1988	1998			
1983	17	1993	2005			
1982	15	1992	2003			
1981	16	1990	2000			
1980	15	1984	1990			
1979	14	1984	1989			
1978	15	1985	1990			
1977	15	1982	1990			

Older vintages	0 to 20 rating	drink from	cellaring potential	Market Value	
				U.S. $	F. frs
1976	16	1985	1995		
1975	15	1990	2005		
1973	13	1982	1990		
1971	15	1980	1990		
1970	14	1982	1992		

Auction prices realized in the last four years

year	U.S. $	F. frs	year	U.S. $	F. frs	year	U.S. $	F. frs
1985*	26.00	149						
1983*	35.00	199						
1978*	15.00	86						
1975	16.00	91						
1966*	27.00	156						
1962*	20.00	111						

Auction prices since the last two years. For an indication of value and quality of the missing vintages until 1928, see category III, page 34/35.

Château La Mission Haut-Brion
Pessac, CRU CLASSÉ DE GRAVES

Comments
In 1983 this château was sold to the neighbor opposite, Château Haut-Brion. Monsieur Woltner, who until the mid-seventies was in charge of this château for almost half a century, was an extremely competent winemaker. He was the propriétaire who as early as the 1920s understood that temperature control during fermentation was of the utmost importance. A vinification technique that was to take 30 to 40 years before being employed all over Bordeaux. In 1987 a new ultra modern fermentation cellar was put into use at the Château, giving rise to expectations for an increase in quality in the near future.

Type Indication
An unprecedented deep, rich, meaty wine since 1928. A forerunner of the modern oenology in Bordeaux. Even the La Mission Haut-Brions from before the war are rich in fruit and finesse which they have retained thanks to a well-controlled temperature during the fermentation process.

Technical data

Owner	: Domaine Clarence Dillon S.A.		
Director	: La Duchesse de Mouchy		
Régisseur	: Jean-Bernard Delmas		
Vineyard acreage			: 44 acres
Grape varieties:	Cabernet Sauvignon	:	60%
	Cabernet Franc	:	5%
	Merlot	:	35%
	Other :		
Average age of vines			: 25 years
Average annual production (cases of 12 bottles)			: 8,000

Specifications

Vintage	Assessment and Development			Market Value Summer 1995		Change in % since '93
	0 to 20 rating	drink from	cellaring potential	U.S. $	F. frs	
1993	16	2000	2015	45.00	203	25%
1992	15	1997	2002	40.00	183	51%
1991	15	1994	2000	42.00	189	4%
1990	17	1996	2010	84.00	380	17%
1989	19	1997	2010	182.00	831	100%
1988	18	1997	2015	69.00	312	10%
1987	15	1991	1997			
1986	16	1995	2010	72.00	326	0%
1985	16	1993	2010	81.00	367	4%
1984	15	1989	1995	37.00	167	-24%
1983	16	1995	2005	81.00	367	4%
1982	16	1987	1997			
1981	15	1988	1998	89.00	408	9%
1980	14	1984	1990			
1979	15	1985	1995			
1978						
1977	12	1983	1990	48.00	217	-17%

Older vintages	0 to 20 rating	drink from	cellaring potential	Market Value	
				U.S. $	F. frs
1973	16	1978	1985		

Auction prices realized in the last four years

year	U.S. $	F. frs	year	U.S. $	F. frs	year	U.S. $	F. frs
1989*	61.00	347	1976*	53.00	299	1949*	493.00	2801
1986*	50.00	282	1975*	306.00	1736	1947	403.00	2286
1985*	84.00	479	1971*	63.00	359	1945*	845.00	4797
1983*	38.00	214	1970*	127.00	718	1938	133.00	754
1982*	127.00	718	1966*	175.00	993	1929*	214.00	1216
1981*	47.00	269	1961*	358.00	2035	1928	199.00	1128
1979*	44.00	251	1959*	495.00	2812	1918	207.00	1178
1978*	78.00	441	1955*	282.00	1599	1877	512.00	2906

Auction prices since the last two years. For an indication of value and quality of the missing vintages until 1928, see category I, page 30/31.

Château Montrose
Saint-Estèphe, 2ME CRU CLASSÉ DU MÉDOC

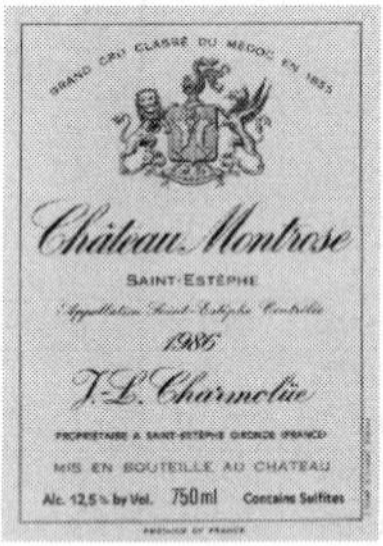

Comments
A 2me Cru which does not compete in the front lines of this category. The list of ratings show changeability in quality. The real top wines are more of a coincidence than with the leaders of the 2me Cru classification. It is a Cru, however, which scores high now and again. In successful vintages certainly, Montrose is a Cru which offers prospects of a top wine against a reasonable price.
Second wine: La Dame de Montrose

Type Indication
In spite of a generous percentage of Merlot (25%) Montrose is, especially in early youth, a tough, somewhat hard wine. A characteristic which can be tied in with the very traditional vinification. The Montrose is mostly rich in color and tannin. Its character is a little coarse, but in good years Montrose has the class of a distinguished 'seigneur'.

Technical data

Owner	: Jean-Louis Charmolüe		
Régisseur	: Bruno Lemoine		
Cellar master	: Jean-Louis Papot		
Oenologist	: Prof. Pascal Ribéreau-Gayon		
Vineyard acreage		:	168 acres
Grape varieties:	Cabernet Sauvignon	:	65%
	Cabernet Franc	:	10%
	Merlot	:	25%
	Other	:	
Average age of vines		:	27 years
Average annual production (cases of 12 bottles)		:	20,000

Specifications

Vintage	Assessment and Development			Market Value Summer 1995		Change in % since '93
	0 to 20 rating	drink from	cellaring potential	U.S. $	F. frs	
1993	17	2000	2015	27.00	124	14%
1992	16	1997	2005	25.00	114	36%
1991	15	1994	2000			
1990	16	1995	2005			
1989	18	1998	2015	58.00	264	61%
1988	16	1997	2005	45.00	203	65%
1987	15	1992	1997			
1986	17	1996	2010	58.00	264	85%
1985	16	1994	2004	45.00	203	17%
1984	14	1989	1997			
1983	16	1990	2005			
1982	15	1987	1995	73.00	333	68%
1981	15	1990	2000	45.00	203	27%
1980	11	1983	1989			
1979	14	1985	1995			
1978	17	1987	1997			
1977	14	1984	1988	21.00	94	3%

Older vintages	0 to 20 rating	drink from	cellaring potential	Market Value	
				U.S. $	F. frs
1976	16	1986	1997		
1975	15	1990	2003	73.00	333
1974	12	1977	1985		
1973	12	1977	1981		
1971	11	1976	1981		
1970	18	1987	2000		
1969	12	1975	1983		
1961	15	1979	1990		

Auction prices realized in the last four years

year	U.S. $	F. frs	year	U.S. $	F. frs	year	U.S. $	F. frs
1989*	31.00	176	1979	25.00	144	1962	68.00	383
1988*	24.00	135	1978*	27.00	155	1961*	151.00	857
1987*	18.00	100	1976*	27.00	151	1959	128.00	724
1986	29.00	163	1975*	31.00	174	1945*	79.00	447
1985*	23.00	132	1971	24.00	137	1943*	116.00	658
1983*	22.00	123	1970*	86.00	490	1929	169.00	958
1982*	45.00	255	1967	26.00	149	1928	199.00	1128
1981*	23.00	131	1966*	44.00	251	1893*	490.00	2783

Auction prices since the last two years. For an indication of value and quality of the missing vintages until 1928, see category II, page 32/33.

Château Mouton-Rothschild
Pauillac, 1ER CRU CLASSÉ DU MÉDOC

Comments
The seventies were not convincing for Mouton. It is the decade in which Mouton graduated from the 2mes Crus to the 1ers Crus. It looked as though, after struggling for so long, Mouton was suffering a relapse.

However, since the early eighties the quality has increased considerably. The improvement in quality is continuing till this day and in recent years Mouton has produced once again one of the best Bordeaux wines.

Type Indication
One of the few Médocs with almost 100% Cabernet grapes on the base. Mouton is an extremely nuanced, deep, rich Pauillac. Especially when fully ripe, Mouton can be recognized by its bouquet, pure Cabernet. In good vintages, a wine which can be cellared long.

Technical data

Owner	: Baronne Philippine de Rothschild	
Technical director	: Patrick Léon	
Cellar master	: Michel Bosq	
Vineyard acreage		: 185 acres
Grape varieties:	Cabernet Sauvignon	: 80%
	Cabernet Franc	: 10%
	Merlot	: 8%
	Other	: 2%
Average age of vines		: 45 years
Average annual production (cases of 12 bottles)		: 25,000

Specifications

Vintage	Assessment and Development			Market Value Summer 1995		Change in % since '93
	0 to 20 rating	drink from	cellaring potential	U.S. $	F. frs	
1993	17	1999	2015	63.00	285	18%
1992	**17**	1996	2005	66.00	299	44%
1991	**17**	1995	2005	92.00	421	71%
1990	**17**	1996	2010	107.00	490	30%
1989	**19**	2000	2030	133.00	606	24%
1988	**18**	1998	2020	98.00	449	0%
1987	**17**	1991	1997	107.00	490	-8%
1986	**18**	1995	2015	272.00	1240	100%
1985	**19**	1995	2020	152.00	694	25%
1984	**16**	1990	2000	66.00	299	0%
1983	**18**	1992	2010			
1982	**18**	1990	2010	451.00	2059	67%
1981	**18**	1990	2010	205.00	933	111%
1980	**16**	1984	1990			
1979	**15**	1986	1998			
1978	**16**	1985	1995	175.00	797	8%
1977	**14**	1985	1993			

Older vintages	0 to 20 rating	drink from	cellaring potential	Market Value U.S. $	F. frs
1976	**18**	1985	2000		
1975	**17**	1999	2010	235.00	1070
1974	**14**	1979	1989		
1973	**16**	1978	1989		
1970	**18**	1987	2000	362.00	1650
1962	**18**	1975	1988		
1961	**19**	1977	1995		
1959	**19**	1973	1982		

Auction prices realized in the last four years

year	U.S. $	F. frs	year	U.S. $	F. frs	year	U.S. $	F. frs
1990*	96.00	546	1979*	63.00	359	1953*	569.00	3232
1989*	93.00	531	1978*	74.00	419	1949*	822.00	4669
1988*	79.00	449	1970*	150.00	850	1947*	897.00	5095
1986*	120.00	682	1968*	190.00	1077	1945*	1811.00	10285
1985*	83.00	473	1966*	180.00	1022	1929*	598.00	3396
1983*	69.00	392	1961*	569.00	3232	1928*	759.00	4310
1982*	194.00	1102	1959*	612.00	3474	1916*	923.00	5241
1981*	60.00	341	1955*	172.00	977	1864*	3629.00	20608

Auction prices since the last two years. For an indication of value and quality of the missing vintages until 1928, see category I, page 30/31.

Château Olivier
Léognan, GRAND CRU CLASSÉ DE GRAVES

Comments
The castle adorning the labels of Château Olivier is an authentic 12th century fortress. The vineyard itself dates from the 18th century and from the beginning of this century was leased and managed by the firm of Louis Eschenauer. The owners, the Bethmann family, took over management in 1981 and since 1984 they have also marketed the wine. Maître de Chai is Christian Dubile, and Advising Oenologist is Guy Guimbertau. Fermentation takes place at temperatures of 25 to 32 °C (77 to 89°F).

A white Graves is also produced at the Château, which is not taken into consideration here.

Type Indication
In fair vintages Olivier is light and elegant, but lacks the texture of a Grand Cru. In top vintages Olivier can be a pleasant surprise. Overall it is not consistent.

Technical data

Owner	: De Bethmann Family
Director	: Jean-Jacques de Bethmann
Cellar master	: Christian Dubile
Oenologist	: Prof. Guy Guimberteau

Vineyard acreage		:	57 acres
Grape varieties :	Cabernet Sauvignon	:	65%
	Cabernet Franc	:	15%
	Merlot	:	20%
	Other	:	
Average age of vines		:	25 years

Specifications

Vintage	Assessment and Development 0 to 20 rating	drink from	cellaring potential	Market Value Summer 1995 U.S. $	F. frs	Change in % since '93
1993	15	1999	2012	19.00	84	26%
1992	**15**	1996	2002			
1991	**14**	1994	2000	17.00	77	26%
1990	**16**	1995	2005	23.00	102	38%
1989	**16**	1996	2005			
1988	**16**	1994	2005			
1987	**15**	1990	1996			
1986	**15**	1994	2005			
1985	**17**	1992	2005			
1984	**14**	1989	1997	15.00	69	0%
1983	**14**	1989	2000			
1982	**14**	1995	2005			
1981						
1980						
1979						
1978						
1977						

Older vintages	0 to 20 rating	drink from	cellaring potential	Market Value U.S. $	F. frs

Auction prices realized in the last four years

year	U.S. $	F. frs	year	U.S. $	F. frs	year	U.S. $	F. frs

* Auction prices since the last two years. For an indication of value and quality of the missing vintages until 1928, see category IV, page 36/37.

CHATEAU OLIVIER

Château Palmer
Margaux, 3ME CRU CLASSÉ DU MÉDOC

Comments
The Dutch family, Mähler-Besse, of the Dutch/French wine firm by the same name, owns the majority of the Palmer stocks. The Sichel family also holds a small block of stocks. Palmer is distributed by Mähler-Besse and the importer for Sichel. As a result, Palmer is a very difficult wine to come by. It is most likely found at auctions.
Second wine: La Réserve du Général

Type Indication
Palmer ranks among the best producers of Bordeaux. The '61 Palmer is one of the highest rated wines of that top year. It is a very compact and intense 'seigneur'. A Cru bringing suppleness, charm and roundness into harmony with a tight, pure intensity.

Technical data

Owner	: Société de Château Palmer	
Director	: Bertrand Bouteiller	
Cellar master	: Yves Chardon	
Oenologist	: Jacques Boissenot	
Vineyard acreage		: 111 acres
Grape varieties:	Cabernet Sauvignon	:
	Cabernet Franc	: 53%
	Merlot	: 45%
	Other	: 2%
Average age of vines		: 30 years
Average annual production (cases of 12 bottles)		: 15,000

Specifications

Vintage	Assessment and Development 0 to 20 rating	drink from	cellaring potential	Market Value Summer 1995 U.S. $	F. frs	Change in % since '93
1993	16	1999	2010			
1992	**15**	1995	2002	39.00	177	
1991	**15**	1994	2000			
1990	**16**	1996	2007	62.00	282	
1989	**17**	1997	2015	72.00	326	2%
1988	**16**	1996	2010			
1987	**15**	1990	1995			
1986	**17**	1993	2010	78.00	353	19%
1985	**17**	1992	2007	76.00	346	9%
1984	**16**	1989	1997			
1983	**17**	1993	2010			
1982	**16**	1992	2010			
1981	**17**	1990	2005			
1980	**15**	1985	1990			
1979						
1978						
1977	**14**	1984	1990			

Older vintages	0 to 20 rating	drink from	cellaring potential	Market Value U.S. $	F. frs
1973	**15**	1978	1995		
1970	**17**	1987	2000		
1969	**14**	1978	1990		
1967	**15**	1974	1985		
1961	**20**	1978	1995		

Auction prices realized in the last four years

year	U.S. $	F. frs	year	U.S. $	F. frs	year	U.S. $	F. frs
1990*	33.00	185	1978*	71.00	400	1959*	261.00	1484
1989*	47.00	268	1975*	84.00	479	1955*	163.00	926
1988*	35.00	196	1973*	22.00	125	1953*	239.00	1356
1986*	39.00	220	1970*	101.00	574	1947*	190.00	1077
1985*	54.00	305	1967*	40.00	227	1943*	99.00	562
1983*	69.00	392	1966*	168.00	951	1928*	447.00	2537
1981*	37.00	212	1964*	59.00	337	1921*	286.00	1622
1979*	58.00	329	1961*	431.00	2449	1918*	113.00	642

Auction prices since the last two years. For an indication of value and quality of the missing vintages until 1928, see category II, page 32/33.

Château Pape Clément
Pessac, GRAND CRU CLASSÉ DE GRAVES

Comments
The château is a well-run company famous for its reliable selection and large annual investment in barrels, all of which are renewed for each harvest. Professor Emile Peynaud stood at the cradle of this renewal and along with Château Léoville-las-Cases this château was one of the first supporters of the Peynaud vinification method. Unfortunately, despite all the good basic factors that are present to produce a top wine, the scores for the early '80s of this Graves are not convincing. However, more recent vintages have seen a rise in the quality curve.
Second wine: Le Clémentin du Château Pape Clément.

Type Indication
A wine with a lot of oak wood in flavor and bouquet, not however always in balance with the texture of the wine, which often gives this Graves a dry and not very supple character.

Technical data

Owner	: Montagne Family		
Director	: Bernard Pujol		
Régisseur	: Etienne Thérasse		
Oenologist	: Prof. Pascal Ribéreau-Gayon		
Vineyard acreage		:	74 acres
Grape varieties:	Cabernet Sauvignon	:	60 %
	Cabernet Franc	:	
	Merlot	:	40 %
	Other	:	
Average age of vines		:	30 years
Average annual production (cases of 12 bottles)		:	13,000

Specifications

Vintage	Assessment and Development			Market Value Summer 1995		Change in % since '93
	0 to 20 rating	drink from	cellaring potential	U.S. $	F. frs	
1993	17	1998	2010	29.00	132	22%
1992	**15**	1996	2002	24.00	107	27%
1991	**16**	1996	2000			
1990	**17**	1995	2005	48.00	217	25%
1989	**17**	1996	2010	42.00	192	15%
1988	**18**	1997	2015	42.00	189	0%
1987	**14**	1990	1997			
1986	**15**	1993	2010	44.00	200	6%
1985	**16**	1990	2005	43.00	196	13%
1984	**15**	1989	1997	22.00	98	-21%
1983	**15**	1992	2002	39.00	176	20%
1982	**14**	1987	1995	43.00	193	-5%
1981	**14**	1987	1997			
1980	**15**	1985	1990	30.00	135	
1979						
1978						
1977	**10**	1982	1988			

Older vintages	0 to 20 rating	drink from	cellaring potential	Market Value	
				U.S. $	F. frs
1975				92.00	421
1974	**16**	1978	1987		
1973	**14**	1977	1982		
1971				78.00	353

Auction prices realized in the last four years

year	U.S. $	F. frs	year	U.S. $	F. frs	year	U.S. $	F. frs
1989*	24.00	135	1975*	40.00	227			
1986*	20.00	113	1974	14.00	81			
1985*	31.00	178	1970*	29.00	164			
1982	33.00	188	1966	43.00	245			
1981*	19.00	108	1961	103.00	584			
1979*	23.00	132	1953*	66.00	373			
1978*	22.00	127	1896*	245.00	1391			
1976*	18.00	100						

Auction prices since the last two years. For an indication of value and quality of the missing vintages until 1928, see category II, page 32/33.

Château Pavie
Saint-Emilion, 1ER GRAND CRU CLASSÉ B

Comments
Pavie embodies, for a Saint-Emilion, the customary composition of the vineyard. The Merlot determines the character, while the cépages Cabernet give the Pavie aging potential. The fermentation cellar installations of cement cuves, date from 1927. At that time they were modern, but now they have been replaced by stainless steel tanks in most châteaux. Even without those latest devices, so useful to the modern oenologist, Jean-Paul Valette and his son Patrick succeed in making Pavie a 'modern' wine. The Valettes are followers of the Peynaud method of vinification.

Type Indication
A depth tasting where the vintages from 1973 through 1979 were compared blind, is surrounded with terms such as: mahogany, balanced, class, firm and reticent with regard to the nose. Regarding the flavor the terms are firm, even, flavorful, round and juicy.

Technical data

Owner	: S.C.A. Consorts Valette	
Director	: Jean-Paul Valette	
Régisseur	: Patrick Valette	
Oenologist	: Prof. Pascal Ribéreau-Gayon	
Vineyard acreage		: 86 acres
Grape varieties:	Cabernet Sauvignon	: 20%
	Cabernet Franc	: 25%
	Merlot	: 55%
	Other	:
Average age of vines		: 45 years
Average annual production (cases of 12 bottles)		: 15,000

Specifications

Vintage	Assessment and Development 0 to 20 rating	drink from	cellaring potential	Market Value Summer 1995 U.S. $	F. frs	Change in % since '93
1993	15	2000	2015	26.00	118	18%
1992	**14**	1995	2002	24.00	110	6%
1991	**13**	1994	2000			
1990	**16**	1995	2005	46.00	207	38%
1989	**17**	1997	2010	46.00	210	26%
1988	**16**	1995	2007	43.00	196	17%
1987	**13**	1991	1997			
1986	**16**	1993	2010	46.00	210	45%
1985	**17**	1992	2015	54.00	244	21%
1984	**14**	1988	1998	28.00	128	6%
1983	**16**	1990	2000			
1982	**17**	1990	2000	85.00	387	45%
1981						
1980	**14**	1984	1990			
1979	**17**	1987	1997			
1978	**15**	1985	1990			
1977	**15**	1980	1985			

Older vintages	0 to 20 rating	drink from	cellaring potential	Market Value U.S. $	F. frs
1976	**16**	1984	1995		
1975				100.00	456
1974	**15**	1980	1988		
1973	**12**	1977	1983		
1970	**15**	1985	1995		

Auction prices realized in the last four years

year	U.S. $	F. frs	year	U.S. $	F. frs	year	U.S. $	F. frs
1989*	22.00	122	1975*	26.00	149	1945*	109.00	620
1988*	35.00	199	1971*	23.00	132			
1985*	33.00	188	1970	34.00	195			
1983*	32.00	180	1966	44.00	251			
1982*	47.00	269	1964	46.00	266			
1981*	28.00	160	1961*	61.00	343			
1979	29.00	164	1955	26.00	148			
1978*	31.00	174	1952	38.00	218			

* Auction prices since the last two years. For an indication of value and quality of the missing vintages until 1928, see category II, page 32/33.

CHATEAU PAVIE
ST ÉMILION
1ᵉʳ GRAND CRU CLASSÉ

Château Pédesclaux

Pauillac, 5ME CRU CLASSÉ DU MÉDOC

Comments
One of the Grands Crus du Médoc which hasn't made much of a name for itself in spite of a production of 8,000 cases per year. The quality of this château is poor. Pédesclaux is a Grand Cru that does not live up to the description and the price is just about what one would expect.
Second wine: Château Belle Rose

Type Indication
Based solely on the 1982 tasting. A healthy, quite light Cabernet wine. Lacks distinctive character. Not a soaring wine, but a tasty '82.

Technical data

Owner	: Jugla Family		
Director	: Bernard Jugla		
Cellar master	: Jean Jugla		
Oenologist	: Bernard Couasnon		
Vineyard acreage		:	49 acres
Grape varieties:	Cabernet Sauvignon	:	70%
	Cabernet Franc	:	7%
	Merlot	:	20%
	Other	:	3%
Average age of vines		:	39 years
Average annual production (cases of 12 bottles)		:	8,000

Specifications

Vintage	Assessment and Development			Market Value Summer 1995		Change in % since '93
	0 to 20 rating	drink from	cellaring potential	U.S. $	F. frs	
1993	14	1997	2005			
1992	12	1995	2000			
1991	12	1994	2000	This Grand Cru is		
1990				not being offered		
1989	15	1995	2005	for sale on the		
1988	16	1995	2008	open market and,		
1987	17	1990	1994	therefore, no exact		
1986	14	1992	2000	prices are available.		
1985	15	1992	2000			
1984	12	1988	1993			
1983	13	1988	1995			
1982	15	1987	1995			
1981						
1980						
1979						
1978						
1977						

Older vintages	0 to 20 rating	drink from	cellaring potential	Market Value U.S. $	F. frs

Auction prices realized in the last four years

year	U.S. $	F. frs	year	U.S. $	F. frs	year	U.S. $	F. frs
1982	18.00	99						
1975	25.00	144						
1970	9.00	48						

* Auction prices since the last two years. For an indication of value and quality of the missing vintages until 1928, see category IV, page 36/37.

CHÂTEAU PÉDESCLAUX
GRAND
CRU CLASSÉ
PAUILLAC - MÉDOC

Château Pichon-Longueville-Baron
Pauillac, 2ME CRU CLASSÉ DU MÉDOC

Comments
Château Pichon-Longueville, which was still one château in 1855, has been split for more than one hundred years in two estates, i.e., Pichon-Longueville of the Comtesse de Lalande and the domain of the Baron. Qualitatively these two châteaux could scarcely be told apart.
However, comparisons of the tasting results of the seventies show that the Baron comes off rather badly.
In 1986, the château was sold to the AXA insurance company. Jean-Michel Cazes, owner of château Lynch-Bages, manages the AXA properties and has made considerable investments in capital and know-how in Pichon-Baron.
Second wine: Tourelles de Longueville

Type Indication
Traditionally the Baron's wine held out longest. It is a definite Cabernet wine, slow in its development and good for cellaring. Since Cazes has taken over, the Pichon-Baron has become stouter and fluffier than the old-style Baron.

Technical data

Owner	: AXA Millésimes		
Director	: Jean-Michel Cazes		
Technical director	: Daniel Llose		
Cellar master	: Patrick Pinto		
Vineyard acreage		:	124 acres
Grape varieties:	Cabernet Sauvignon	:	75%
	Cabernet Franc	:	
	Merlot	:	24%
	Other	:	1%
Average age of vines		:	40 years
Average annual production (cases of 12 bottles)		:	20,000

Specifications

Vintage	Assessment and Development			Market Value Summer 1995		Change in % since '93
	0 to 20 rating	drink from	cellaring potential	U.S. $	F. frs	
1993	17	1999	2012	27.00	121	8%
1992	15	1996	2002	24.00	110	26%
1991	16	1995	2005	28.00	128	23%
1990	18	1998	2015	58.00	264	68%
1989	19	1997	2025			
1988	18	1997	2010	48.00	217	11%
1987	17	1991	1997	30.00	135	29%
1986	18	1993	2015	54.00	244	48%
1985	16	1990	1995	48.00	217	20%
1984	14	1988	1996			
1983	15	1990	1998	37.00	169	0%
1982	14	1990	1998	63.00	285	33%
1981	15	1988	1997			
1980	15	1984	1990			
1979	16	1987	1998			
1978	14	1983	1993			
1977	12	1982	1990			

Older vintages	0 to 20 rating	drink from	cellaring potential	Market Value U.S. $	F. frs
1976	13	1984	1994		
1973	14	1976	1981		
1970	11	1980	1990		
1969	10	1974	1979		
1966	13	1974	1984		
1965	10	1970	1975		
1958	13	1965	1975		

Auction prices realized in the last four years

year	U.S. $	F. frs	year	U.S. $	F. frs	year	U.S. $	F. frs
1989*	40.00	229	1978*	41.00	235	1955	48.00	272
1988*	23.00	131	1976*	23.00	128	1952	77.00	435
1986*	19.00	109	1975*	43.00	243	1949*	72.00	408
1985*	30.00	169	1973*	25.00	144	1947	76.00	431
1983*	22.00	122	1970*	74.00	419	1939	53.00	299
1982*	95.00	539	1966*	34.00	191	1937	70.00	398
1981*	20.00	116	1961*	111.00	629	1878	177.00	1006
1979*	23.00	131	1959	105.00	599			

Auction prices since the last two years. For an indication of value and quality of the missing vintages until 1928, see category II, page 32/33.

Château Pichon-Longueville Comtesse de Lalande

Pauillac, 2ME CRU CLASSÉ DU MÉDOC

Comments

Not Comtesse de Lalande but the energetic Madame de Lencquesaing holds the reins. In close cooperation with Professor Emile Peynaud and Pascal Ribereau-Gayon, she has succeeded in bringing this Cru up to the highest standard. Château Pichon-Comtesse, which before 1900 was still joined with Pichon Baron, was qualitatively far ahead of the Baron in the late seventies and early eighties. In the sixties both Pichons were still well-matched. In the past decade, the château and cuverie underwent considerable renovation.
Second wine: Réserve de la Comtesse

Type Indication

A compact, very concentrated texture. Especially in youth this Cru is reserved, sturdy and a little manly. It is a true-to-type Pauillac, with long aging potential in good vintages. A wine requiring patience.

Technical data

Owner	: S.C.I. du Ch. Pichon-Longueville Comtesse de Lalande
Director	: Mme May-Eliane de Lencquesaing
Technical director	: Thomas Do Chi Nam
Oenologist	: Prof. Pascal Ribéreau-Gayon
Vineyard acreage		: 185 acres
Grape varieties:	Cabernet Sauvignon	: 45%
	Cabernet Franc	: 12%
	Merlot	: 35%
	Other	: 8%
Average age of vines		: 30 years
Average annual production (cases of 12 bottles)		: 17,500

Specifications

Vintage	Assessment and Development			Market Value Summer 1995		Change in % since '93
	0 to 20 rating	drink from	cellaring potential	U.S. $	F. frs	
1993	17	1998	2012	27.00	121	8%
1992	**16**	1995	2003	25.00	114	23%
1991	**16**	1994	2000	34.00	155	24%
1990	**18**	1998	2015	54.00	244	36%
1989	**18**	1996	2015	55.00	251	13%
1988	**18**	2000	2010	50.00	228	13%
1987	**16**	1991	1996			
1986	**17**	1993	2015	76.00	346	7%
1985	**18**	1992	2015	63.00	285	18%
1984	**17**	1990	2000			
1983	**16**	1993	2010	55.00	251	-3%
1982	**18**	1990	2010			
1981	**17**	1990	2005	63.00	285	11%
1980	**16**	1985	1995			
1979	**19**	1987	1997	66.00	299	5%
1978	**18**	1985	1995			
1977	**12**	1982	1990			

Older vintages	0 to 20 rating	drink from	cellaring potential	Market Value	
				U.S. $	F. frs
1976	**17**	1985	1995	60.00	271
1975	**17**	1987	2005		
1973	**16**	1978	1983		
1971	**15**	1978	1990		
1970	**17**	1985	2000		
1967	**13**	1973	1982		
1966	**16**	1976	1990		
1958	**15**	1964	1978		

Auction prices realized in the last four years

year	U.S. $	F. frs	year	U.S. $	F. frs	year	U.S. $	F. frs
1990*	39.00	218	1981*	53.00	299	1953*	131.00	741
1989*	40.00	229	1978*	69.00	392	1952*	73.00	413
1988*	33.00	188	1976*	44.00	248	1947*	197.00	1117
1987*	26.00	147	1970*	93.00	526	1943*	159.00	904
1986*	47.00	269	1966*	105.00	599	1934*	178.00	1012
1985*	50.00	285	1961*	185.00	1048	1929*	166.00	940
1983*	49.00	278	1959*	158.00	898	1928*	197.00	1121
1982*	137.00	778	1955*	83.00	470	1916*	137.00	778

Auction prices since the last two years. For an indication of value and quality of the missing vintages until 1928, see category II, page 32/33.

Château Pontet-Canet
Pauillac, 5ME CRU CLASSÉ DU MÉDOC

Comments
Since 1865, this Cru has been owned by the Cruse family, who also owned the Bordeaux firm of the same name. In 1975 the château was sold to Guy Tesseron, Cruse's son-in-law.

In the sixties and previous to that, Pontet-Canet was known as an extremely well-cared-for Cru that could stand up to comparison with many a 2me Cru. Since that time, its reputation has declined. Pontet-Canet couldn't maintain itself at the top in the seventies. But from 1984 onward, a slow change has been noticed. The quality curve is once again on the upswing.

Second wine: Château Les Hauts de Pontet

Type Indication
A Pontet-Cane old style is hefty, sturdy and excellent for cellaring. The large percentage Cabernet that lies at the base of this wine can give a firm and distinguished flavor and aroma pattern.

Technical data

Owner	: Tesseron Family	
Technical director	: Alfred Tesseron	
Régisseur	: Guy Tesseron	
Cellar master	: Alain Coculet	
Vineyard acreage		: 193 acres
Grape varieties:	Cabernet Sauvignon	: 62%
	Cabernet Franc	: 6%
	Merlot	: 32%
	Other	:
Average age of vines		: 35 years
Average annual production (cases of 12 bottles)		: 22,000

Specifications

Vintage	Assessment and Development 0 to 20 rating	drink from	cellaring potential	Market Value Summer 1995 U.S. $	F. frs	Change in % since '93
1993	16	2000	2015	19.00	87	17%
1992	14	1995	2000	17.00	76	12%
1991	16	1995	2005			
1990	15	1995	2005	28.00	128	21%
1989	18	1995	2010	33.00	148	27%
1988	17	1995	2010	28.00	128	21%
1987	14	1990	1995			
1986	18	1994	2015			
1985	17	1994	2010	36.00	162	16%
1984	15	1989	1997			
1983	13	1988	1998			
1982	15	1987	1995	43.00	196	29%
1981	13	1988	1994	36.00	162	0%
1980	14	1984	1989			
1979	14	1985	1995			
1978	16	1985	1995	57.00	258	3%
1977						

Older vintages	0 to 20 rating	drink from	cellaring potential	Market Value U.S. $	F. frs
1973	14	1976	1980		
1970	14	1975	1983		
1962	11	1970	1978		

Auction prices realized in the last four years

year	U.S. $	F. frs	year	U.S. $	F. frs	year	U.S. $	F. frs
1989*	19.00	105	1975	24.00	138	1928	88.00	500
1986*	25.00	143	1970	28.00	157	1899	289.00	1642
1985*	19.00	105	1966	39.00	219	1874	316.00	1796
1983*	16.00	90	1961*	127.00	718			
1982	26.00	150	1959	84.00	479			
1981*	19.00	108	1953	59.00	334			
1978	25.00	144	1947	113.00	640			
1976	23.00	132	1945	92.00	520			

* Auction prices since the last two years. For an indication of value and quality of the missing vintages until 1928, see category IV, page 36/37.

Château Pouget
Cantenac, 4ME CRU CLASSÉ DU MÉDOC

Comments
The owner of Château Pouget, Monsieur Pierre Guillemet is also owner of Château Boyd-Cantenac, 3me Cru Classé du Médoc.
Both of these Grand Crus are nurtured under the same roof. Until recently, Pouget has been the second wine of Boyd-Cantenac. However, for the last two years this Cru has had its own signature.

Type Indication
The wine is a little stronger that its sister, the Boyd-Cantenac. Pouget is a well-cared-for middle-of-the-road wine with good aging potential.

Technical data

Owner	: Elie-Guillemet Family	
Technical director	: Lucien Guillemet	
Régisseur	: Pierre Guillemet	
Oenologist	: Jacques Boissenot	
Vineyard acreage		: 25 acres
Grape varieties:	Cabernet Sauvignon	: 66%
	Cabernet Franc	:
	Merlot	: 30%
	Other	: 4%
Average age of vines		: 30 years
Average annual production (cases of 12 bottles)		: 3,800

Specifications

Vintage	Assessment and Development			Market Value Summer 1995		Change in % since '93
	0 to 20 rating	drink from	cellaring potential	U.S. $	F. frs	
1993	14	1998	2010			
1992	12	1995	2000			
1991	14	1995	2002			
1990	16	1995	2005			
1989	17	1996	2010	25.00	114	21%
1988	17	1995	2010	24.00	110	20%
1987	13	1990	1995			
1986	17	1993	2010			
1985	16	1990	2005			
1984	15	1988	2000			
1983						
1982						
1981						
1980						
1979						
1978						
1977						

Older vintages	0 to 20 rating	drink from	cellaring potential	Market Value	
				U.S. $	F. frs

Auction prices realized in the last four years

year	U.S. $	F. frs	year	U.S. $	F. frs	year	U.S. $	F. frs
1986	14.00	78						
1984*	11.00	62						
1971	21.00	119						
1969	7.00	38						
1967	62.00	352						

Auction prices since the last two years. For an indication of value and quality of the missing vintages until 1928, see category IV, page 36/37.

CHATEAU POUGET
grand cru classé
MARGAUX

Château Prieuré-Lichine
Cantenac, 4ME CRU CLASSÉ DU MÉDOC

Comments
In 1951 the château was bought by Alexis Lichine, the author of the well-known wine encyclopedia. In 1953 Lichine added his name to that of the château. The vineyards are rather split up and not every section yields grapes of Grand Cru quality. With a stricter selection at the base, this château would be able to attain a higher quality score. This will depend on the decisions of Sacha Lichine, who has been holding the reins since the death of his father Alexis.
The successful vintages of this Cru are quite worth buying.
Second wine: Château de Clairefort

Type Indication
Prieuré-Lichine is a wine consistent with the appellation Margaux type. It is a supple, elegant Cru, which as a rule does not need to ripen for long.
In the big vintages, Prieuré is a little short on intensity.

Technical data

Owner	: Sacha Lichine		
Director	: Sacha Lichine		
Chef de culture	: Etienne Pélissié du Rausas		
Oenologist	: James Palge		
Vineyard acreage		:	178 acres
Grape varieties:	Cabernet Sauvignon	:	55%
	Cabernet Franc	:	2%
	Merlot	:	39%
	Petit Verdot	:	4%
Average age of vines		:	30 years
Average annual production (cases of 12 bottles)		:	36,000

Specifications

Vintage	Assessment and Development			Market Value Summer 1995		Change in % since '93
	0 to 20 rating	drink from	cellaring potential	U.S. $	F. frs	
1993	17	1998	2012	19.00	87	20%
1992	16	1996	2003	19.00	87	49%
1991	14	1994	2000			
1990	15	1995	2005	39.00	176	88%
1989	15	1995	2005			
1988	17	1995	2010			
1987	13	1991	1995			
1986	16	1995	2010			
1985	16	1990	2000			
1984	13	1989	1997			
1983	15	1988	2000			
1982	15	1987	1995			
1981	13	1988	1995			
1980	13	1984	1990			
1979	14	1985	1994			
1978	15	1987	1997			
1977	16	1984	1989			

Older vintages	0 to 20 rating	drink from	cellaring potential	Market Value	
				U.S. $	F. frs
1976	16	1985	1995		
1975	15	1986	1996		

Auction prices realized in the last four years

year	U.S. $	F. frs	year	U.S. $	F. frs	year	U.S. $	F. frs
1989*	18.00	101	1971	25.00	144			
1986*	21.00	118	1970	42.00	239			
1983*	23.00	132	1966	32.00	180			
1982*	25.00	139						
1981	21.00	118						
1979	19.00	107						
1978	30.00	168						
1975*	20.00	114						

Auction prices since the last two years. For an indication of value and quality of the missing vintages until 1928, see category III, page 34/35.

Château Rausan-Ségla
Margaux, 2ME CRU CLASSÉ DU MÉDOC

Comments
Since 1994, Rausan-Ségla belongs to Chanel, the perfume and fashion company. In early 1960, a rigorous replanting of the vineyards was started at Rausan-Ségla, which meant that this 2me Grand Cru was slightly anemic for some time. In 1987 the château invested heavily in the cuverie. Investments in the wine itself involved a rigorous cellar selection. For example, the total 1987 vintage was declassified as a second wine. The management focuses on quality, and the scores for the last vintages testify to this. The Wertheimer family, the owner of Chanel, Inc., wants to continue this policy, not just by means of large investments, but through step-by-step adjustments and improvements. The final goal is to restore the former reputation of Rausan-Ségla as "first among the second crus". Second wine: Château Ségla

Type Indication
A well-cared-for, although an insufficiently textured Margaux. A wine with charm and finesse but with too little substance for its class as a deuxième Cru. Reasonable aging potential.

Technical data

Owner	: Société Holt Frères et Fils		
Director	: Jacques Théo		
Régisseur	: Michel Bruzaud		
Cellar master	: Henry de Ruffray		
Vineyard acreage		:	121 acres
Grape varieties:	Cabernet Sauvignon	:	65%
	Cabernet Franc	:	2%
	Merlot	:	33%
	Other	:	
Average age of vines		:	17 years
Average annual production (cases of 12 bottles)		:	16,500

Specifications

Vintage	Assessment and Development 0 to 20 rating	drink from	cellaring potential	Market Value Summer 1995 U.S. $	F. frs	Change in % since '93
1993	16	2000	2015	25.00	114	1%
1992	**13**	1995	2000	22.00	101	33%
1991	**15**	1994	2000	25.00	112	14%
1990	**16**	1995	2005	46.00	210	
1989	**17**	1997	2010	44.00	200	
1988	**17**	1996	2015	45.00	203	
1987	Harvest has been declassified					
1986	**17**	1993	2010			
1985	**15**	1995	2000			
1984	**15**	1989	1997			
1983	**16**	1990	2005			
1982	**15**	1988	2000			
1981	**13**	1988	1998			
1980	**11**	1984	1990			
1979						
1978						
1977						

Older vintages	0 to 20 rating	drink from	cellaring potential	Market Value U.S. $	F. frs
1973	**15**	1977	1983		
1970	**16**	1988	2000		
1967	**11**	1972	1978		

Auction prices realized in the last four years

year	U.S. $	F. frs	year	U.S. $	F. frs	year	U.S. $	F. frs
1988	32.00	180	1975*	15.00	84	1949	38.00	217
1986*	34.00	193	1971*	19.00	109	1929	405.00	2299
1985	18.00	104	1970*	33.00	188	1899	361.00	2050
1983*	33.00	188	1966	44.00	251	1865	557.00	3161
1982*	24.00	136	1961	73.00	414			
1981*	22.00	122	1959	52.00	296			
1978	23.00	133	1955	36.00	204			
1976	16.00	88	1952	23.00	131			

* Auction prices since the last two years. For an indication of value and quality of the missing vintages until 1928, see category III, page 34/35.

1981
CRU
CHÂTEAU
RAUSAN SEGLA
2ᵐᵉ cru classé en 1855

Château Rauzan-Gassies

Margaux, 2ME CRU CLASSÉ DU MÉDOC

Comments

In recent decades, the management by the Quié family, which also owns Croizet-Bages, has not been very dynamic. Although considerable renovation took place on this domain in the early seventies, it yielded few results. The renovation was limited to the buildings and cellars, so that Rauzan-Gassies continues to lag qualitatively behind other 2me Crus.

At the start of the 1992 vintage, the château boasted a new, extensive cuverie, so that different types of grapes can now be vinified separately and the assembly of the wine can occur with greater care.

Type Indication

Beautifully perfumed and pure of bouquet. Often finely-tuned and well-balanced. Most years a Cru with class, but it has insufficient structure for a 2me Cru.

Technical data

Owner	: P. Quié Family	
Technical director	: Jean-Michel Quié	
Régisseur	: Marc Espagnet	
Oenologist	: Jacques Boissenot	
Vineyard acreage		: 74 acres
Grape varieties:	Cabernet Sauvignon	: 40%
	Cabernet Franc	: 23%
	Merlot	: 35%
	Other	: 2%
Average age of vines		: 30-35 years
Average annual production (cases of 12 bottles)		: 10,000

Specifications

Vintage	Assessment and Development 0 to 20 rating	drink from	cellaring potential	Market Value Summer 1995 U.S. $	F. frs	Change in % since '93
1993	13	1997	2007	18.00	83	24%
1992	12	1995	2000	17.00	75	3%
1991	11	1994	2000			
1990	14	1995	2005	24.00	110	11%
1989	16	1995	2005	27.00	121	16%
1988	15	1997	2007	24.00	107	3%
1987	12	1989	1995			
1986	14	1995	2005			
1985	16	1993	2003			
1984	13	1988	1995			
1983	17	1993	2010			
1982	15	1987	1995			
1981	16	1990	2000	28.00	128	
1980	10	1983	1987			
1979	16	1985	1995			
1978	16	1983	1990			
1977						

Older vintages	0 to 20 rating	drink from	cellaring potential	Market Value U.S. $	F. frs
1973	15	1977	1982		
1970	14	1980	1990	63.00	285
1967	12	1972	1981		
1964				57.00	258

Auction prices realized in the last four years

year	U.S. $	F. frs	year	U.S. $	F. frs	year	U.S. $	F. frs
1990*	23.00	133	1971*	14.00	78	1952*	73.00	413
1989*	20.00	115	1970*	24.00	134	1947	42.00	238
1985	15.00	86	1966	38.00	217	1940	88.00	500
1983*	20.00	112	1962	34.00	192	1921	130.00	739
1982*	20.00	111	1961*	47.00	269			
1981*	16.00	91	1959*	41.00	232			
1978	25.00	144	1955	37.00	209			
1975	21.00	119	1953	32.00	180			

* Auction prices since the last two years. For an indication of value and quality of the missing vintages until 1928, see category III, page 34/35.

Château Saint-Pierre

Saint-Julien, 4ME CRU CLASSÉ DU MÉDOC

Comments

Until 1982, a rather 'dusty' Grand Cru which in both senses of the word lay in the shadow of Château Beychevelle. In July 1982, the château was bought by the old and reputable winemaker Henry Martin. This veteran, who died in 1991, and who also owned Château Gloria and was advisor to the 1er Cru Latour, had as objective to bring the quality of the Saint-Pierre once again up to Grand Cru standards. In the last years of his life, this famous advocate of quality succeeded in achieving his goal. The future will show whether his successors will be able to maintain this level.

Type Indication

The last years are impressive, intense in color and flavor. Perfectly cared-for, well-harmonized wines. Its sturdy, and since 1982 well-cared-for character, makes Saint-Pierre a high-class wine, with good aging potential.

Technical data

Owner	: Domaines H. Martin	
Management	: Jean-Louis Triaud / Emmanuel Cassagne	
Régisseur	: Isidore Elichégaray	
Cellar master	: Jean-Marie Galey	
Vineyard acreage		: 42 acres
Grape varieties:	Cabernet Sauvignon	: 70%
	Cabernet Franc	: 10%
	Merlot	: 18%
	Other	: 2%
Average age of vines		: 30 years
Average annual production (cases of 12 bottles)		: 8,000

Specifications

Vintage	Assessment and Development			Market Value Summer 1995		Change in % since '93
	0 to 20 rating	drink from	cellaring potential	U.S. $	F. frs	
1993	16	2000	2015	19.00	87	17%
1992	**15**	1995	2000			
1991	**15**	1994	2000			
1990	**16**	1995	2005	29.00	132	29%
1989	**16**	1997	2010	30.00	135	6%
1988	**16**	1995	2015	30.00	135	30%
1987	**15**	1991	1996			
1986	**17**	1996	2015			
1985	**17**	1993	2008			
1984	**17**	1992	2005			
1983	**17**	1990	2000	39.00	176	4%
1982	**16**	1987	1997	51.00	230	14%
1981	**16**	1990	2000			
1980						
1979						
1978						
1977						

Older vintages	0 to 20 rating	drink from	cellaring potential	Market Value	
				U.S. $	F. frs
1973	**14**	1978	1983		
1970	**15**	1976	1985		
1966	**14**	1974	1983		

Auction prices realized in the last four years

year	U.S. $	F. frs	year	U.S. $	F. frs	year	U.S. $	F. frs
1989*	23.00	133						
1986*	19.00	110						
1985*	20.00	112						
1982	23.00	132						
1981	21.00	119						
1975	30.00	169						
1970	35.00	196						

* Auction prices since the last two years. For an indication of value and quality of the missing vintages until 1928, see category III, page 34/35.

CHATEAU SAINT-PIERRE
GRAND CRU CLASSÉ
ST JULIEN (FRANCE)

Château Smith Haut Lafitte
Martillac, GRAND CRU CLASSÉ DE GRAVES

Comments
Until the middle of this century, Smith-Haut-Lafitte was the plaything of speculators. In 1958 the property fell into the hands of Société Eschenauer, a Bordeaux mercantile house which in turn was owned by investors from London, the Holt Group. At the end of 1990, its was purchased by Daniel Cathiard.

The image and also the quality of this Graves fall thus far below average. With stricter cellar selection, the new owner could quickly score much higher. The production methods are traditional.

The château produces also a dry white Graves, not taken into consideration here.

Second wine: Les Hauts de Smith

Type Indication
Smith Haut Lafitte is a delicate and elegant wine lacking, however, a little body and texture. Nevertheless, in top vintages this Graves can have a distinctive rich constitution.

Technical data

Owner	: Daniel Cathiard
Régisseur	: Jean-Jacques Guérin
Cellar master	: Gabriel Vialard
Oenologists	: Prof. Pascal Ribereau-Gayon, Michel Rolland

Vineyard acreage		: 136 acres
Grape varieties:	Cabernet Sauvignon	: 55%
	Cabernet Franc	: 10%
	Merlot	: 35%
	Other	:
Average age of vines		: 28 years
Average annual production (cases of 12 bottles)		: 23,000

Specifications

Vintage	Assessment and Development 0 to 20 rating	drink from	cellaring potential	Market Value Summer 1995 U.S. $	F. frs	Change in % since '93
1993	16	2000	2015	20.00	92	23%
1992	**16**	1997	2003			
1991	**16**	1995	2005	19.00	84	
1990	**16**	1995	2005	27.00	124	
1989						
1988	**14**	1995	2005			
1987	**13**	1990	1995			
1986						
1985	**17**	1992	2007			
1984	**12**	1987	1994			
1983	**14**	1990	2000			
1982	**13**	1988	1995			
1981	**12**	1987	1995			
1980	**12**	1984	1988			
1979						
1978						
1977						

Older vintages	0 to 20 rating	drink from	cellaring potential	Market Value U.S. $	F. frs

Auction prices realized in the last four years

year	U.S. $	F. frs	year	U.S. $	F. frs	year	U.S. $	F. frs
1985*	13.00	72						
1983*	15.00	86						
1982*	20.00	111						
1978*	19.00	108						
1970	41.00	230						
1891*	170.00	963						
1878	261.00	1479						

Auction prices since the last two years. For an indication of value and quality of the missing vintages until 1928, see category III, page 34/35.

CHATEAU
SMITH HAUT LAFITE

Château Talbot
Saint-Julien, 4ME CRU CLASSÉ DU MÉDOC

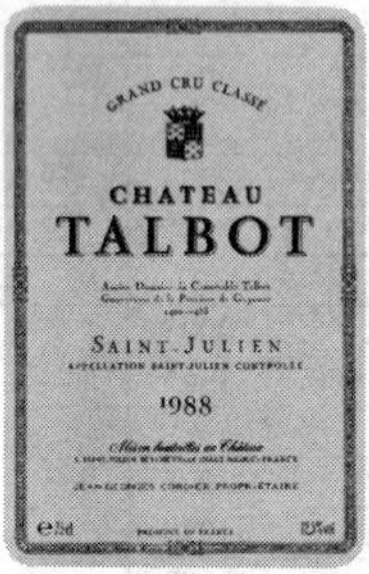

Comments
The Talbot vineyard belongs to the largest in the Médoc. Since 1993 the domaine is once again entirely in the hands of the Cordier family. As in other former Cordier properties, the very competent Georges Pauli is in charge of enology at Talbot. His style of vinification is also recognizable at Gruaud-Larose, Cantemerle and Château Meyney. Especially in poor and average years, Georges Pauli succeeds in achieving fine results. After the takeover by Cordier and the death of Jean Cordier at the end of 1993, responsibility for the vinification was transferred to Thierry Rustmann. Professor Pascal Ribéreau-Gayon acts as consulting enologist.

Château Talbot also produces a small amount of white wine for which five hectares have been planted with Sauvignons and one hectare with Sémillons.

Second wine: Connétable de Talbot

Type Indication
The vinification style of Georges Pauli is recognizable by the intense deep color, even in poor vintages. The flavor of the Talbot is also mostly deep and intense.

Technical data

Owner	: Nancy Bignon-Cordier and Lorraine Rustmann-Cordier	
Régisseur	: Thierry Rustmann	
Cellar master	: Ramon Jorajuria	
Oenologist	: Prof. Pascal Ribéreau-Gayon	
Vineyard acreage		: 264 acres
Grape varieties:	Cabernet Sauvignon	: 66%
	Cabernet Franc	: 3%
	Merlot	: 24%
	Other	: 7%
Average age of vines		: 35 years
Average annual production (cases of 12 bottles)		: 45,000

Specifications

Vintage	Assessment and Development 0 to 20 rating	drink from	cellaring potential	Market Value Summer 1995 U.S. $	F. frs	Change in % since '93
1993	15	1998	2010	23.00	103	18%
1992	17	1995	2002	26.00	116	31%
1991	16	1995	2005			
1990	16	1995	2005	32.00	144	
1989	19	1998	2015	29.00	132	
1988	18	1995	2010	30.00	137	-25%
1987	16	1991	1996	26.00	116	-24%
1986	16	1995	2015			
1985	17	1995	2015			
1984	16	1988	2000	27.00	122	24%
1983	16	1990	2005			
1982	18	1990	2005			
1981	16	1989	2005			
1980	15	1984	1990			
1979	17	1986	1996			
1978	16	1988	1998			
1977	16	1982	1990			

Older vintages	0 to 20 rating	drink from	cellaring potential	Market Value U.S. $	F. frs
1976	16	1982	1992		
1975	16	1988	2000		
1974	14	1978	1988		
1973	14	1978	1985		
1972	15	1977	1984		
1971	16	1980	1985		
1970	16	1983	1995		
1966	14	1975	1990		

Auction prices realized in the last four years

year	U.S. $	F. frs	year	U.S. $	F. frs	year	U.S. $	F. frs
1989*	25.00	143	1978*	30.00	168	1960	23.00	132
1988*	24.00	135	1976	26.00	150	1949*	100.00	569
1986*	38.00	215	1975*	46.00	263			
1985*	24.00	136	1970*	47.00	269			
1983*	25.00	143	1967	18.00	99			
1982*	45.00	254	1966*	58.00	328			
1981*	22.00	124	1964*	61.00	347			
1979*	27.00	156	1961	103.00	583			

* Auction prices since the last two years. For an indication of value and quality of the missing vintages until 1928, see category III, page 34/35.

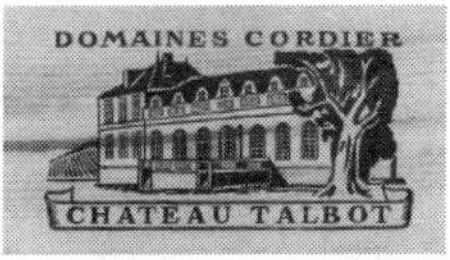

Château du Tertre

Arsac, 5ME CRU CLASSÉ DU MÉDOC

Comments

In 1960, this was still a run-down château with hardly any vineyards. Philippe Gasqueton, the owner of Château Calon-Ségur has been manager here for 30 years.

He has scarcely troubled himself with the château or buildings, but the vineyards are in a fine condition. Monsieur Gasqueton is a 'gentleman farmer'. He owns a few splendid vineyards in the Médoc. He is a propriétaire with a strong affinity with the soil. A royalist, true to tradition, and a perfectionist.

Second wine: Hauts du Tertre, Margaux Réserve

Type Indication

Du Tertre comes under the appellation Margaux, a district from which one expects charming and supple wines. With the large percentage of Cabernet grapes, as much as 85%, du Tertre is the exception. Because Philippe Gasqueton's vinification is also very traditional, this wine has a tough character in youth. With sufficient ripening, a Cru develops with a broad and subtle spectrum of flavors.

Technical data

Owner	: Philippe Capbern-Gasqueton	
Régisseur	: Alain de Baritault	
Cellar master	: David Fennely	
Oenologist	: Prof. Pascal Ribéreau-Gayon	
Vineyard acreage		: 124 acres
Grape varieties:	Cabernet Sauvignon	: 85%
	Cabernet Franc	: 5%
	Merlot	: 10%
	Other	:
Average age of vines		: 29 years
Average annual production (cases of 12 bottles)		: 16,000

Specifications

Vintage	Assessment and Development			Market Value Summer 1995		Change in % since '93
	0 to 20 rating	drink from	cellaring potential	U.S. $	F. frs	
1993	16	1997	2008	23.00	103	27%
1992				17.00	77	6%
1991	**14**	1994	2000			
1990	**14**	1995	2005			
1989	**15**	1995	2005	23.00	105	8%
1988	**16**	1998	2010			
1987	**12**	1990	1995			
1986	**14**	1993	2010			
1985	**16**	1992	2005			
1984	**13**	1989	1997			
1983	**15**	1990	2000			
1982	**14**	1987	1995			
1981	**16**	1990	2000	28.00	128	21%
1980	**13**	1983	1988			
1979	**16**	1986	1996			
1978	**16**	1985	1995			
1977	**14**	1982	1988			

Older vintages	0 to 20 rating	drink from	cellaring potential	Market Value U.S. $	F. frs
1976	**14**	1983	1990		
1975	**13**	1983	1990		
1974	**14**	1979	1985		
1973	**14**	1976	1983		
1972	**11**	1975	1979		

Auction prices realized in the last four years

year	U.S. $	F. frs	year	U.S. $	F. frs	year	U.S. $	F. frs
1988*	12.00	65	1970	27.00	153			
1986*	12.00	65	1966*	30.00	171			
1985	27.00	154	1916	47.00	267			
1983*	19.00	105						
1982*	21.00	118						
1981*	14.00	81						
1979	43.00	245						
1978	45.00	253						

* Auction prices since the last two years. For an indication of value and quality of the missing vintages until 1928, see category IV, page 36/37.

Château La Tour Carnet
Saint-Laurent, 4ME CRU CLASSÉ DU MÉDOC

Comments
La Tour Carnet was a run-down and neglected property. The Lipschitz family who bought the château in 1962 have been at great pains to bring this Grand Cru up to the old standard. More than the half of the vineyards have been replanted and are now in their prime. With good prospects of grapes from a mature vineyard as basis material, it looked as though the eighties were very promising for this château. Unfortunately, the figures do not substantiate this.
Second wine: Sire de Carmin

Type Indication
In spite of the quite large percentage of Merlot grapes, the character of La Tour Carnet is quite rigid and reserved. It is often a somewhat tight wine showing finesse and élan instead of roundness.

Technical data

Owner	: Pelegrin-Lipschitz Family	
Management	: Marie-Claire Pelegrin-Lipschitz	
Oenologist	: Bernard Couasnon	
Vineyard acreage		: 104 acres
Grape varieties:	Cabernet Sauvignon	: 53%
	Cabernet Franc	: 10%
	Merlot	: 33%
	Other	: 4%
Average age of vines		: 30 years
Average annual production (cases of 12 bottles)		: 16,000

Specifications

Vintage	Assessment and Development			Market Value Summer 1995		Change in % since '93
	0 to 20 rating	drink from	cellaring potential	U.S. $	F. frs	
1993	13	1998	2008	16.00	73	8%
1992	**14**	1995	2000	14.00	64	3%
1991	**12**	1994	1996			
1990	**15**	1995	2005	20.00	90	
1989	**16**	1995	2005	21.00	95	
1988	**14**	1994	2000			
1987	**13**	1990	1994			
1986	**13**	1990	2000			
1985	**16**	1992	2005			
1984	**13**	1989	1997			
1983	**13**	1988	1998			
1982	**16**	1987	1997			
1981	**15**	1988	1998			
1980	**13**	1983	1988			
1979	**14**	1985	1995			
1978	**14**	1983	1993			
1977	**14**	1982	1989			

Older vintages	0 to 20 rating	drink from	cellaring potential	Market Value	
				U.S. $	F. frs
1976	**15**	1983	1993		
1975	**16**	1985	2000		
1974	**13**	1972	1987		
1967	**11**	1972	1977		

Auction prices realized in the last four years

year	U.S. $	F. frs	year	U.S. $	F. frs	year	U.S. $	F. frs
1982*	16.00	93						
1981	39.00	220						
1978	19.00	107						
1975	14.00	78						
1970	21.00	118						

Auction prices since the last two years. For an indication of value and quality of the missing vintages until 1928, see category IV, page 36/37.

Château La Tour Haut-Brion
Talence, GRAND CRU CLASSÉ DE GRAVES

Comments
Since 1924, the 'little brother' of La Mission Haut-Brion, the second wine really, has been in the hands of the same family Woltner that exploited La Mission Haut-Brion and has profited from the same modern approach. The three Haut-Brion vineyards benefit from the close proximity of the city of Bordeaux: temperatures a fraction higher, thousands of students available for fast picking at the right moment in time. The wines of La Mission Haut-Brion and those of La Tour Haut-Brion are vinified in the same cellars. La Tour Haut-Brion is inferior to La Mission Haut-Brion, in price and in quality.

Type Indication
La Tour Haut-Brion is a rich, supple wine in successful vintages. In terms of color and robustness La Mission Haut-Brion is superior.

Technical data

Owner	: Domaine Clarence Dillon S.A.
Director	: La Duchesse de Mouchy
Régisseur	: Jean-Bernard Delmas

Vineyard acreage		: 20 acres
Grape varieties:	Cabernet Sauvignon	: 100%
	Cabernet Franc	:
	Merlot	:
	Other	:
Average age of vines		: 25 years
Average annual production (cases of 12 bottles)		: 3,200

Specifications

Vintage	Assessment and Development			Market Value Summer 1995		Change in % since '93
	0 to 20 rating	drink from	cellaring potential	U.S. $	F. frs	
1993	15	2000	2010	22.00	101	23%
1992	**14**	1996	2001	21.00	94	33%
1991	**13**	1994	2000			
1990	**15**	1995	2005	36.00	162	10%
1989	**16**	1994	2000	36.00	162	2%
1988	**16**	1996	2010	36.00	162	10%
1987	**14**	1990	1995	30.00	135	21%
1986	**16**	1995	2010			
1985	**16**	1992	2000	43.00	196	-16%
1984	**15**	1988	1993	23.00	103	-21%
1983				45.00	203	
1982	**16**	1987	1997			
1981	**15**	1988	1998			
1980	**14**	1984	1990			
1979	**15**	1985	1995			
1978						
1977						

Older vintages	0 to 20 rating	drink from	cellaring potential	Market Value	
				U.S. $	F. frs

Auction prices realized in the last four years

year	U.S. $	F. frs	year	U.S. $	F. frs	year	U.S. $	F. frs
1982*	46.00	263	1949	135.00	765			
1981	27.00	156	1929*	278.00	1580			
1979*	23.00	131	1919	120.00	683			
1978	40.00	229						
1975	91.00	519						
1970	47.00	268						
1963	36.00	206						
1959	103.00	583						

Auction prices since the last two years. For an indication of value and quality of the missing vintages until 1928, see category III, page 34/35.

Château La Tour Martillac

Martillac, GRAND CRU CLASSÉ DE GRAVES

Comments

The small property of La Tour Martillac has been run by the Kressmann family since 1930. The wine is sold exclusively by the firm of the same name in Bordeaux. Characteristic are a number of very old vines, some of which were planted more than 100 years ago and which date from before the phylloxera. The production process has been highly modernized, although only cow manure is used, artificial fertilizer being resorted to as little as possible.

A dry white Graves is also produced by the château, which is not taken into consideration here.

Second wine: Château La Grave Martillac

Type Indication

Through the employment of new production methods (long cuvaison, high temperature, 30 to 50% new barrels) the primary aromas dominate. In comparison with the older vintages, this Graves new style has more color and texture and can be aged better.

Technical data

Owner	: Kressmann Family	
Régisseur	: Tristan Kressmann	
Cellar master	: Loïc Kressmann	
Oenologist	: Valerie Miqueu	
Vineyard acreage		: 84 acres
Grape varieties:	Cabernet Sauvignon	: 60%
	Cabernet Franc	: 3%
	Merlot	: 35%
	Other	: 2%
Average age of vines		: 20 years
Average annual production (cases of 12 bottles)		: 10,000

Specifications

Vintage	Assessment and Development			Market Value Summer 1995		Change in % since '93
	0 to 20 rating	drink from	cellaring potential	U.S. $	F. frs	
1993	16	2000	2015			
1992	**14**	1997	2003			
1991	**15**	1994	2000	Maison Kressmann in		
1990	**15**	1995	2005	Bordeaux has the sole		
1989	**17**	1997	2010	exclusivity to market		
1988	**14**	1995	2005	La Tour Martillac.		
1987	**13**	1991	1997	Therefore, this wine		
1986				is not listed on		
1985	**16**	1990	2005	the open market.		
1984						
1983	**16**	1988	1995			
1982	**15**	1990	2000			
1981	**14**	1988	1996			
1980	**10**	1983	1988			
1979	**14**	1984	1990			
1978	**12**	1982	1988			
1977						

Older vintages	0 to 20 rating	drink from	cellaring potential	Market Value	
				U.S. $	F. frs

Auction prices realized in the last four years

year	U.S. $	F. frs	year	U.S. $	F. frs	year	U.S. $	F. frs
1988*	14.00	77						
1975	10.00	54						
1970*	13.00	74						

Auction prices since the last two years. For an indication of value and quality of the missing vintages until 1928, see category IV, page 36/37.

Château Trotte Vieille
Saint-Emilion, 1ER GRAND CRU CLASSÉ B

Comments
The château is the property of the family Castéja. The wine is distributed exclusively by the mercantile firm of Borie-Manoux. Because of this exclusivity contract, Trotte Vieille is isolated from the other 'Grands Crus' quoted on the open market. For some years now Combescaud, who originally came from Algeria, has been the maître du chai and there is evidence of a new style: cement tanks, automatic cooling, fermentation at higher temperatures for the color and, last but not least, more plantings of Merlot. All of this leads to expectations for the future.

Type Indication
Tasting results show improvement. During the last few years, Trotte Vieille has grown into a well textured, warm St.-Emilion, fitting in with the good wines of the classification.

Technical data

Owner	: Castéja Family		
Director	: Philippe Castéja		
Cellar master	: Jacques Combescaud		
Oenologist	: Prof. Pascal Ribéreau-Gayon		
Vineyard acreage		:	25 acres
Grape varieties:	Cabernet Sauvignon	:	5%
	Cabernet Franc	:	45%
	Merlot	:	50%
	Other	:	
Average age of vines		:	40 years
Average annual production (cases of 12 bottles)		:	4,000

Specifications

Vintage	Assessment and Development			Market Value Summer 1995		Change in % since '93
	0 to 20 rating	drink from	cellaring potential	U.S. $	F. frs	
1993	14	1998	2008			
1992	**13**	1995	2000			
1991	**12**	1994	1998	This Grand Cru is		
1990	**16**	1995	2005	not being offered		
1989	**17**	1997	2015	for sale on the		
1988	**16**	1995	2010	open market and,		
1987				therefore, no exact		
1986	**16**	1995	2010	prices are available.		
1985	**15**	1993	2005			
1984						
1983	**16**	1992	2005			
1982	**15**	1990	2000			
1981	**14**	1985	1995			
1980	**13**	1985	1995			
1979						
1978						
1977						

Older vintages	0 to 20 rating	drink from	cellaring potential	Market Value	
				U.S. $	F. frs
1973	**14**	1976	1980		

Auction prices realized in the last four years

year	U.S. $	F. frs	year	U.S. $	F. frs	year	U.S. $	F. frs
1989*	19.00	110						
1986*	20.00	116						
1983*	12.00	67						
1982*	20.00	113						
1978*	13.00	74						
1966	28.00	157						

* Auction prices since the last two years. For an indication of value and quality of the missing vintages until 1928, see category III, page 34/35.

Supplement

Château Le Bon Pasteur
Pomerol

Comments
Château Le Bon Pasteur belongs to the Rolland family. Michel Rolland is a very capable, driven and passionate winemaker whose career took off after his studies in enology at the University of Bordeaux. Now he is one of the enologists most sought after by the top châteaux.

After his father died in 1978, he took charge of Le Bon Pasteur and turned it into a model domaine. The vineyards are receiving first class care. Harvesting is done by hand, and the wine is vinified separately for each parcel in small cuves of 75 hl. Thanks to the lengthy cuvaison and strict temperature control during fermentation, Rolland squeezes the most out of every harvest.

Type Indication
Le Bon Pasteur combines the finesses of a generous Pomerol with the strong structure of a Saint-Emilion. The deep cherry-red color, the creamy, fruity bouquet and the concentrated flavor with refined tannins, make this one of the best wines of the appellation.

Technical data

Owner	: Michel Rolland Family
Régisseur	: Dany and Michel Rolland
Oenologist	: Michel Rolland

Vineyard acreage		: 17 acres
Grape varieties:	Cabernet Sauvignon	:
	Cabernet Franc	: 25%
	Merlot	: 75%
	Other	:
Average age of vines		: 30 years
Average annual production (cases of 12 bottles)		: 3,500

Specifications

Vintage	Assessment and Development			Market Value Summer 1995		Change in % since '93
	0 to 20 rating	drink from	cellaring potential	U.S. $	F. frs	
1993	18	1998	2015	30.00	137	31%
1992	**16**	1996	2002	28.00	128	21%
1991	**14**	1994	2000			
1990	18	1995	2005	43.00	193	
1989	**17**	1994	2003			
1988	**17**	1994	2008			
1987	**15**	1992	1997			
1986	**16**	1992	2005			
1985	**17**	1989	1996			
1984	**15**	1987	1992			
1983	**17**	1989	1997			
1982	**18**	1990	2005			
1981						
1980						
1979						
1978						
1977						

Older vintages	0 to 20 rating	drink from	cellaring potential	Market Value	
				U.S. $	F. frs

Auction prices realized in the last four years

year	U.S. $	F. frs	year	U.S. $	F. frs	year	U.S. $	F. frs
1989*	24.00	135						
1988*	18.00	102						
1983	23.00	132						
1982	58.00	329						
1981	20.00	111						

* Auction prices since the last two years. For an indication of value and quality of the missing vintages until 1928, see category III, page 34/35.

Château Chasse-Spleen
Moulis, CRU GRAND BOURGEOIS EXCEPTIONNEL

Comments
Owners of this reputable castle are two companies and a bank. The castle was managed very professionally by Madame Bernadette Villars until she died in a hiking accident in the Pyrenees at the end of 1992. After her tragic death, the management was taken over by her daughters Claire and Céline Villars.
The 'Eminence Grise' is Monsieur Jacques Merlaut, a wealthy wine merchant from Bordeaux and grandfather of Claire and Céline Villars. The château is a matter of prestige for Merlaut, with which he wants to show that the designation Grand Cru is not sacred. He invests liberally in quality and succeeds in embarrassing many a Grand Cru producer. The wine ripens in oak barrels, half of which are renewed after each harvest.

Type Indication
High-class wine, rivaling many a Grand Cru; very good too in poor vintages. Consistent in quality and a good aging wine.

Technical data

Owner	: S.F. du Château Chasse-Spleen		
Management	: Claire and Céline Villars		
Technical director	: Mr. Sutré		
Oenologist	: M. Boissonen		
Vineyard acreage		:	124 acres
Grape varieties:	Cabernet Sauvignon	:	60%
	Cabernet Franc	:	
	Merlot	:	35%
	Petit Verdot	:	5%
Average age of vines		:	25 years
Average annual production (cases of 12 bottles)		:	25,000

Specifications

Vintage	Assessment and Development 0 to 20 rating	drink from	cellaring potential	Market Value Summer 1995 U.S. $	F. frs	Change in % since '93
1993	16	1998	2010	19.00	87	15%
1992	**14**	1996	2002	19.00	86	35%
1991	**15**	1994	2000			
1990	**17**	1995	2005	30.00	135	38%
1989	**18**	1996	2010	30.00	135	13%
1988	**17**	1998	2010	36.00	162	47%
1987	**14**	1990	1995			
1986	**17**	1993	2012	48.00	217	43%
1985	**17**	1991	2010			
1984	**12**	1988	1995			
1983	**17**	1992	2010			
1982	**16**	1987	1995			
1981	**17**	1990	2000			
1980	**16**	1984	1990			
1979	**17**	1985	1995			
1978	**16**	1986	1996			
1977	**16**	1983	1990			

Older vintages	0 to 20 rating	drink from	cellaring potential	Market Value U.S. $	F. frs
1976	**16**	1985	1995		

Auction prices realized in the last four years

year	U.S. $	F. frs	year	U.S. $	F. frs	year	U.S. $	F. frs
1990*	21.00	117	1979*	18.00	99	1960	19.00	108
1989*	33.00	188	1978*	52.00	298	1957*	13.00	75
1988*	20.00	116	1976	21.00	122	1953*	40.00	226
1986*	26.00	147	1975*	23.00	129	1898	167.00	950
1985*	19.00	109	1971	34.00	195	1890	348.00	1975
1983*	24.00	136	1970*	38.00	217			
1982*	27.00	155	1966	24.00	138			
1981*	19.00	106	1961*	63.00	359			

Auction prices since the last two years. For an indication of value and quality of the missing vintages until 1928, see category IV, page 36/37.

Château La Conseillante
Pomerol

Comments
A traditional, sound Pomerol, with a modern vinification. The list of evaluation scores shows a constant and consistent quality.

La Conseillante is, like the other top wines of the Pomerol, Pétrus and Vieux Château Certan, difficult to come by. The 'Première-Tranche' of this wine is very often sold out within a day.

Type Indication
La Conseillante is a deep, very intense wine with a luxurious color. La Conseillante differentiates itself from the other three top Pomerols by its suave, strikingly creamy bouquet which announces itself at a young age. The soft tannins too, which this wine has in abundance, are surrounded in such a way by fruit and roundness that even in youth this Pomerol is extremely pleasant to drink.

Technical data

Owner	: Sté Civile Héritiers Nicolas	
Oenologist	: Prof. Pascal Ribéreau-Gayon, Michel Rolland	
Vineyard acreage		: 32 acres
Grape varieties:	Cabernet Sauvignon	:
	Cabernet Franc	: 30%
	Merlot	: 65%
	Malbec	: 5%
Average age of vines		: 35 years
Average annual production (cases of 12 bottles)		: 5,000

Specifications

Vintage	Assessment and Development 0 to 20 rating	drink from	cellaring potential	Market Value Summer 1995 U.S. $	F. frs	Change in % since '93
1993	18	1998	2012			
1992	15	1994	1999	36.00	162	4%
1991	14	1994	2000	51.00	233	
1990	17	1996	2010	114.00	518	48%
1989	19	1997	2010			
1988	16	1995	2008			
1987	16	1990	1996			
1986	17	1993	2010			
1985	17	1992	2020	110.00	503	100%
1984	15	1990	2000	39.00	176	-10%
1983	18	1990	2005	66.00	299	17%
1982	18	1990	2005	127.00	578	60%
1981	15	1988	1998			
1980	16	1985	1993			
1979	16	1987	1995			
1978				92.00	421	-9%
1977	16	1985	1995			

Older vintages	0 to 20 rating	drink from	cellaring potential	Market Value U.S. $	F. frs
1975	17	1982	1997		
1974	10	1976	1980		
1973	16	1978	1984		
1972	10	1975	1980		
1971	15	1977	1985		
1970	15	1978	1990		

Auction prices realized in the last four years

year	U.S. $	F. frs	year	U.S. $	F. frs	year	U.S. $	F. frs
1989*	62.00	352	1976	28.00	161	1916	86.00	489
1986*	33.00	188	1975*	32.00	183			
1985*	55.00	310	1971	34.00	192			
1983*	29.00	165	1970*	68.00	387			
1982*	73.00	415	1966*	60.00	343			
1981*	41.00	232	1961	173.00	983			
1979*	36.00	204	1947	131.00	741			
1978	53.00	299	1934	89.00	506			

Auction prices since the last two years. For an indication of value and quality of the missing vintages until 1928, see category II, page 32/33.

Château Gloria
Saint-Julien, CRU BOURGEOIS DU MÉDOC

Comments
Henri Martin, who died in 1991, bought Gloria in 1940 with a 2 acre vineyard! During the following 30 years he expanded it, by cleverly buying and exchanging with neighbors and friends, to its present size of 111 acres. He turned Château Gloria into the most renowned Cru Bourgeois of the Médoc, which is sold at Grand Cru prices. Vinification takes place in steel tanks and ripening in small wooden barrels which are renewed depending on the structure of the harvest.
Second wine: Château Peymartin

Type Indication
A firm wine, rich in fruit. Bouquet and flavor have depth and finesse and attest to having been cared for well and with skill. Good aging potential.

Technical data

Owner	: Triaud Family		
Technical director	: Emmanuel Cassagne		
Régisseur	: Jean-Louis Triaud		
Cellar master	: Jean-Marie Galey		
Vineyard acreage		:	111 acres
Grape varieties:	Cabernet Sauvignon	:	65%
	Cabernet Franc	:	5%
	Merlot	:	25%
	Petit Verdot	:	5%
Average age of vines		:	37 years
Average annual production (cases of 12 bottles)		:	20,000

Specifications

Vintage	Assessment and Development 0 to 20 rating	drink from	cellaring potential	Market Value Summer 1995 U.S. $	F. frs	Change in % since '93
1993	15	1998	2008	18.00	80	1%
1992	13	1996	2000	15.00	69	-3%
1991	15	1994	2000			
1990	17	1997	2005	30.00	135	64%
1989	17	1995	2005			
1988	16	1995	2008			
1987	13	1990	1995			
1986	16	1995	2005	28.00	128	0%
1985	15	1993	2010			
1984	16	1991	2005			
1983	13	1988	1995			
1982	16	1987	1995	48.00	217	30%
1981	13	1986	1994	28.00	128	
1980	15	1985	1990			
1979	14	1985	1990			
1978						
1977	12	1983	1989			

Older vintages	0 to 20 rating	drink from	cellaring potential	Market Value U.S. $	F. frs
1976	16	1984	1994		
1975	17	1987	1997		
1974	10	1978	1985		
1973	14	1978	1982		
1972	9	1976	1980		
1971	14	1978	1985		
1970	16	1978	1985		
1969	14	1978	1985		

Auction prices realized in the last four years

year	U.S. $	F. frs	year	U.S. $	F. frs	year	U.S. $	F. frs
1986*	22.00	124	1971	27.00	153			
1985*	20.00	114	1970	38.00	215			
1983*	19.00	106	1961	76.00	431			
1982*	31.00	177						
1981	21.00	118						
1979	21.00	120						
1978	34.00	190						
1975*	34.00	192						

Auction prices since the last two years. For an indication of value and quality of the missing vintages until 1928, see category IV, page 36/37.

Château
Gloria
St JULIEN (FRANCE)

Château Pétrus
Pomerol

Comments
The château is managed and distributed exclusively by the firm of Moueix, which also owns a number of châteaux in Saint-Emilion and Pomerol. Pétrus is the jewel in the crown of the Moueix domains. This miniature château is surrounded by the greatest care and attention. To gather the grapes the most ideal weather conditions are waited for. The grape gatherers of the other Moueix estates are then immediately redirected to this small vineyard, where they bring in the harvest in one or at the most two days. Pétrus is the most expensive Bordeaux. The demand for this Pomerol is much larger than the supply.

Type Indication
Pétrus is one of the most rich, voluminous and luxuriant wines of Bordeaux. The luxuriance and roundness Pétrus gets from the grape; the depth and finesse from the infinite care and attention given by the owner. A top Merlot wine, with long aging potential, exceptional for this variety of grape.

Technical data

Owner	: Madame Lacoste / Jean-Pierre Moueix		
Technical director	: Christian Moueix		
Régisseur	: Michel Gillet		
Cellar master	: François Veyssières		
Vineyard acreage		:	28 acres
Grape varieties:	Cabernet Sauvignon	:	
	Cabernet Franc	:	5%
	Merlot	:	95%
	Other	:	
Average age of vines		:	40 years
Average annual production (cases of 12 bottles)		:	4,000

Specifications

Vintage	Assessment and Development			Market Value Summer 1995		Change in % since '93
	0 to 20 rating	drink from	cellaring potential	U.S. $	F. frs	
1993	18	2000	2020			
1992	**17**	1998	2010			
1991	Harvest has been declassified			Maison Moueix in		
1990	**18**	2000	2025	Bordeaux has the sole		
1989	**19**	2000	2020	exclusivity to market		
1988	**18**	1998	2010	Pétrus. Therefore,		
1987	**17**	1995	2005	this wine is not listed		
1986	**18**	2000	2025	on the open market.		
1985	**18**	1995	2020			
1984	**15**	1989	1995			
1983	**18**	1995	2010			
1982	**18**	1995	2015			
1981	**19**	1990	2005			
1980	**17**	1985	1993			
1979						
1978						
1977						

Older vintages	0 to 20 rating	drink from	cellaring potential	Market Value	
				U.S. $	F. frs
1976	**18**	1990	2000		
1973	**15**	1978	1983		
1970	**19**	1987	2005		
1969	**13**	1974	1982		
1967	**19**	1972	1988		

Auction prices realized in the last four years

year	U.S. $	F. frs	year	U.S. $	F. frs	year	U.S. $	F. frs
1990*	317.00	1799	1980*	157.00	893	1959*	846.00	4804
1989*	337.00	1911	1979*	252.00	1433	1953*	531.00	3017
1988*	211.00	1197	1978*	242.00	1373	1949*	633.00	3592
1986*	232.00	1317	1975*	397.00	2257	1948*	405.00	2299
1985*	364.00	2065	1970*	531.00	3017	1947*	1347.00	7650
1983*	330.00	1873	1966*	569.00	3232	1945*	2596.00	14740
1982*	576.00	3268	1962*	405.00	2299	1943*	506.00	2873
1981*	346.00	1962	1961*	1898.00	10775	1934*	197.00	1116

* Auction prices since the last two years. For an indication of value and quality of the missing vintages until 1928, see category I, page 30/31.

Vieux Château Certan
Pomerol

Comments
Owned by the Belgian family Thienpont since 1924. A perfectly groomed little château and vineyard, where a wine is produced which must be ranked among the 'Prévendus' of the Bordeaux wines. That this Cru is part of the Prévendus, that is to say it is already sold before the wine is offered for sale on the open market, is not so surprising for such a quality wine from such a small crop.

The yearly offer of only 5000 cases is too small to meet our demand certainly when we compare it to the Grands Crus from the Médoc which offer on the average 20,000 cases for sale each year.

Second wine: La Gravette de Certan

Type Indication
Vieux Château Certan is a deep, creamy wine full of fruit, displaying intense color and velvety aroma in successful vintages. The wine is not always clearly recognizable, as the owner improvises annually. Changeability is therefore no stranger to this château.

Technical data

Owner	: Thienpont Family		
Régisseur	: Alexandre Thienpont		
Cellar master	: Yannick Favereau		
Oenologist	: Laboratoire C.B.C., Libourne		
Vineyard acreage			: 32 acres
Grape varieties:		Cabernet Sauvignon	: 15%
		Cabernet Franc	: 35%
		Merlot	: 50%
		Other	:
Average age of vines			: 35 years
Average annual production (cases of 12 bottles)			: 5,000

Specifications

Vintage	Assessment and Development			Market Value Summer 1995		Change in % since '93
	0 to 20 rating	drink from	cellaring potential	U.S. $	F. frs	
1993	16	1998	2010	40.00	183	37%
1992	13	1995	2000	28.00	128	15%
1991						
1990	17	1995	2005	69.00	312	47%
1989	17	1996	2010	58.00	264	0%
1988	15	1994	2005			
1987	16	1990	1995			
1986	16	1993	2010	72.00	326	2%
1985	18	1992	2020	75.00	339	20%
1984	16	1990	2000	30.00	135	-9%
1983	17	1990	2005			
1982	18	1990	2005			
1981	17	1990	2000			
1980	14	1984	1990			
1979	15	1985	1990			
1978	16	1987	1997			
1977						

Older vintages	0 to 20 rating	drink from	cellaring potential	Market Value	
				U.S. $	F. frs
1976				72.00	326
1975	18	1985	2000		
1974	11	1977	1982		
1973	14	1976	1982		
1972	12	1977	1982		

Auction prices realized in the last four years

year	U.S. $	F. frs	year	U.S. $	F. frs	year	U.S. $	F. frs
1989*	53.00	302	1978*	42.00	236	1966	69.00	391
1988*	43.00	243	1976*	20.00	113	1964	44.00	251
1986*	41.00	233	1975*	47.00	266	1959*	127.00	718
1985*	36.00	203	1973*	14.00	80	1955*	96.00	545
1983*	36.00	202	1971*	40.00	226	1952*	53.00	299
1982*	57.00	321	1970*	47.00	266	1947*	379.00	2151
1981*	31.00	178	1969	28.00	158	1945	218.00	1237
1979*	31.00	174	1967*	22.00	122	1943	94.00	534

Auction prices since the last two years. For an indication of value and quality of the missing vintages until 1928, see category II, page 32/33.

ISBN 0-932664-94-6

TASTING NOTES

TASTING NOTES

TASTING NOTES